THE KITCHEN GARDEN

CHARLES LYTE

THE OXFORD ILLUSTRATED PRESS

THE OXFORD ILLUSTRATED PRESS

© 1984, Charles Lyte
Printed in Great Britain by J. H. Haynes & Co Limited
ISBN 0 946609 03 9
The Oxford Illustrated Press
Sparkford, Yeovil, Somerset,
England

Distributed in North America by Interbook Inc.,
14895 E. 14th Street, Suite 370, San Leandro, CA 94577, USA.

British Library Cataloguing in Publication Data

Lyte, charles
The Kitchen garden.
1. Vegetable gardening —History
I. Title
635'.09   SB320.8.G7
ISBN 0–946609–03–9

This book is dedicated, with very great affection, to my parents-in-law, Peggy and George Carey-Foster.

Acknowledgements

I would like to acknowledge my very great gratitude for all the help I have received in preparing this book, especially from the Chief Librarian of the Royal Horticultural Society Lindley Library, Dr. Brent Elliott, and Barbara Collecott. I am also deeply indebted to the staffs of the Imperial War Museum Library; the Botanical Library of the Natural History Museum, Kensington; Miss Suzanne Kew and the staff of the Ministry of Agriculture, Fisheries and Food Library; the Linnaean Society; the Royal Geographical Society, and The London Library. And, of course, my wife, Sarah, whose help and encouragement made the book possible, and the patience of my children.

I am grateful to Harry Smith, Hyde Hall, Rettenden, Chelmsford; The Iris Hardwick Library, Cerne Abbas, Dorset, and Tania Midgley for their photographs. To Mrs. Ruth Duthie for the cover photograph, and to Eileen Tweedie for photographing William Hooker's paintings of fruit, and the plates from Elizabeth Blackwell's *A Curious Herbal*. My thanks also to the Royal Horticultural Society for permission to reproduce the paintings and plates. I would also like to thank Penguin Books, for permission to reprint from Leslie Thomas's *The Magic Army*. Mr. J. C. H. Bibby of Rutland Gallery, St. George Street, London, for permission to reproduce the still-life 'Kitchen Garden'. Mr. E. Pearson, secretary, Bordesley Green Ideal Allotment Holders Association. David Zahller, Community Garden Co-Ordinator, U.S. Department of the Interior, Washington D.C.

Contents

Introduction

The kitchen garden is a place to browse in; to breathe deeply of the scent of fruit blossom or the crushed leaves of herbs, to taste the absolute freshness of fruit and vegetables plucked straight from the soil or branch. It should never be a purely functional area for food production.

It was walls that brought the kitchen garden to perfection, with fruit trees trained against the brick or stone, changing with the seasons: first the delicate new leaves and blossom, and later the rich, strong colours of the ripening fruit.

Vegetables too are beautiful to look at; the black and white, sweetly scented flowers of the broad bean, and the scarlet, pink and white flowers of runner beans produced in brilliant profusion; the huge yellow trumpets of marrows and pumpkins, and the little gold cornets of squashes and cucumbers. Onions and leeks with their elegant grey-green foliage, and the bright green of lettuces. The deep wine reds of beetroot and orache; the slender, cane-like stems of Jerusalem artichokes, and the statuesque splendour of globe artichokes, with their grey-blue leaves and magnificent thistle heads. The green and white marble of Swiss chard; the delicate, feathered fronds of carrots. Radishes, black, scarlet, white and pink, and all the form and colour of the herb bed.

Even the cabbage family, so familiar and so much taken for granted, enriches the kitchen garden with its wide range of colour and beauty. The bloom on the succulent leaves of summer cabbages, and the crinkled dark green of savoys. The strong stems of Brussels clustered with the hard buttons of the sprouts. The deep purple-red of red cabbage, the chalk-white curds of cauliflowers, the green heads of calabrese, and the white and purple spikes of sprouting broccoli.

Shrubby gooseberries become laden with fruit like jade teardrops, while the currants are beaded with tassles of white, red and black fruit. Rubies grow on raspberry canes and in the strawberry bed. Rhubarb grows like a jungle plant, and the new growth of asparagus is like an emerging bamboo thicket. Plants bubble and writhe out of cold frames, and fill the greenhouse, where the smells and atmosphere are of other countries.

There is a comfortable peaty earthiness in the potting shed, where in wet, cold weather peaceful hours are spent preparing for better days. Even in the winter months when much of the kitchen garden is lying fallow it is an aesthetically rewarding place, for like the austere, meticulously raked sand gardens of Japan, there is a great beauty in well dug soil.

Even if the colour and scents of the kitchen garden fail to make an impression, then the food it is producing must. There is a delightful sense of greedy anticipation in rows of vegetables ready to be gathered, cooked and served in a variety of delicious ways. I confess to deriving the greatest pleasure from picking my own Brussels sprouts on Christmas morning, even if the hard, round buttons are iced with frost, and my hands throb and ache with the cold.

Of course a kitchen garden does not need to be walled to be beautiful. It can be 'fenced in' with espalier fruit trees, or with a strong protective hedge of beech or hornbeam. Or it can be an allotment, bright, busy and lovingly tended in the midst of some urban sprawl.

This book is, if you like, a celebration in history of the kitchen garden, from the most remote times when men and women hacked at the virgin soil with deer-antler picks and stone adzes, and pierced the unused soil with pointed sticks to set their seeds, to today with its cultivators, miniature tractors, and sprays in aerosol canisters.

But the eighteenth-century vogue for landscaping relegated the kitchen garden to a kind of servant class; essential, but ideally kept out of sight. This down-grading was to some extent reflected in the poor quality of vegetable cookery which dragged on into the nineteenth and twentieth century. Fortunately there have always been enlightened cooks and writers of cookery books who have kept alive the art of good vegetable cookery.

Introduction

It is still all too easy to find very badly prepared vegetables, but perhaps because of the high price of meat, and the increasing interest in health, and healthy eating, vegetables and fruit are enjoying a new popularity, which seems set to stay.

As far as possible I have told the story in chronological order from the hunter-gatherer's crude beginnings as cultivators to modern times. I have tried to show how fruit and vegetables fitted in with the great civilisations which flowered in Egypt and the Near East, Greece and Rome.

In Britain there can be no doubt that the Romans made an enormous impact on vegetable and fruit culture. When they built their villas and settlements they introduced their favourite plants, because they were vital to so much of their elaborate cuisine which made great use of vegetables, herbs and fruit in sauces, stuffings, salads and individual dishes.

The Roman Empire crumbled and the invaders left, but even in the dark decades that followed, vegetable and fruit culture continued, albeit at a simpler level. The real or imagined medicinal powers of herbs and vegetables kept them in cultivation, particularly in the gardens of the religious houses, where monks and nuns grew them for treating the sick of the neighbourhood.

In the sixteenth and seventeenth centuries the salad in many forms became an essential part of diet, and in turn resulted in the cultivation of many plants for their roots and leaves, and even their stalks and seeds.

The following centuries saw an increasingly sophisticated approach to vegetable and fruit production. Selection and hybridizing turned a trickle of new varieties into a torrent, and gardeners tuned and polished their skills so that the humble pot-herb became the prize specimen on the show bench. One thing this story tells us is that neither storm nor blight, war or social upheavals have been able to still the art of kitchen gardening.

1
First Find Your Vegetables

The dependence of mankind on vegetables is as ancient as it is true. Even if there was an incarnation of the species which was wholly meat-eating, those people would anyway have come at the end of a food chain that started with vegetable matter in some form. But all the evidence points clearly to the fact that man the hunter was also man the gatherer and harvester, although it seems likely that it was the women and children who searched the forests and savannas for roots, tubers, bulbs, grains and fruits. There is also an unlovely theory, but plausible for all that, that when plant food was scarce, ancient peoples ate the partly digested vegetable matter in the stomachs of the game they killed. Gathered fruits and vegetables were soaked in water until soft enough to be chewed.

Palaeobotany, the study of identification of prehistoric food plants, has discovered that ancient peoples enjoyed a quite varied vegetable and fruit diet. Evidence has been gathered from the sites of prehistoric settlements: carbonised seeds, and the impression of seeds picked up in the wet clay of pots which were made and baked by the cooking fires. Seeds have also been found in the remains of mummies, in the area of the stomach cavity of skeletons unearthed from burial grounds. The autopsy on The Tollund Man, the 2,000-year-old corpse recovered from a Danish peat bog in an almost perfect state of preservation, revealed that his last meal was a gruel or broth made from a variety of seeds, including those of dock, bindweed and chamomile. Other discoveries in Denmark have shown that Iron Age Danes made a drink from cranberries.

Palaeobotanists working on prehistoric settlements in Switzerland have discovered that the inhabitants' diet included raspberries, cherries, sloes, hazelnuts and the Cornelian cherry.

Almonds in an excellent state of preservation were found in a fourth-century shipwreck off Kyrenia in Cyprus, but long before that period food crops were being cultivated. Seeds found on Neolithic sites have included field peas, lentils and horse beans, as well as the more predictable wheat and barley.

Horse beans have been found on the early Iron Age sites at Glastonbury in Somerset. They were probably used for making flour and porridge. Certainly the Romans used them for flour making. Although they go back to neolithic times, lentils did not arrive in Britain until the invasion by the Romans, who used them with peas to make broth.

Fruit clearly played an important part in the prehistoric diet, and included apples, pears, figs, grapes, bullace or wild plums, as well as walnuts and almonds.

Prehistoric vegetables included cabbage, orache (a spinach-like vegetable, rarely grown these days except as an ornament), white mustard, sorrel, coriander, and fenugreek, a clover-like plant which was a popular vegetable for centuries, but which I cannot find even in the most adventurous modern seed catalogue. While some of these plants may have been cultivated under crude garden conditions, it seems more likely that they were gathered in the wild along with couch grass, shepherd's purse, fat hen, plantain, dock, chickweed and wild carrots, but they were in the vanguard of kitchen gardening.

As the hunter-gatherers wandering in tribes or even in small family groups, began to settle, so they exchanged hunting for a pastoral life. Instead of depending on a purely wild source of vegetable food, they began to collect the plants they ate and cultivated them, saving the seed from the most productive, and thus starting a process of selection which would continue for centuries.

Among the more primitive communities the first gardens were no more than a patch of roughly cultivated soil, crudely fenced to keep out animals, while the advanced civilisations brought vegetable culture to a fine art. In 3500 B.C. the Sumarians in the Euphrates Valley built irrigation systems for their vegetable crops. The Ancient Egyptians grew onions (which they venerated), chicory, melons, radishes and lentils to perfection. Their doctors grew caraway, colchicum, dill, elderberry, gentian, lettuce, mint and poppies for medicines.

In Israel the Jews cultivated almonds, leeks, onions, garlic, cucumbers, melons and lentils, and in Ancient Greece vegetables, herbs and fruit played an important part in public and religious ceremonies. Heroes were crowned with wreathes of parsley (which was also planted around graves) and lettuce and fennel were grown as offerings to Adonis; the apple was dedicated to Aphrodite, and mint to Pluto. Cabbages were said to have sprung from the tears of Lycurgus.

The Persians transformed grafting into an art, and are credited with inventing the so-called family tree in which several varieties of a fruit are grafted to a single stock.

Meanwhile in Britain vegetable and fruit gardening could hardly be said to be developing at any great pace: it was little more than subsistence cultivation of pulses and grains that could be dried and stored to fend off starvation during the lean months of winter and early spring. British gardening, in a recognizable form, had to wait for the Roman invasion, and the settlement of the country as a colony of the Empire.

Apart from conquest, the Roman's loved their food. They brought cooking to an exceptional art, so it is naturally inconceivable that throughout their three hundred years of occupation they would have existed on a diet of porridge. To satisfy the demands of their complex and ingenious cuisine they introduced vegetables, herbs and fruit and grew them in the gardens cultivated around their British villas.

Apicius, who lived at the time of Tiberius in the first century A.D., wrote a classic cookery book which gives a clear picture of the demands of the Roman table. Indeed, his own history illustrates the importance of food in Roman life. It is said that when, doing his accounts, he discovered he had spent one hundred million sesterces on food, and only had another ten million sesterces left; he poisoned himself rather than face starvation.

Since one of the skills of Roman cookery was to alter the flavour of the basic ingredient of a dish, vegetables, herbs, spices and fruit were an important part of the Roman cook's arsenal. At a Roman meal the hors d'oeuvre, which was called *gustum, gustatio* or *promulsis* involved a variety of vegetables eaten raw or cooked, and included asparagus, cucumbers, pumpkins, lettuce, mushrooms and herbs, all of which were served with *mulsom*, a mixture of grape juice and honey.

Vegetables were always served with meat and fish, and sauces played an important part in providing a rich array of flavours. The base to sauces was *liquamen*, a liquid produced from the fermenting entrails of fish, and whole small fish such as sprats and anchovies, mixed with water, wine or vinegar. Since *Liquamen* was very strongly flavoured it was used sparingly with cumin, lovage, parsley, mint, bay leaves, caraway, dill, spikenard (a variety of elecampane), alecost (costmary), coriander, rue, thyme, savory and fennel.

The dessert was largely fruit, and in many cases even the cheese owed its origins to vegetables, when the flowers of wild thistle, artichokes, saffron seeds or the sap of the fig tree were used as a rennet substitute in the making of cheese.

Vegetables were appreciated by the richest and the poorest Romans. Pliny the Elder wrote: 'The garden constituted of itself the poor man's field, and it was from the garden that the lower classes procured their daily food.'

Rich Romans, on the other hand, went to great trouble and expense to raise rare vegetables and fruits in their gardens. Tiberius was said to be so fond of cucumbers that his gardeners found ways of providing him with a supply the year round. They developed forcing techniques, and introduced the first greenhouses, which were hot-bed pits roofed with sheets of talc or mica. Some of the greenhouses were heated by fires set around the walls.

Cabbages and turnips were highly regarded by Romans of all classes, not merely as delicious vegetables, but also as an aid to good health. Columella urged the abundant growing of turnips, arguing that any surplus could be fed to animals. Some considerable care must have gone into their culture since Pliny writes of roots weighing as much as forty pounds.

Apart from cabbages and turnips, the Roman kitchen garden was also stocked with leeks, onions, garlic, beets, radishes, artichokes, endive, lettuce, carrots, parsnips, skirrets, beans, peas, lentils, marrows, cucumbers, melons, celery (which was also grown for its seed), alexanders (a form of wild celery), fenugreek, shallots, orache and chicory.

Numerous herbs were grown, many of them as popular today as they were then: thyme, mint, parsley, bay, as well as fennel, dill, rue, hyssop, savory, saffron, cumin, coriander, lovage, oregano, caraway, myrtle (for its berries), chervil, borage, mustard, southernwood, and sweet marjoram.

They also lavished attention on their orchards of apples (twenty-two varieties), pears (thirty-six kinds), plums, peaches (four types), quinces (three), eight cherries, damsons and apricots, as well as their walnut trees, sweet chestnuts, nut bushes, almonds, and grapes.

Most, if not all these plants were brought to Britain by the Roman occupiers, and introduced into the national diet. Even the Dark Ages which followed the collapse of Roman rule could not destroy such hardy vegetables as cabbage, lettuce, leeks, onions, radishes, garlic, mint, garden cress, orache and parsley. Even the rose and cherry survived fire and sword, and it is more than possible that other fruits and herbs escaped from ruined, deserted gardens and survived in the wild. According to Pliny, cherries were introduced into Britain in 42 B.C., although other sources claim the arrival to be in the year A.D. 55. The medlar, which used to be found growing wild, is another Roman escape, as was the quince, which at one time was naturalised in the Sussex Weald; and if the walnut was brought by the Romans (opinions differ) it too took to the open countryside.

Although some of the food plants brought by the Romans did survive, the art of gardening all but died during the dark years following those of Roman enlightenment.

2

Marigolds and Cabbages

With the Romans gone, their forts, villas and cities were laid waste by neglect and tribal warfare within the country, and marauding Saxons from without. The Saxons, with the Angles and Jutes they had absorbed into their nation, were brutish invaders, but like most predators, once they had settled, they turned to the more peaceful occupation of feeding themselves. They continued to cultivate at least some of the vegetables and fruits that the Romans and Romanised British had grown to such perfection. Gardening was sufficiently important to have its own Saxon vocabulary. The *wyrtzerd* or *wyrttun* was a plant enclosure; *oortzerd* or *orcead*, an orchard. Some plants and fruit were grown in their own special gardens; the *appletun* or *applezerd* for apples, *cherryzerd* for cherries, and the *leac tun*, an exclusive enclosure for leeks, which were clearly a vegetable of considerable importance. The word *wurt* attached to a plant indicated that it was valued for food or medicine, and in most cases for both.

But it was the spread of Christianity and the establishment of monasteries that ensured the future of the kitchen garden and orchard, despite the Viking savagery that was eventually to almost wipe out the religious houses. Gardening played a crucial role in monastic life. Physical labour was regarded as an exercise that refined the spirit. St. Jerome urged young monks to 'hoe your ground, set out cabbages, convey water to them in conduits'. It was essential advice since the communities were self-supporting, and certainly could not rely on outside supplies. St. Benedict ruled that vegetables should be part of the main meal of the day in his Order's houses.

When plans were drawn up for the monastery of St. Gall, named after the shy Irish monk who accompanied St. Columba on his missionary expedition to England and Europe in the sixth century, they included what was to become the blueprint for monastery gardens. The great religious house on the shores of Lake Constance included a large kitchen garden, and an orchard which was also the burial ground for the monks. The specifications listed the fruit trees to be planted: apples, pears, plums, service tree (*sorbus*), quinces, peaches, mulberries, figs, almonds, hazelnuts, walnuts, chestnuts and bay trees.

As monks were physicians of the body as well as the soul, the gardens included a large variety of herbs. Indeed nuns taught housewives how to grow medicinal plants and use them to treat the sick and injured.

They planted vineyards and cider apple orchards, and developed and improved their crops. The Warden pear, which remained popular for centuries, was raised by the monks of Warden Abbey in Bedfordshire, and brought them such fame that three Warden pears were included in their coat of arms. Francis Bacon rated it among the essential fruit in the gardens of princes, and Robert Herrick lists the aroma of a baked Warden among the arousing scents of jasmine, carnations, roses, almond blossom and orange flowers. Like so many of the old varieties of fruit, it has now disappeared.

Albert Magnus, a Cistercian who wrote authoritatively about plants, re-introduced the greenhouse, and was accused of witchcraft for his pains.

The Dissolution of the Monasteries during the reign of Henry VIII was another set-back for vegetable and fruit growing, but fortunately by then large private gardens were being established.

Throughout the Middle Ages warring and feuding were such constant threats that ruling classes found it necessary to live within the relative safety of the castle or the fortified manor house. The result was that there was little opportunity for serious gardening. Orchards were planted outside the castle walls, but if the building came under attack the orchard was usually destroyed by the attackers. Space within the fortifications was so limited that little more than a few essential medicinal herbs could be grown, along with the more strongly flavoured culinary herbs used to mask the unpleasant taste of preserved, and sometimes rotting, meat.

As society became more peaceful and orderly, so gardens were planted, and the kitchen gardens in particular were well stocked. By the fifteenth century, Master John Gardener was able to set out in his poem *The Feate of Gardening*, the first how-to-do-it gardening book in English, what should be grown in the kitchen garden.

Cabbages or *wortys* were so important that he devotes a special section to them:

Wurtys we most have
Both to Mayster & to knave
Ye schul have mynde here
To have wurtys yong all tyme of ye yere
Every moneth hath his name
To set & sow without any blame.
May for some ys all the best
July for eruyst (harvest) ys the nexst
November for wynter mate the thyrde be
Mars for lent so make y the . . . .
The land mote well y dygnyd (dunged) be.

The advice is practical and sound. Master John advises sowing for spring, summer and winter cabbages, which suggests that there were even then different varieties of cabbages available, and not merely greens little removed from the wild cabbage. He urges gardeners to keep the land in good heart, and reminds them that it was a vegetable relished at both the rich and poor man's table.

Parsley, which was an important pot-herb and flavouring, he said should be cut hard during the growing season, but left alone in the winter. The rule still stands.

His list of herbs for cooking and sauces, contains many familiar kitchen garden plants, and some that would be regarded with trepidation by the modern cook.

Master John's ideal kitchen garden contained: pelitory, rue, sage, clary, thyme, hyssop, orache, mint, savory, town cress, spinach, lettuce, calamint, avens, borage, fennel, southernwood, wormwood, ribwort,

St. John's wood, stinking robert, walwort (*sedum acre*), hart's tongue, polypodium, comfrey, gromwell, woodruff, hindheal, betony, *Iris foe-tidissima*, valerian, scabious, spearwort, vervain, wood sour (wood sorrel), water lily, liverwort, mousear, agrimony, honeysuckle, bugloss, century, horsehele, adder's tongue, bugle, henbane, chamomile, teasle, groundsel, alysaunder (Alexanders), bruisewort, stitchwort, lavender, radish, sanicle, mustard, periwinkle, violet, cowslip, lily, strawberry, motherwort, ox-tongue, tansy, fieldwort, orpine (sedum), nep, hore-hound, campion, Narcissus, pseudo-narcissus (wild daffodil), primrose, salvia verbena, red rose, white rose, foxglove, pimpernel, hollyhock, coriander and paeony.

Of course these were not all for the pot, and some would be extremely dangerous to use at random, for in Master John's kitchen garden, vegetables, culinary herbs and medicinal herbs were grown together to be at hand for the housewife who was as tutored in cooking as she was in curing.

His epic gardening poem also gives detailed instructions on planting and rearing trees, grafting, vine culture, seed sowing, and growing saffron. All proof that the art of gardening was on the mend after so many dark years.

The kitchen garden developed as a separate entity not only for practical reasons, but because it was regarded as bad form to mingle fruit and vegetables, and particularly vegetables and flowers.

As late as 1626 readers of *The Country Housewife's Garden* were being told 'your garden flowers shall suffer some disgrace, if among them you intermingle Onions, Parsnips etc... that which is for your kitchen's use must yield daily roots, or other herbs, and suffer deformity.' Once again the poor kitchen garden was being treated as a second class citizen. On the other hand orchards were regarded as romantic places, filled with the scent and sight of blossom and later of ripening fruit; a place for trysting, for love and dalliance.

Although kitchen gardening was making advances, it suffered two setbacks in the fourteenth and fifteenth centuries. The first was the Black Death – which wiped out nearly one-third of the population – and the second the Wars of the Roses. After the plague had abated, the able-bodied had to turn to farming to provide enough food for the shattered nation. Gardens were neglected. And between 1399 and the Battle of Bosworth Field in 1485 the country was rocked by civil war and confusion, and again gardening became the victim of neglect.

Perhaps because of this the diet of the rich became meat-based, whilst the poor had to make do with bread and vegetables. Flesh – beef, mutton, veal, venison and fowls – became the food for gentlemen. William Forrest in his *The Pleasaunt Poesye of Princelie Practise*, which he wrote in 1548 declared:

> Owre Englische natur cannot lyue by Rooats,
> by water, herbys or suche beggerye baggage . . . .

It was even argued that fruit and vegetables were positively harmful. But if the Tudors, who came out with all the prizes from the Wars of the Roses, scorned vegetables, they did not despise gardening. As the peace became established so there was time to consider the more pleasant aspects of life, and the wealthy laid out pleasure grounds – knot gardens, mazes, labyrinths, mounts, turf seats set in arbors, and shady walks. Love and romance were in the air after the cruel decades of violence.

While the kitchen garden was pushed into the background, it was not forgotten. Hampton Court Palace kitchen garden grew vegetables for Henry VIII's table, as well as melons and cucumbers. Its orchards were well stocked with pears, apples, damsons, cherries and medlars. Nonesuch Palace at Ewell in Surrey was famed for its large kitchen garden and in particular for its apricots and soft fruit: strawberries, raspberries (which were then called hindberries), gooseberries and barberries (berberis). At Beaulieu the gardeners produced green vegetables, roots, salads and fruit.

With the accession of Elizabeth I to the throne the renewed interest in gardening spread to the kitchen and fruit gardens. The art of cooking was developing, and with it the demand for a wide variety of ingredients. Spinach was used in rich tarts filled with chopped veal, kidney, herbs, spices, sugar and dried fruit. Asparagus and peas were sought-after vegetables, and strawberry flan served with fresh cream, just as it is today, was a favourite Elizabethan pudding. In the more ordinary homes boiled beef would be surrounded by mounds of carrots, cabbages and turnips.

In 1573 Thomas Tusser listed what he regarded as essential fruit in a good garden: apples, apricots, barberries, bullace (black and white), cherries (red and black), cornel cherries (*Cornus*), damsons, plums, peaches, pears, quince, medlars, mulberry, service tree, raspberries, currants, strawberries, whortleberries, sweet chestnuts and filberts. Fruit was so greatly valued in Tudor times that a statute of 1545 decreed that anyone caught barking or damaging trees should have their ears cropped as well as paying heavy damages.

Vegetable gardening received an added boost in Elizabeth's reign by the arrival of Protestant refugees from France, Italy and Holland, all countries where vegetable and fruit growing had been held in high esteem for centuries. They brought their gardening skills with them.

Salads played an important part in the Elizabethan meal. Lettuce was eaten at the beginning of a meal to sharpen the appetite, and at the end of the meal as an antidote to drunkenness. Quantities of herbs were used in the salads, which included pre-cooked vegetables, and the flowers of marigolds, violets, primroses, mallows and strawberry leaves were added to give them colour.

The kitchen garden was coming back into its own, but it was still regarded as unsightly in comparison with the pleasure grounds, and was tucked out of sight behind brick or mud walls, a lattice fence or a quick-set hedge. But this did not mean that it lacked the same kind of care and attention given to the knots and bowers. An Elizabethan starting a new herb garden was instructed to thoroughly dig the soil, and remove all roots. Then he must soak the earth with scalding water to kill off weed seed and any remaining roots, before the turf paths were laid and the beds planted.

It did not end there. Gardening was steeped in lore, often bizarre and completely fallacious, which nevertheless must have added greatly to the work in the kitchen and fruit garden. To get red apples the trees had to be planted close to mulberry or rose trees, or the grafts dipped in Pike's blood. To breed red peaches, seven days after planting you had to dig up the stone and pour vermilion into the now open shell. The same effect was supposed to come from grafting a peach to a red rose or an almond tree. Rue had to be grafted to fig bark to sweeten its taste and aroma, and cuttings were said to grow better if they were set in a bean or an onion.

Pest control has some even more remarkable rules. You should bury the stomach of a sheep to attract pests, which you presumably then destroyed. An owl with its wings outstretched was fastened to a pole to ward off hail. A toad in an earthenware pot buried in the ground was a defence against lightning and thunder. Smoke was used as a treatment for the various blights, and bay trees were planted as they were believed to act as a magnet to draw disease from other plants.

But not all the techniques were outlandish. Straw and ashes were spread on tender plants to protect them from frost; small bonfires were lit to dispel mist and fog, and wheat or barley grains soaked in wine and hellebore were set out to drug birds that attacked crops. Snails were discouraged, if not killed, by a mixture of oil and soot, and caterpillars were sprayed with ashes of burnt vine shoots mixed with water.

Grafting was regarded as a fine science, indeed an art. The family tree of three or four different types of apples or pears (a skill which had been developed by the ancient Persians) were extremely popular, and it is a technique of great value to owners of small gardens today. But the Elizabethan propagator believed that if fruit trees were grafted on to different stocks this would regulate the times of fruiting. Peaches grafted to mulberries were supposed to fruit and ripen early. For the same effect vines were grafted on to cherries; medlars on to gooseberries or mulberries. There must have been a lot of disappointed Elizabethan propagators!

Attempts at engineering the performance of fruit trees did not end at grafting. Stoneless cherries, it was believed, would be produced from cuttings which had had the pith removed, and if you filled the hollow with a laxative, then the fruit would have laxative properties, which most fruit does have if you eat enough of it. Grafts dipped in honey and spices would produce fruit tasting of the spice selected. Shell-less nuts would grow from kernals wrapped in wool or vine leaves before planting.

To grow peaches and almonds with words written on the fruit, the stones destined for planting were opened and the message engraved on the kernel with a brass stylus. Young fruit was placed into moulds on the branch and left to grow into strange shapes, or bear some design or stamp.

The day-to-day care and running of the kitchen garden was normally left to women, and indeed the weeding women were a familiar sight in English gardens in the early part of this century. It was a sensible arrangement since it was women who had to understand the use of vegetables, fruit and herbs in the kitchen, and also how to use herbs in the treatment of the sick. They also had to grow large quantities of sweet herbs such as lavender, thyme and rosemary to strew on the floors of the great hall and the private apartments.

The dividing line between the physic herb for medicine and the pot-herb for cooking was often indistinguishable since many of the common vegetables, such as cabbages, played a dual role as food and medicine. Red coleworts (cabbages) were an ingredient in a treatment for the bite of a mad dog. Cabbage was also regarded as being good for arresting failing sight, for treating coughs and breathlessness, and the juice was used as an antidote to fungi poisoning. Lettuce was given to insomniacs, and cucumbers were recommended as a cure for red noses.

Onion juice was used as a hair restorer; turnips for hoarseness, coughs, and gout, and the juice was used to temper steel for knives, daggers and swords. Leeks and radishes were an antidote for drunkenness, and asparagus and garlic for toothache. There was little in the kitchen garden which the Elizabethans could not turn to some virtuous use, and this view was to be shared by succeeding generations.

Despite the influence of the old folk lore on gardening practice, enquiring minds turned towards food plants, and the sixteenth and seventeenth centuries saw the publication of a number of books that excited the interest of the educated minority. Many of them were herbals, and therefore concentrated largely on medicinal plants, but they also had the effect of putting into some order the vegetables, herbs and fruits that could and should be cultivated.

The Rev. William Turner published a herbal in 1568, and ten years before Thomas Tusser gave good gardening advice in *One Hundred Pointes of Good Husbandrie*. The great Elizabethan, Francis Bacon, wrote on gardening, and recommended the fruits to be planted in the 'royal ordering of gardens'.

Henry Lyte was a practical gardener, as well as a scholar, and developed a famous herb and botanic garden, and an orchard at his home,

Lytes Cary in Somerset. He also produced an English translation, from the French, with his own additions, of Rembert Dodoens' herbal, which had originally been written in Flemish. It remained a popular book until John Gerarde published his *The Herbal or General Historie of Plantes* in 1597. He too was a practical man and grew many of the plants he described in his own garden. He grew sweet corn and remarked that it ripened in hot summers, and advised that onions should be grown on 'a fat ground well digged and dunged', and gave an insight into the appearance of Elizabethan kitchen gardens when he wrote: 'It is now and then in beds sown alone, and many times mixed with other herbs, as with lettuce, parsnip and carrots.'

But without doubt the essential seventeenth-century reading was John Parkinson's great work, *In Paradisi in Sole Paradisus Terrestris*, in which, apart from dealing with the plants for the pleasure garden, he wrote of 'A Kitchen garden of all manner of herbs, rootes & fruits, for meat or sauce used with us, and An Orchard of all sorte of fruitbearing Trees and shrubbes fit for our land together with the right orderinge planting and preserving of them and their uses and vertues...'

Although he, too, recommended that the kitchen garden should be on one or other side of the house, and away from the best rooms as 'the many different sents that arise from the herbes, as Cabbages, Onion &c. are scarce well pleasing to perfume the lodgings of any house...', he nevertheless accorded it the respect it deserved as he approached the subject of kitchen gardening:

I now proceede to your herbe garden, which is not of the least respect belonging to any man's house, nor utterly to be neglected for the many utilities are to be had from it, both for the Masters profit and pleasure, and the meyneis content and nourishment...

He urged the liberal manuring of kitchen gardens so that the soil should be 'fat, fertill and good'.

In Tudor Britain there were no glossy seed catalogues, and gardeners had to grow and collect their own seed. According to Parkinson the best radish, lettuce, carrot, parsnip, turnip, cabbage and leek seed was grown in England, but he urged kitchen gardeners not to ignore imported seed.

Orchards, he insisted, should take a formal shape and should be planted to protect the pleasure gardens from north-east and north-west winds. The well-ordered estate should have its own nursery for raising fruit trees, and he urged gentlemen to learn the skills of budding and grafting, recommending a kit of instruments for the purpose which would have done credit to a surgeon.

Parkinson's *Theatrum Botanicum: The Theatre of Plantes: or An Universal and Compleate Herbal*, published eleven years later, was a perfect companion volume to *In Paradisi*, providing the kitchen gardener with a difinitive list of plants for the herb beds.

Nicholas Culpeper's *The English Physician* followed in 1652 and was enormously successful, despite the fact that it reeked somewhat of the occult, and was hardly any advance on what had been written before.

If Parkinson set the tone for gardening at the beginning of the seventeenth century, John Evelyn certainly signed off the century with his horticultural output. Apart from translating de la Quintinye, whose work he published under the title of *The French Gardener*, he wrote two small works that can hardly have left the pockets of gardeners who wanted to succeed: *Kalendarium Hortense: or the Gard'ners Almanac*, and *Acetaria. A Discourse of Sallets*. He combined a deep and profound scholarship with a sensitive, almost passionate love of gardening.

Acetaria could, perhaps, be regarded as the first specialist gardening book, since it was devoted to the growing of salad plants. A salad, he said, was '... a particular Composition of certain crude and fresh Herbs, such as usually are, or may safely be eaten with some Acetous Juice, Oyle, Salt, &c. to give them a grateful Gust and Vehicle.' Nothing much has changed.

Salads in his day were varied concoctions, but he spread the net wider than most, reminding his readers that the French and Italians gathered for their salads 'anything almost that's Green and Tender, to the very Tops of Nettles; so as every Hedge affords a Sallet...'

Salad plants, Evelyn directed, should be eaten fresh when they are young and succulent. He had no time for some of the fads perpetuated by Culpeper, for sowing and reaping crops according to the phases of the moon and the position of stars.

Marigolds and Cabbages

The early Spring and ensuing Months (till they begin to mount, and prepare to Seed) is certainly the most natural, and kindly Season to collect and accommodate them for the Table. Let none then consult Culpeper, or the figure-flingers, to inform them when the governing Planet is in its Exaltation; but look upon the Plants themselves, and judge of their Vertues by their own Complexions.

Evelyn was one of the new breed of men who were taking the first tentative steps towards a more modern scientific study of the natural world. He was a Fellow of the Royal Society, which was busy trying to brush away the cobwebs of superstition and quackery. While the French in Burgundy were refusing to eat potatoes because they believed they caused leprosy, simply because the knobbly tubers looked like leprous hands and feet, the Royal Society was urging its Fellows to grow potatoes to test whether they could produce a crop that would be a hedge against food shortage and famine.

3
Hot-Beds and Pine-Pits

Throughout the seventeenth century noblemen like Sir Robert Cecil, the first Lord Salisbury, Charles Villiers, Duke of Buckingham, Sir Edward Wotton, and Sir Dudley Digges, were laying out great gardens, and seeking new plants, including those for the kitchen garden and orchard. Cecil sent John Tradescant the Elder, the first of the botanist gardeners, to the continent to acquire plants for him. He also collected the Portugal quince for Lord Burleigh in 1611.

Tradescant became an addicted collector; his remarkable collection of curiosities was the basis of the Ashmolean Museum in Oxford. He travelled to Russia and found new varieties of red, white and black currants, bilberries, and strawberries. He joined an expeditionary force as a gentleman volunteer to fight Barbary pirates in the Mediterranean, simply so that he could collect the Algerian apricot, and came back with two varieties. His son, John the Younger, worked in Virginia, and is credited with introducing the Evening Primrose (*Oenothera biennis*), which at the beginning of this century was still being eaten as a vegetable.

The interest in establishing kitchen and fruit gardens was such that it supported commercial nursery-men. Arnold Banbury, who ran a nursery garden at Westminster between 1598 and 1665 exported a complete orchard to one John Percivalle in Ireland. He sent twelve apricot trees, four cherries, four nectarines, fourteen peaches, eighteen pears, and twenty-four plums.

Charles I attached the royal seal of approval to gardening, as did his wife, Queen Henrietta Maria. After the Civil War, when Commonwealth government agents were making an inventory of the Queen's Wimbledon estate in 1649 they found a superbly run garden. Orange, lemon and pomegranate trees were fruiting, the orchard supported a large collection of fruit trees, and the kitchen garden was well stocked with herbs and vegetables, and flourishing musk melon beds. There was even a separate artichoke garden.

In keeping with the severe and gloomy mood of the times, the Cromwellian puritans eschewed the frivolity of pleasure gardens, and turned their energies towards economic plants. Vegetable and fruit gardening was officially important. In 1649 Walter Blith in his book *The English Improver, or a New Survey of Husbandry* urged the planting of orchards and vineyards, and the growing of vegetable crops such as cabbages, carrots, onions, parsnips, artichokes and turnips.

A gardening writer of the 1650s, Ralph Austen, tried to discredit and eliminate the old superstitions and folklore surrounding the growing of fruit and vegetables. He tried to encourage the cultivation of Jerusalem artichokes for human consumption, and not just for feed for poultry and pigs. Almost alone, for it was scarcely a popular view, he recognised the value of potatoes in the making of bread, cakes, pastry and pies.

The eighteenth century was a period of excitement, curiosity and enquiry. New lands were being discovered and explored, Britain was building an empire. Every vessel that docked brought new wonders, not least those of the vegetable kingdom. At the same time science was being prised out of the alchemist's den and placed where it belonged, in the laboratory.

Improvement was the order of the day. New methods and technologies were being tried out in industry and agriculture, and gardening was not ignored. It became a past-time for servant and dilettante alike. The art of kitchen and fruit gardening became much more orderly. Although haphazard, the process of selection had improved vegetable types. Instead of the hotch-potch of wild and cultivated plants recommended by Master John Gardener, eighteenth-century kitchen gardens were cropped very much as they are today. Old saws were being abandoned. Grafting, sowing and planting no longer had to be carried out according to a strict observance of the phases of the moon. Indeed in the century before the great master de la Quintinye said of the theory: 'I perceive it was no weightier than Old Wives Tales, and that it has been advanced by unexperienced gardeners.'

At the beginning of the eighteenth century, George London and Henry Wise, in their book *The Retir'd Gard'ner*, which was a translation of *Le Jardinier Solitaire*, to which they added their own expertise, established the pattern of future kitchen gardening.

The book assumes that a man of means is establishing a modest country estate. Four acres are set aside for the kitchen and fruit garden: eight blocks for vegetables, and eight for fruit, with each block being ninety-four feet long and fifty-eight feet wide. A large water basin was set in the centre, for both decorative and practical use. Paths from two feet to seven feet wide divided the beds, and the whole garden was surrounded by a three-foot wide border edged with aromatic herbs: lavender, savory, thyme, hyssop, marjoram, balm, rosemary, double and single violets.

London and Wise recommended vegetables which are quite typical of a good kitchen garden today; long and round turnips, yellow, orange and red carrots, parsnips, skirret, scorzonera, salsify, black and white spanish radishes, Strasbourg parsley, London radish, onions, London and French leeks, rocambole, shallots, garlic, potatoes, asparagus, artichokes, celery, plain and curled endive, cardoons, chicory, red, white and Roman beets, Italian fennel, cauliflower, English, Dutch and Russian cabbage, Dutch and yellow savoys, borecole and colewort.

Strangers in a modern garden would be skirret, a small, parsnip-like root vegetable, rocambole, a type of leek used mainly for flavouring, colewort and cardoons.

Salad vegetables, which were an important part of eighteenth-century kitchen garden produce, included some unexpected bed-mates, such as marrows and spinach. Well-stocked salad beds grew lop lettuce, common, broad and curled cress, turnips, common and white mustard, prickly spinach, chervil, purslane, lamb's lettuce, Sandwich radish, rocket, nasturtium, cabbage lettuce (Brown, Dutch, Silesian, and Red Spanish), cos and Roman lettuce, tarragon, mint, long, short and prickly cucumbers, melons, gourds, pompions (marrows) scurvey-grass and chives.

And in the beds of sweet and pot-herbs would be found thyme, winter and summer savory, winter and summer marjoram, plain and curled parsley, rosemary, hyssop, sorrel, beet, borage, buglos, bloodwort, marigolds, columbine, orache, tansy, alecost (costmary), and sweet maudlin (a type of *Achillea*).

Peas and beans were grown, and London and Wise list four types of kidney beans (large and small, white and speckled), and twenty-one varieties of peas (Edward's Early, Flanders Early, Green's Early, Barnes Hotspur, Sandwich and Reading peas, grey, blue, green and white Rouncivals, large, small and dwarf sugar peas, egg peas, Dutch Admiral's peas, Crown or Rose peas, Hotspur, Gosport, Spanish and Windsor).

The big blocks were subdivided into beds four feet wide with twelve-inch paths between them. Vegetables such as sorrel, beet, parsley, chervil and spinach were sown in drills drawn with a stick, but others were broadcast: 'sow 'em in an even bed and rake the bed lightly after it'. After sowing the vegetable beds were mulched with an inch of manure.

Cabbage, lettuce, celery, cucumbers, Spanish cardoons and pumpkins were germinated in hot-beds before transplanting.

Hot-beds were essential to eighteenth-century gardening, not only were they used to start plants we would now sow in greenhouses or heated frames, but they were used to produce melons and cucumbers.

According to London and Wise they should be constructed from horse manure built into beds four feet high, and four feet broad, and covered with eight or nine inches of mould. About eight days after making they would have generated enough heat for planting, and when necessary were re-heated with fresh dung.

The Reverend Gilbert White, best known for his classic work, *The Natural History of Selborne*, was an indefatigable builder of hot-beds in his garden at Wakes in Selborne village.

His *Garden Kalendar*, which he kept between 1751 and 1773, records the prodigious quantities of dung he used for his beds on which he raised melons and cucumbers. On 12 March 1752 he wrote a memorandum: 'Seven *very full* cart-loads of dung make an exact suitable hot-bed for my great two-light frame: & five for my four hand-glasses.'

So great were the quantities required that he had an arrangement to borrow fresh dung from a neighbouring farmer called Parsons. Presumably it was returned, well-rotted to be spread on the fields. In the spring of 1755 he borrowed seven cart loads, and in March and April of the following year he borrowed eight loads, and in May and June of that year he went to another farmer, John Berriman, and borrowed a total of eleven loads.

Gilbert White and his family lived well off the Wakes garden, for apart from melons, both musk and cantaloup, and cucumbers, he grew broad beans, cabbages, sweet corn, skirret, scorzonera, seakale, the Chilean strawberries, which were introduced in 1714, carrots, parsnips, beets, radishes, lettuce, leeks, onions, salsify, cardoons, artichokes, celery, celeriac, asparagus, garden cress, endive, broccoli, peas, French beans, Spanish radishes (which he called turnip radishes), spinach, rhubarb, gooseberries, currants and the usual orchard fruits.

Philip Miller, the irascible, but brilliant gardener at the Chelsea Physic Garden, which in his time was the foremost botanical garden in the country, in his *Gardener's Dictionary*, underscored the importance of the hot-bed, when he wrote:

> Hot-beds are of general use in these Northern Parts of Europe, without which we could not enjoy so many of the Products of warmer Climes as we do now; nor could we have the Tables furnished with the several Products of the Garden, during the Winter and Spring months, as they are at present in most parts of England, better than in any other Country in Europe; for altho' we cannot boast of the Clemency of our Climate, yet England is better furnished with all Sorts of esculent Plants for the Table, much earlier in the Season, and in greater Quantities, than any of our Neighbours; which is owing to our skill in Hot-beds.

In January, Miller said, the beds produced crops of salad herbs such as cresses, turnips, radish, rape, mustard, coriander, chervil, tarragon, burnet and mint; and asparagus was ready on beds made in November. The following months there were salad vegetables, as well as pot-herbs and aromatic herbs such as winter savory, hyssop, thyme, lavender, rosemary, marjoram, and Swiss Chard. By March the hot-beds were producing cucumbers, asparagus, peas, kidney beans and purslane, along with the usual salads and herbs. The need for well fertilised land for good vegetable crops was well understood in the eighteenth century.

Stephen Switzer, a gardener and seedsman who lived and worked in Westminster, made a close study of fertilisers and the soil. A man of some learning, he described himself as having 'tasted both rough and smooth (as we plainly call it) from the best Business and Books, to the meanest Labours of the Scythe, Spade, and Wheel-barrow.' In 1742 he published an important book, *Ichonographis Rustica: or, the Nobleman, Gentleman, and Gardener's Recreations* in which he gave quite intricate recipes for different types of soil, which he said should be made up into 'Heaps or Lestals, or Magazines'.

Cold clay land needed: 'Three load of natural mould, two load of good rotten dung, one load of sand, if it be had aplenty, the sea-kind, or sharp sand, two loads of the top spit turf in meadows or other kind of rich turf land, and half a load of coal ashes or the sweepings of streets, a small sprinkling of pigeon, sheep or other hot dungs.' It could be further improved with malt dust, coal ashes, wood and straw ashes, and pigeon droppings.

Loose sandy soil was given heart with: 'Three load of natural soil, three load of pond earth, or the scouring of ditches, three load of strong loamy earth, and two load of dung.'

He was a great believer in the scourings of deep ditches and ponds as a general top dressing, but also wrote enthusiastically about the virtues of blood, urine, dung, shavings of horns and hooves, hair, wool, feathers, shells, lees of wine and beer, ashes of all sorts, vegetable matter, leaves, straw roots and stubble. He particularly recommended horse manure for cabbage and cauliflowers.

Ashes were stored undercover for use as a top dressing and included those of coal, wood, kilns, straw, furze, peat fires, leaves, prunings, grass, weeds, and burnt turf. Sand and crushed shells were also used, and rags and tanners bark were composted.

Like so many authorities of the time, Switzer was partly right on a number of things. On the subject of water, he quoted Francis Bacon: 'That for the Nourishment of Vegetables, the Water is all in all; and that the Earth doth keep the Plant upright, and save it from the Extremities of either of Heat or Cold.' Soil analysis was yet to come.

But interesting experiments were being carried out. Lettuces were used to discover the effect of air, and the lack of it, on germination and growth. The experiment proved, not surprisingly, that without air the seeds did not germinate, but when air was allowed into their sealed container, they did.

Air was generally regarded as a source of nutriment for plants, as Switzer explained:

> ... it does not only insinuate itself into the Earth, and amongst the Liquids thereof, and by its own Elastick Quality, and the Genial Force of the Sun, cause that Ascendant Motion or Fermentation, (call it which you will) but also that there is a Nitrous Aliment that enters the Pores of the Tree or Plant, whereby it is wonderfully nourish'd and encreas'd ...

He also advanced the theory that vegetables and fruits need elements in the soil, peculiar to them, to create their individual characteristics and flavours. 'If therefore the Soil, wherein any vegetable or seed is planted, contains all or most of these ingredients, and those in due quantity, 'twill grow and thrive there: Otherwise 'twill not.'

Switzer also subscribed to the popular belief in the spontaneous growth of plants; that the soil itself contained the ingredients that made up seeds, rather than the seeds themselves. He explained: 'That every Earth is endued with a peculiar Faculty of producing Plants peculiar to it; and that it had a seminal Power communicated at the first Creation of things; is, I think, very obvious to the least Observer; Because, if Earth is digged out of the deepest pit, or Well, and carried up to the Top of the highest mountain, it will produce Plants proper to the Country where they grow (though not dug out at the Time when Plants seed).'

But experience taught the eighteenth-century gardener to follow rules as sound today as they were then. When judging soil you should look to the state of the weeds. The best ground was rich in mallows, nettles, docks, hemlock, daisies, clover, charnock and mustard. His general rule was 'Where Weeds and Grass do naturally grow strong and big, that Earth is undoubtedly most rich and fruitful.'

He knew nothing of stratifying seeds, but ruled that hard-shelled seeds such as walnuts and plums should be sown in the autumn, arguing that such seeds needed a long time to swell and break, and it was better for that to happen during the winter months so that the seedlings would get away early in the spring.

While being unaware that legumes fix nitrogen, he recognised that freshly broken ground benefited from a first crop of peas and beans.

Unlike the great landscape gardeners of the eighteenth century, Switzer declared that the kitchen garden should be, reasonably enough, next to the kitchen, but separated from the pleasure grounds by espaliers of apples and pears, which he contended made better windbreaks than walls for the protection of 'tender greens'.

But the fruit garden, he believed should be separate and private, and set on higher ground than the kitchen garden. It had to be walled, and the ideal measurements were forty yards long by twenty-four yards wide, or, if you were doing things on the grand scale, one hundred and sixty yards long and sixty yards wide. However in his opinion the smaller area was sufficient 'to contain the most delicate fruit' which would grow against the brick walls 'being not only the handsomest, but the warmest and kindest for ripening of Fruit, besides the most convenient for nailing.' In Northamptonshire and Leicestershire fruit garden walls were constructed of mud and straw, and said to be superior to brick for ripening.

On the south-facing walls Switzer planted peaches. He recommended a dozen varieties. Against the east- and west-facing walls apricots were grown, either the Orange apricot or the Masculine. Figs, pears and plums were also to be trained against the walls. The beds in the walled fruit garden were planted with strawberries, artichokes and salad vegetables.

The orchard again was to be set separately from the rest of the garden and great care taken in its preparation. The soil had to be ploughed and manured for two years before the trees were planted, and the site open to the south, south-east and south-west, but sheltered from the north winds by woods or espalier trees. There must not be less than eight yards or more than fourteen yards between the trees which should be planted between October and the end of November.

To give it 'the utmost Beauty and Magnificence' the orchard must have a broad walk round it, a grand one through it, and a spacious one across it. The middle walk was through lofty pear trees, the cross walk shaded by apple trees, one end walk was lined with the Golden Pippin, one of the oldest and best loved dessert apples (Muriel Smith in the *National Apple Register* of the United Kingdom says it was recorded in 1625, while George Lindley in his *A Guide to the Orchard and Kitchen Garden* used John Ray's reference of 1688. Certainly the apple still existed when Lindley published his book in 1831).

The other walks in Switzer's orchard were lined with cherries, codlins, and fruit trees forming hedges to '... render your Orchard as delightful as a Grove or little wood'. In its immature state he suggested planting beans or peas between the young trees.

Like John Evelyn before him, Switzer had a great love of trees, and urged landowners to plant small woods dotted around their estates. He had a charming idea of using the small fields surrounded by woods as fruit gardens planted with currants, raspberries, gooseberries and strawberries. Hedgerows, he said, should be planted with filberts, hazelnuts, damsons, crab apples and pears, and while the saplings were establishing themselves, turnips could be grown between them to keep down the weeds. Later the roots could be fed to sheep.

His ideal garden was situated near Bath, where the kitchen garden and orchard were set either side of the house, and there was a greenhouse stocked with orange and lemon trees in tubs which were carried out on to a terrace in the summer.

With the expansion of the Empire and increasing support for exploration the trickle of new plants into the country grew to a torrent, but most of them were either ornamental or of potential use as commerical crops at home and in the colonies. There was precious little interest in new vegetables, although exotic fruits had their enthusiasts.

Sir Joseph Banks, the wealthy Lincolnshire landowner and botanist who had travelled and collected in Newfoundland and Labrador, and had, at his own expense, signed on as botanist with Captain James Cook on the circumnavigation of the world between 1768 and 1771, reflected the current attitude in a paper he wrote on '*Hints on the Subject of Gardening suggested to the Gentlemen who attend the Embassy to China, 1792*'. At the time of writing Sir Joseph was President of the Royal Society, and the unofficial director of the Royal Botanic Garden at Kew, which he had developed into the international clearing house for new plants.

He wrote: 'The delicious flavour of fruit will always induce the rich to pay an exorbitant price for their cultivation and flowers will be supported at a considerable charge, but it is not so with the other esculent vegetables that supply our tables. The Chinese have carrots, cabbage, radishes etc., etc., as may be learned from their paper hangings, but unless these are superior in their flavour to those of the same in Europe, little attention will be paid to them here, we have, in short, so many varieties of cabbages, carrots, turnips etc., that we want no addition for the sake of change. It is intrinsic merit only that will use our gardening to add to the number.'

In short he was saying don't waste your time and valuable cargo space on collecting vegetables that will be little different from those at home.

If they did collect, Sir Joseph cautioned the gentlemen: 'It must be remembered, however, that if particular sweetness is met with in any of these short-lived productions of the earth that it may possibly depend on the soil in which they grow, of the nature of which, if any attempt is made of transporting them to Europe, especial remark must be made.' He was calling for field notes as well as a parcel of seeds.

Despite Bank's interest in new vegetables for human consumption, they were still considered by many to be more suitable food for animals. This was made clear by the agriculturist and writer, Arthur Young, in a book published in 1771 describing his six-month tour of the north of England. He found turnips, cabbages and kohl-rabi being grown to feed cattle and sheep, and carrots for pigs.

Charles Turner, a farmer of Kirkleatham in Cleveland, fed his sheep on broccoli in the spring, and fed his pigs and dairy herd on carrots. Young observed 'several hogs, porkers of six stone, were fatted on them: No pork could be finer, they fatted quick and exceedingly well: The carrots were given raw.'

Potatoes were fed boiled to pigs and poultry, and raw to young cattle. Christopher Crowed of Kiplin cultivated acres of Jerusalem artichokes for his animals. Simon Scroope of Danby grew magnificent 5-lb savoys, and fed them to his cattle. He also grew a cabbage called Anjou, which soared to seven feet tall.

Scroope's carrots were eighteen inches long and eleven inches in circumference. 'They were given to pigs, who fatted so well on them, that a few pease finished them, and the fat was very fine and firm'. And Mr. Scroope went even further, he cultivated onions, celery, endive, garden peas, cos lettuce, cauliflowers and carrots in his fields, declaring to Arthur Young that his experiments were 'a proof that garden stuff may be cultivated to a greater perfection in the fields than in the garden, and to be had there, when they were not to be gained in the latter.'

It was clear that kitchen gardening, indeed gardening of any kind, was not practised with much enthusiasm in the north in the eighteenth century. Young, who was the most assiduous of observers, only mentions one particular kitchen garden in a journey that took him from Bedfordshire to the north and back to Kensington, and that was when he called on Sir Walter Blackett at Wallington, and remarked: 'The new kitchen gardens are excellently disposed, kept in admirable garden husbandry, and the convenience of water very great.'

What he did find were numbers of market gardens; carrot gardens at Sandy in Bedfordshire, asparagus and other vegetables in the Vale of Evesham, and commercial gardening at Hammersmith and Kensington.

Commercial vegetable growing, which had started in medieval times with noblemen selling the surplus from their kitchen gardens and orchards from stalls near St. Paul's Cathedral, and become more organised with the building of Covent Garden market in 1632, grew rapidly in the eighteenth century. Nurseries and market gardens flourished around London at Bromley, Chertsey, Chiswick, Kennington, Hackney and Walworth. At Walworth, James Maddock was selling three hundred and twenty varieties of gooseberries raised from seed in Lincolnshire, which he graded as amber, black, green, red, yellow and white. Elsewhere in the country vegetable and fruit markets were flourishing in Norwich, Bristol, Salisbury, Plymouth, Derby, Birmingham, Leeds, Huddersfield, Manchester, Glasgow, and Cardiff. The growth of industry and the pollution it brought with it was ringing out the death knell for the great gardens of London and manufacturing cities.

But in the country and suburbs kitchen and fruit gardening grew in popularity, and with it a demand for seeds. Apart from selling fruit trees, Henry Woodman, who traded as a seedsman at Strand on the Green, Chiswick, issued a catalogue offering a wide variety of vegetable seeds: early turnip, red, green and yellow top turnips, parsnip, orange carrot,

Welsh onion, Strasburgh and white Spanish onions, Italian celery, London leeks, red and white beet, large nasturtium, Dutch asparagus, cauliflower, yellow savoy, green savoy, true borecole, broccoli, Silesian lettuce, curled endive, red cabbage, early cucumber, ten varieties of melons, scozonera, salsify, Battersea cabbage, bush basil, sweet marjoram, winter marjoram, cardoons, purslane and black Spanish radishes.

Great ingenuity was exercised in the production of fruit. Throughout the century greenhouses were greatly improved, and were used for forcing vegetables as well as growing fruit and rare, tender decorative plants.

Hot walls, which were being used to grow apricots and grapes as early as the 1660s, remained popular. They were considerably cheaper than glass-houses, and remarkably effective. At its most basic it was the utilisation of a wall backed by a fire. The wall backing the kitchen fire was ideal because the heat was pretty constant. But another method was to pile fresh dung against a wall and let that generate heat. The beds in front of the fruit trees were used to force early vegetables under hand lights, or covers made from oiled paper; the latter were widely used in growing melons.

Philip Miller describes in his *Gardener's Dictionary* how fruit was ripened out of season under movable glass screens, and artificial heating, confirming Sir Joseph Bank's assertion that 'The delicious flavour of fruit will always induce the rich to pay an exorbitant price for their cultivation...' Writing in the 1750s, Miller said that as a means of ripening fruit 'it is now pretty much practis'd in England'. To provide for what he described as 'a middling family', presumably not a particularly princely establishment, it was necessary to build a wall ten feet high, and eighty to one hundred feet long. But this was the bare minimum: '...where a person is desirous to have the Fruit in Perfection, and the Trees to continue in a good Condition many years, there should be three times this Quantity of Walling built; so that by dividing it into Three Parts, there will be two Years for the trees to recover their Vigour between the Times of their being forc'd.' The walls were threaded with flues which were heated by boilers at each end, and the trees themselves were protected by lean-to glass screens which could be moved along the wall each year. In the borders in front of the cherries, plums, peaches, nectarines, and apricots, dwarf peas and beans were brought on for early crops. The first cherries were picked in April, and the remainder of the fruit followed in May.

A cheaper system was to build a wooden plank wall, and stack fresh manure against the back to create the heat. But the steam from the dung heaps tended to cause condensation and spoil the fruit.

The lean-to-glass screens were also used against ordinary walls, with a blanket of dung laid at the back of the wall to produce the heat. These sloping hot buttresses of manure, which were built to within four inches of the top of the ten foot walls, had to be changed three times to keep up sufficient heat to ripen cherries by April. But they did produce gooseberries for tarts in February, currants in April, as well as early grapes, apricots, nectarines, peaches, plums, and strawberries.

Heated and glassed pine-pits for growing pineapples were built, and the rich put up huge greenhouses. Lord Petre had three in 1736 on his estate at Thornden Mill, Essex, in which he grew cocoa, coffee, date palms and bananas.

Great care was lavished on the culture of grapes, and there were some magnificent vines to be found around the country. In 1781 one produced a bunch of grapes weighing nineteen and a half pounds; another vine at a house at Northallerton was measured in 1789 and found to cover 137 square yards of wall.

While the wealthy were spending fortunes producing tropical fruits for their tables, the poor exercised their skill in producing giant gooseberries for exhibition. Gooseberry clubs were started in 1740, and some prodigious fruits the size of ping-pong balls, and weighing as much as two ounces each, were exhibited.

The increasing sophistication of vegetable and fruit gardening was reflected in the more imaginative ways of preparing and serving them at the table. Gone were the days of the Anglo-Saxons dressing their vegetables with lumps of bacon fat or lard; disappearing too were the thick, stodgy pottages made mainly from dried peas and beans, flavoured with herbs and cabbage, and occasional pieces of meat, which was the staple of the working people. Rural workers with gardens were growing a wider variety of vegetables than in the past, but where the Enclosure Acts had robbed them of land, and in the towns, the diet of the poor was deplorable. Bread was their staple and fresh vegetables were a rarity.

But not so with the rich. One wealthy landowner had this to say of his kitchen garden:

My salads, roots, and pot-herbs, my own garden yields in plenty and perfection; the produce of the natural soil, prepared by moderate cultivation. The same soil affords all the different fruits which England may call her own, so that my dessert is every day fresh-gathered from the tree.

The eighteenth century saw the introduction of Continental Cuisine, in which vegetables had always played a much more prominent role than in Britain. They were served with practically every meal in well-heeled homes. Even taverns and cookshops began to dish them up with meat pies and joints. One traveller described how he was served cabbage, cucumber and salad with his mutton. But English vegetable cooking certainly was not up to Continental standards. Charles Moritz, a Swiss traveller in England, noted disgustedly: '. . . cabbage-leaves, boiled in plain water; on which they pour a sauce made of flour and butter, the usual method of dressing vegetables in England.'

There was really no excuse for vegetables to be badly cooked since the popular cookery books of the day contained a dazzling display of recipes involving a great variety of vegetables. Carrots were used to make puddings as well as being served with meat, and vegetables and herbs were used extensively in sauces for fish and meat. Artichokes, potatoes, skirrets, parsnips and lettuce were all used to make elaborate pies.

Perhaps the most significant development of the century was the realisation of the health value of vegetables, particularly as an anti-scorbutic. For centuries scurvy had been a recurring scourge, on land as much as at sea. By the end of the winter, and in the early spring, when there was little or no green stuff to be had, scurvy, with all its horrible symptoms, was a common disease. Despite the fact that the Irish, who had been using the potato increasingly in their main diet since the late sixteenth century, were remarkably free of scurvy, the connection between a lack of vegetables in diet and scurvy was a long time being made. Indeed, the only observation made about the Irish and potatoes was that it was proof that the potato was an aphrodisiac, otherwise why did the Irish have such large families!

Dr. Johannes Bachstrom of Leyden is credited with spotting the link in 1734. The Navy took the discovery to heart, and 1768 Captain Cook fed the crew of the Endeavour sauerkraut, a highly effective anti-scorbutic, and concoctions of carrots, celery, oranges and lemon. Admiral Sir Thomas Pasley, in the 1770s, had salads grown in boxes of earth on the deck of his 28-gun frigate, *Sybil*. In 1775 the admiralty ordered that all the seamen were to be given green and root vegetables in their rations, as well as boiled dried peas.

Forty-five years later, when the *Hecla* and *Gripper* were frozen into Winter Harbour, Melville Island, during the 1819–20 expedition to find a north-west passage from the Atlantic to the Pacific, the Commander, William Edward Parry, had to cope with an outbreak of scurvy.

He recorded in his journal: 'I began about this time to raise a small quantity of mustard and cress in my cabin in small shallow boxes filled with mould and placed along the stove pipe; by these means, even in the severity of winter, we could generally ensure a crop at the end of the sixth or seventh day after sowing the seed, which by keeping several boxes at work, would give two or three scorbutic patients nearly an ounce of salad each daily.' Because they were grown in virtual darkness the plants were colourless, but effective for all that. Thus the salad garden went to sea.

Vegetables were even introduced into the rations supplied in hospitals, workhouses and prisons, and in 1776 people were advised to eat more vegetables to counteract obesity – 'we should eat in great moderation and make vegetables the principal part of our food' was the advice given.

By the turn of the century vegetable gardening was firmly established, and the kitchen garden was not only an essential department of every garden, but it was back in its rightful place, close to the house.

In 1829, when the great radical, William Cobbett, published *The English Gardener* he railed against the eighteenth-century fashion for banishing the kitchen garden to a part of the estate sometimes so remote that one visitor to a great house remarked that you needed a guide to find it.

Cobbett turned his withering scorn on one Sir Robert Rich, who bought Waverley Abbey, where there had been a kitchen garden in 'the finest situation for a kitchen garden that I ever saw' until Sir Robert got his hands on it.

Sir Robert Rich tore everything to atoms, except the remaining wall of the convent itself. He even removed the high hill at the back of the valley; actually carried it away in carts and wheelbarrows; built up a new-fashioned mansion-house with grey bricks, made the place look as bare as possible; and, in defiance of nature, and of all the hoar of antiquity, made it very little better than the vulgar box of a cockney.

I must be excused for breaking out into these complaints. It was the spot where I first began to learn to work, or, rather, where I first began to eat fine fruit, in a garden; and though I have now seen and observed upon as many fine gardens as any man in England, I have never seen a garden equal to that of Waverley.

Cobbett firmly adds 'it is most miserable taste to seek to poke away the kitchen-garden, in order to get it out of sight. If well managed, nothing is more beautiful than the kitchen-garden: the earliest blossoms come there: we shall in vain seek for flowering shrubs in March, and early in April, to equal the peaches, apricots and plums; late in April, we shall find nothing to equal the pear and the cherry; and, in May, the dwarf, or espalier, apple-trees, are just so many immense garlands of carnations. The walks are unshaded: they are not greasy or covered with moss, in the spring of the year, like those in the shrubberies: to watch the progress of the crops is by no means unentertaining to any rational creature; and the kitchen-garden gives you all this long before the ornamental part of the garden affords you anything worth looking at. Therefore, I see no reason for placing the kitchen-garden in some out-of-the-way place, at a distance from the mansion house, as if it were a mere necessary evil, and unworthy of being viewed by the owner. In the time of fruiting, where shall we find anything much more beautiful to behold than a tree loaded with cherries, peaches, or apricots, but particularly the two latter? It is curious enough, that people decorate their chimney-pieces with imitations of these beautiful fruits, while they seem to think nothing at all of the originals hanging upon the tree, with all the elegant accompaniment of flourishing branches, buds, and leaves.'

While Sir Robert Rich was everything that Cobbett found objectionable in a gardener, Henry Drummond of Albury in Surrey, came in for his unstinting approval for his kitchen garden, which, he declared, was nearly perfection.

It seems to have been influenced by the guidelines laid down in *The Retir'd Gard'ner*, with its broad walks, and basin of running water.

It is an oblong square; the wall on the north side is close under a hill, that hill is crowned with trees which do not shade the garden. There is a flat, or terrace, in the front of this wall. This terrace consists, first of a border for the fruit-trees to grow in, next of a broad and beautiful gravel walk, then, if I recollect rightly, of a strip of short grass. About the middle of the length, there is a large basin supplied with water from a spring coming out of the hill, and always kept full. The terrace is supported, on the south side of it, by a wall that rises no higher than the top of the earth of the terrace. Then comes another flat, running all the way along; this flat is a broad walk, shaded completely by two rows of yew-trees, the boughs of which form an arch over it: so that, here, in this kitchen-garden, there are walks for summer as well as for winter: on the gravel walk you are in the sun, sheltered from every wind; and, in the yew-trees walk, you are completely shaded from the sun in the hottest day in summer...

The mansion-house stands at a little distance opposite the garden, on the other side of the brook; and, though all the grounds round about are very pretty, this kitchen-garden constitutes the great beauty of the place.

Throughout the nineteenth century the kitchen garden grew in stature with the increasing demand for vegetables, although curiously this part of the national diet was largely denied to children. Vegetables rarely appeared at school meals; according to *Tom Brown's Schooldays* the boys' breakfast was cold beef and pickles. Vegetables and fruits were considered an unnecessary luxury for children, indeed almost to the end of the century it was asserted that fruit and vegetables were actually bad for children, causing stomach upsets and diarrhoea. Some doctors also held the belief that fruit eroded the surface of the teeth.

Quite early in the century vegetarianism made its appearance. From time to time there had been passing fashions for fruit juice cures for obesity, but it was not until 1847 that the Vegetarian Society of England was formed. Its members were regarded as distinctly odd, even suspect, and were ridiculed by the medical profession.

But it was not the vegetarians that boosted kitchen and fruit gardening, but the boom in new varieties available to gardeners.

Up until the nineteenth century relatively few new varieties of vegetables and fruit appeared, and those that did were the product of chance seedlings, and a fairly haphazard selection. Gardeners saved their own seed, and would choose the most robust plants as their seed source. Inevitably from time to time a particularly good strain would emerge. This was especially true of fruit, much of which was raised from seed, the Ribstone Pippin is a classic example of this. Indeed the word pippin means literally a pip, or from a pip.

But in the first quarter of the nineteenth century hybridizing became all the rage, and the enthusiastic endeavours of professionals and amateurs resulted in hundreds of fruit and vegetable introductions.

Thomas Andrew Knight, a friend of Sir Joseph Banks, bred cherries, apples, pears and plums, as well as melons, pineapples, nectarines, strawberries and potatoes. Wild strawberries collected in Virginia and Chile were crossed to produce the parents of our large modern berries.

John Goss and Thomas Laxton worked on peas, and Archibald Finlay, much later in the century, began breeding new varieties of potatoes.

Activity throughout Europe was intense, and some clear idea of the wealth of choice that became available can be gleaned from *The Vegetable Garden* translated from the French and first published in English by William Robinson in 1885. Twenty-eight varieties of carrots are named (nine in a modern seed catalogue); twenty-three pumpkins (three today). No less than ninety-two different cabbages; and an amazing one hundred and ninety-seven peas, which even allowing for the likelihood of synonyms, is a real choice compared with the average of twenty or so offered by today's seedsmen.

The invention of sheet glass, and great advances in the technique of constructing iron frames, and hot water heating, transformed the glasshouse from a novelty to almost a commonplace in nineteenth-century gardening. While the majority of the houses were built for the growing of tropical decorative plants, they ranged from the vastness of the Great Stove at Chatsworth in Derbyshire, which was large enough for Queen Victoria to drive through in an open carriage, to the more modest, but essential status symbol of the newly rich industrialists; many were built to ensure a regular supply of peaches and nectarines, melons and grapes.

The century saw the art of gardening brought to a very fine degree of perfection. Labour was cheap, scientific advances improved methods of cultivation, and for the middle and upper classes money was plentiful. Two world wars have largely ended private gardening on the grand scale, but social changes have made it available to far more people. The twentieth century has brought many gains to the kitchen and fruit garden, and some sad losses. But these are the subject of a later chapter.

4

Of Melon Masters
and The Russian Globe

One of the fruits of adventure and exploration was, quite literally, fruit. Adventurers brought back melons, oranges, lemons, pomegranates and pineapples, and although quite unsuitable for culture in the British climate, the rich and powerful were determined to have them on their tables, freshly picked from their gardens.

The first to test the ingenuity of the gardener was the melon. It was not an entirely unfamiliar fruit, since it was widely grown on the Continent, and had been a favourite of the Romans. Apicius describes a sauce containing pennyroyal which was used to dress the fruit, and it is an interesting area of speculation as to whether the Romans did grow melons at their villas in Britain. If they did the practice certainly did not survive their departure.

George Lindley asserts that 'the melon appears to have been brought into England as early as the year 1570.' Certainly the Elizabethans were growing them for there is a cooking tip of the period which recommends putting a slice of melon into a pot with meat to make it boil faster. They treated them rather like cucumbers, serving them sliced and dressed with pepper and salt.

In his herbal John Gerarde mentions four kinds of musk melon or million, while Henry Lyte refers only to the melon, and says that: 'Melons are sowen in gardens, and they require a fat and well dunged ground, and also a dry ground, standing well in the Sunne, for otherwise you scarce see them proper in this country.'

John Parkinson in *Theatrum Botanicum* mentions only two types, and in *In Paradisi in Sole Paradisus Terrestris* made it clear at the time of publishing, in 1629, that they were relative newcomers, and none too successful in English gardens. He recommended high raised beds of well-rotted stable manure on a south-facing slope. Plants should be raised from Spanish seed, as he said that home-grown seed was rarely effective, and certainly not after the third generation. The seedlings were raised on a hot-bed before being planted out under glass bells, or protected by straw like strawberries. Clearly fruiting depended on a good hot summer.

By the time John Evelyn wrote *Kalendarium Hortense* in 1685 it was evident that melons were raised and fruited on hot-beds, which he said should be made in February.

When Philip Miller wrote his *Gardener's Dictionary* he was able to name eight varieties of melons, of which, in his view, only three were worth growing; the Portugal or Pocket melon, it was also known as King Charles's Pocket melon, which was a musk melon, the Cantaloup and Zatta melons. The Zatta must have been a variety of Cantaloup, for the Italian word for a Cantaloup is Zatta. Not only had the varieties increased in numbers, but growing techniques had become more sophisticated. Nevertheless the culture of melons in the eighteenth century was an expensive, exacting and time-consuming process.

In the first place it was necessary to make sure that your seed came from a reliable source. There was a tendency to go for size, and Miller complained that 'this has occasioned so great a Scarcity of these Fruits, which are tolerable: for it is not only in England, but most parts of Europe, that from the great Quantity of these Fruits which are annually raised, not one in a hundred of them are fit to eat.' The best Cantaloup seed came from Armenia 'where the best Melons in the world grow'. It was never to be sown until it was three years old, and Miller recommended carrying it around in your pocket as it matured.

As well as condemning the practice of growing giant, but tasteless fruits, he was also scornful of people who forced melons. 'It is common to hear many Persons valuing themselves upon having two or three early Melons; which, when brought to the Table, are not so good as a Turnep; and these are procured at a great Expense, and with much Trouble.'

The good melon grower expected his first fruit in June, and would continue cutting until September, or even October. But it was a harvest reaped at the expense of constant care and attention. A compost of two-thirds fresh loam, and one part rotted cows dung, had to be prepared a year ahead, being turned regularly to expose it to sun and frost, and kept absolutely weed free. A trench about eighteen inches deep, and wide enough to accommodate lights was dug and filled with fresh dung (fifteen wheelbarrow loads to each light), covered and allowed to heat. Getting the heat right was a tricky job. Often the dung would get so hot that it would burn the earth laid over it. The knack was to achieve just the right temperature and then lay on a covering of about two inches of the prepared compost. The melon plants were then set into the top of a fifteen-inch-high cone of soil. Watering had to be carefully controlled, because if the plants were over-watered they tended to rot off at the root.

If lights were not used, melons were raised under glass bells, or oiled paper, which was stretched over frames. This latter method was a good deal cheaper than glass, and if properly managed was very effective. But it did mean glueing sheets of paper together and then treating them with linseed oil. When glass bells were used, the beds were covered with matting at night to conserve heat and protect the plants, and whatever system was adopted the melon beds were sheltered from the wind by high reed fencing. The supply of fresh air to the plants had to be constantly monitored, for plants would die if there was too much, or too little air admitted to them. In fact, Miller insisted, melon growing was a one man job, and brought the title of Melon Master. There should be a gate in the reed fence with a lock on it 'and this should be kept locked, that no Persons should be allowed to go in, but those who have Business; for ignorant Persons, having often Curiosity to look into the Beds, open the Glasses, and let the cold Air to the Plants!'

A friend of Philip Miller, who devoted a great deal of his time to growing melons, was the Rev. Gilbert White, and he has left the most detailed accounts of his triumphs and failures in his *Garden Kalender*. It was the record of a constant battle with the hostile British climate, even in his sheltered garden at Wakes in Hampshire. In 1754 violent storms destroyed his oiled paper covers and damaged the melon plants, but with justifiable pride he was able to record on August 7th: 'Cut first Melon, weight $4\frac{1}{2}$ lbs. It was firm and thick fleshed and better tasted than could be expected after such a continuance of shade and wonderful wet weather.'

In March 1755 he was making a six-light bed with no less than twenty loads of dung. The weather was appalling, cold and wet, but proof of Gilbert White's skill was that he was cutting Cantaloups in September weighing over three pounds. In December he had new glass lights made for a bed over thirty feet long. The next year he made a melonry forty-five feet long, and in the March sowed twelve pots of melons, and cut his first fruits in August, but not all of them were good. One from some seed given to him by Philip Miller 'tho' it promised well was very abominable; being about an inch thick in the rind, without any flesh or flavour.' That was on August 29, and on September 11 he cut the second Miller Cantaloup which 'turned out as execrable as the former'.

By 1757, Gilbert White had become a considerable melon expert and was conducting experiments with new varieties, including a Dutch cantaloup that had never been grown in England before. The following year he was testing out new ingredients for his hot beds, making a bed thirty-six feet long and six feet wide from eighteen cart loads of dung and eighty bushels of fresh tan. It heated up so violently that it had to be torn apart to cool it down. Even when it was re-made it generated a tremendous heat, which he concluded was caused by the tan.

I find a moderate thickness of tan, when laid on a good strong bed of dung, to occasion a very dangerous & unequal Heat, so that there is scarce any judging when the earth is free from burning. For in shady weather it will appear very mild; but on a hot morning will rage again as fierce as when it first came to its full heat. Tan gives a mild & lasting heat by itself, but does not seem suitable with dung.

Despite the difficulties, by the beginning of August he had set forty melons, and by the twenty-second he was cutting the first of them. Although Gilbert White's interest turned increasingly to natural history, and his enthusiasm for gardening seemed to dwindle, he nevertheless continued to cultivate melons.

George Lindley was another melon enthusiast, so much so that he was moved to write in 1831 '. . . it stands so high in general estimation for the richness of its flavour, independent of its magnificent appearance, that no dessert can be considered as complete without it, so long as it continues in season.' He named twenty-four different varieties, under the headings of summer and winter melons. Winter melons had to be kept for some months before eating. Hot-beds were still the main method of cultivation, although frames were being increasingly used.

Forty-one years later William Rhind, in his *History of the Vegetable Kingdom* recorded that the *Fruit Catalogue* of the Horticultural Society listed no less than seventy-one varieties. The increase in the numbers was due to the more certain cultivation under glass, rather than the tricky business of hot-beds.

Techniques had so improved that by the time *The Vegetable Garden* was published in English, the varieties recommended for British gardens had grown to ninety. Greenhouse culture was the choice of experts, and one writing in a gardening magazine told gardeners to grow them like cucumbers. 'Melons grown like Cucumbers, and in a house with them if need be, will be continually gaining strength, and, almost incredible as it may appear to some, will set fruit naturally and at different times.'

Cheap bulk imports of melons have largely banished them from the kitchen garden, although there are still a good number of enthusiasts cast in the Gilbert White mould, who prefer to take the trouble to grow their own.

Virtually contemporary with the melon as a new introduction into English gardens was the orange, which was even more taxing to skill and ingenuity, and to the purse, because you could not get away with a hot-bed and glass lights. Oranges had to be sheltered for much of the year and this necessity produced some of the most beautiful and elegant garden architecture – orangeries.

Oranges, and in fact all the citrus fruits, originated in China and south-east Asia. From China oranges travelled to India where the Arabs found them and are said to have brought them through Iran to Syria, from where they eventually reached Italy and France. The bitter, so-called Seville oranges were introduced to Spain from North Africa. Many centuries were to pass before they were brought into England, probably during the early part of the sixteenth century. Sir Walter Raleigh is credited with importing the first fruit, and Sir Francis Carew, who married Sir Walter's niece, is said to have planted the seeds from these oranges and raised the first orange trees on British soil.

Whether or not this is true, Sir Francis certainly did grow oranges with great success at Beddington in Surrey. In 1695 it was recorded that there had been orange trees on the estate for one hundred years and that they always fruited. Remarkably they were planted in the open ground, but had a moveable cover to protect them during the most bitter months of the year. At the beginning of the eighteenth century the trees in this remarkable orchard had grown eighteen feet tall, and in 1738 a permanent glass-house-like structure was built to completely enclose the trees, but to no avail, for an intense, deep frost the following year destroyed them.

It must have been a particularly bitter frost to have killed trees that were so well protected, for in 1629 John Parkinson's instructions seemed to afford only relatively slight protection. If you did not have an orangery, then the orange trees were planted against a wall, and covered in the winter with boards and cloth.

Lemon and citron trees were even more sensitive to the British winter, although Rhind asserts that 'for a hundred years, in a few gardens of the south of Devonshire, they have been seen, trained as peach trees against walls, and sheltered only with mats of straw during the winter. The fruit of these is stated to be as large and fine as any from Portugal.'

Oranges in any quantity were probably first seen by Englishmen fighting in the Crusades, and they generated many fanciful beliefs. Some declared them to be the fruit that brought about the downfall of Adam and Eve, to others they were the Golden Apples of the Hesperides, which grew in the garden in the land of the sunset, guarded by a dragon and the nymph daughters of Hesperus.

Lemons and citrons were not grown as extensively as oranges, although certainly the lemon was being cultivated at the Oxford Botanic Garden in 1648, and the Duke of Argyle grew the trees against a heated wall at Whitton. Towards the end of the nineteenth century London nursery gardens were offering twelve varieties, as well as five types of lime.

Quite apart from their fruit, oranges were valued for their beauty. The most usual way of growing them was in large square tubs which were hauled out on to a terrace or into a special orange garden in the summer where the beauty and scent of the flowers combined with the growing and ripening fruit.

During the eighteenth century it became increasingly popular to try to grow them in the open. Philip Miller reported: '... and some curious Persons have planted these Trees in the full Ground, and have erected moveable Covers over these Trees in Winter, which are so contrived as to be taken away all Summer: where these have been well executed, the Trees have made great Progress in their Growth, and produced a much larger Quantity of Fruit, which have ripened so well, as to be extremely good for eating.'

Miller lists twenty varieties of oranges which were grown by eighteenth-century enthusiasts, some of them such as the Horned orange, the Large-Warted orange and the Distorted orange being grown as curiosities. But the so-called Common orange was most generally cultivated, with the best plants being imported from Italy, although the keenest gardeners raised their own stocks from pips potted and plunged in a hot-bed, on to which they budded their favourite varieties.

The citron was also grown, and Miller lists seven varieties, and twelve of lemon, and two limes.

Thomas Mawe and John Abercrombie in their successful book, *Every Man his Own Gardener*, published in 1794, considered citrus trees a useful addition to the orchard, despite the fact that they needed the most constant and careful attention throughout the year. When they were under-cover they had to be given air whenever the weather allowed. They should never be allowed to dry out, but never over-watered. When the trees flowered the blossoms had to be thinned, but nothing was wasted because the thinnings were made into orange flower water, which was widely used in eighteenth-century cooking and perfumery. The soil in the cases had to be regularly refreshed, and the fruit thinned. An interesting use was made of orange seedlings as a salad plant.

Another fruit tree to arrive in the sixteenth century was the pomegranate. Although it was well known by reputation as an ancient fruit (Solomon grew orchards of them), it was not introduced into England until 1596, when John Gerarde grew trees in his London garden. It was something of a disappointment, because while the trees appeared to survive quite well out of doors, and even to produce their beautiful flowers, they would not set fruit. Rhind says it grows well out of doors, but normally trees had to be protected in the winter with wooden structures with windows, or giant straw bee hives. Pomegranates were fruited in greenhouses, where their large fruits remained on the trees throughout the winter as a much admired ornament.

But of all the exotic fruits, none excited the enthusiasm and ingenuity of the British gardener more than the pineapple. In the eighteenth and nineteenth century, and even into the present century, the dining tables of the great houses were incomplete without their home-grown *ananas* among the dessert. It was a fruit considered worthy on more than one occasion of being presented as a gift to a reigning monarch. Despite being expensive and demanding to grow, even people of quite modest means installed pine-pits in their kitchen gardens.

The pineapple is a native of South America, and was said to have been introduced to Britain in 1690, probably by way of Holland, although there is some dispute about the actual date of its arrival. The famous painting of King Charles II being presented with the first pineapple grown in this country by his gardener is open to some doubt, and it has been suggested that the fruit was actually grown in Holland.

A painting by T. Netscher, dated 1720, of a pineapple grown in the garden of Sir Matthew Decker at Richmond in Surrey, is also claimed to be the first pineapple grown in this country, and it is interesting that in 1716, when she was on her way to Constantinople, the highly observant Lady Mary Wortley Montagu was served pineapple as a dessert in Hanover and remarked that she had never seen the fruit before, and believed it was unknown in England.

While there may be arguments about exactly who it was who first grew pineapples in Britain, the fact is that by the nineteenth century gardeners had become extraordinarily expert in the culture of this luscious fruit. Rhind wrote that the English-produced fruit was regarded as superior to those grown in hot climates 'because the English gardeners may, by skilful treatment and choice of sorts, more than make up for the want of sun and the deficiency of natural temperature.'

Philip Miller, who listed six varieties, which included the Sugar-loaf-pine, the pineapple with smooth leaves, and the pineapple with shining-green leaves, further confused the origin of the fruit by saying that it probably came from Africa 'where, I have been informed, they grew in uncultivated places in great Plenty'. He also casts some further doubt on the claim that the plant was introduced to British gardens in the seventeenth century, when he wrote in the 1750s that 'it hath been very lately that it was introduced into the European Gardens, so as to produce fruit.' Coming from a man regarded at home and abroad as a leading expert on plants and horticulture (even Linnaeus travelled to England to meet him), this statement is important.

He said that the first man to successfully produce fruit in Europe was one Monsieur Le Cour of Leyden in Holland, and then only after many trials and failures.

> ... and it is to this worthy Cultivator of Gardening, who did not spare any pains or Expence to accomplish it, that all the Lovers there of are obliged, for introducing this King of Fruits amongst them; and it was from him that our Gardens in England were first supplied...

Following these first introductions, large numbers of plants began to arrive from America, but they did not produce very high quality fruit, and even worse were the carriers of an aphid which spread to the orange and lemon trees growing in gardens, particularly around London, which involved gardeners in having to sponge the leaves of infected plants with a wash made from a strong infusion of tobacco stalks and water.

When pineapples first appeared they were grown in hot-beds made from tanners bark and kept under lights, but improved knowledge and techniques, and the enormous popularity of the fruit, led to the development of pine-pits, a special greenhouse heated by hot-air flues for growing the mature plants and ripening the fruit. A small house was used to raise the young plants, so that a well organised garden could ensure a steady supply of fruit.

By the early nineteenth century gardeners were producing fruit of prodigious size. In June 1820, a Mr. John Edwards of Rheola in Glamorganshire, presented King George IV with a fruit of a variety called New Providence which weighed nine pounds, four ounces, and a year later in the *Transactions of the Horticultural Society* another of the same variety was recorded as weighing in at ten pounds, eight ounces. It was grown by Lord Cawdor's gardener, Mr. Buchan, at Stackpool Court, Pembrokeshire, stood ten and a half inches high, and was part of the dessert at the Coronation banquet.

By 1831 George Lindley was able to list no less than thirty-seven varieties of pineapple cultivated in Britain, and suggested eight that should be grown in the small garden: Black Antigua, Black Jamaica, Enville, New Black Jamaica, Queen, Ripley, Russian Globe and White Providence.

Methods of cultivation had changed little from those established in the mid-1700s, with the young plants being raised in hot-beds, and the mature plants finished and fruited in tan-beds in a pine-pit, which had to be kept hot and moist; seventy degrees in the winter, and allowed to rise to one hundred degrees or more in the summer.

5

Cottagers, Doctors, Bus Drivers and Opera Singers

While the wealthy enjoyed the produce of their walled kitchen gardens, orchards, hot-beds and greenhouses, lavishing money and labour on the production of exquisite fruits and vegetables, the scene in the cottage gardens of the labouring poor was very different.

In medieval times the cottage was often little more than a flimsy shelter soused in smoke and soot (the fireplaces had no chimneys), and an earth floor that would become churned into a quagmire in wet weather. The garden or close was an enclosure in which the occupier grew cabbages, leeks, onions, garlic, mustard, peas, beans, shallots, parsley and chervil. He usually had some apple and pear trees, and sometimes a cherry. But gardening had to be fitted in between farm work for the local lord of the manor, or, if he was lucky enough, on his own strip of land. The demands of the local magnate came first, and the growing of grain to support stock and family, came before the vegetables could be tended, despite the fact that they were vital to the main diet of the peasants (this was bread and pottage, a thick soup made from dried peas and beans, to which cabbage and the other vegetables and herbs were added). Beans and peas were also ground and added to grain flour for bread making.

As time passed the cottage garden evolved towards something closer to that charmingly, if perhaps a little romantically, immortalised by the artists William Coleman, Helen Allingham and Myles Birket Foster, and later still so assiduously cultivated by middle-class 'cottagers'.

Cottage women were educated in the use of medicinal herbs by the nuns who grew them in the convent gardens, and soon began to grow their own in their own gardens. The culinary skills of the manor kitchen spread, and sweet and pot-herbs joined the more basic vegetables: violets, marigolds, primroses, strawberries and roses, so widely used in salads, brought colour to the small enclosures. Apricots and grapevines appeared on cottage walls, and as new vegetables were grown in the kitchen garden of the great house so, inevitably, they found their way into cottage gardens.

William Cobbett, who did not have too much time for fancy things (he regarded tea and potatoes as particularly pernicious introductions), did, in his book *Cottage Economy*, recommend growing maize in cottage gardens. Indeed, he went so far as to call it Cobbett's Corn; it was a dwarf variety which his eldest son had introduced and, he said, would always ripen in the British climate. He grew it at his market garden in Kensington, and claimed that it would ripen perfectly even in the coldest summers. It would, he said, make excellent flour for bread and puddings, but best of all it should be used to fatten the labourer's hog. He also urged the growing of swedes and turnips, partly for the pot, but mainly to fatten animals. Cobbett was definitely a beer and beef man.

Cottages and cottage gardens rarely occupied the best land, and the cottagers exercised considerable skill to get the best from their soil. Arthur Young in his travels through the north of England was greatly impressed by the produce of a turnpike keeper on the road to Brough in Yorkshire: 'The turnpike keeper in his little garden, which is taken from the waste, shews what might be done with this land: He raises excellent potatoes, good garden beans, and admirable turnips.'

At Swinton a mine-owner and farmer, William Danby, enclosed plots of moorland for the miners so that they might grow vegetables for their families and feed for a cow or two, or pigs and poultry. One of his miners, James Croft, took advantage of the extra land. He worked a shift from midnight to mid-day in the mine, and cultivated his land during the day, only allowing himself four hours sleep out of the twenty-four, and through his hard work he ultimately became a successful tenant farmer.

Despite the fact that Cobbett would have preferred cottagers to brew and bake, and fatten hogs, and eschew such alien things as tea and potatoes, cottage gardeners did take to the new and unusual, as much from necessity as anything else. Before the potato became generally accepted, the working classes found it an agreeable and valuable source of protein, and they became expert producers of them, particularly the early varieties such as Broughton's Dwarf, Ash-leaved Kidney, Fox's Seedling, Early Mule, Nonsuch and Goldfinger. And their skill paid off, for by the 1870s potatoes were well and truly in fashion, and there was a tremendous demand for earlies to grace the most elegant dining tables. A new cottage industry grew up raising them in beds of light, rich soil protected against frost with turf walls, and screens of reeds and straw. A contemporary observer wrote that 'as much as £70 had been offered by local dealers for the produce of a little cottage garden, not large enough for the support of a cow.'

Cottage gardens were too small, however pretty and charming the crowded, rampant vegetation might have appeared to the passer-by, to do the job of yielding a large part of the food for the families. In fact they were no more than the uneven-handed pay off for the loss of common land which started as a trickle with the enclosures in the reign of Queen Elizabeth I, and grew to a torrent between 1760 and 1818.

The enclosures transformed Britain, physically as well as socially, and had a most dramatic effect on gardening. On the one hand it enabled the landowners to gain almost complete control of the land (no more common land to interfere with grand plans) so that they could develop their farms, and also lay out their great gardens and parks, with their kitchen and fruit gardens, orchards, greenhouses, hot-beds, pine-pits, orangeries and melonaries; on the other it enabled them more easily, and in too many cases too ruthlessly, to manipulate the rural workforce. The peasants who had enjoyed a small measure of independence through their stake in common-land were now squeezed into their cottages set on an 'ideal' eighth of an acre of land. To survive and feed their families they had to work for the land-owner and do as the land-owner directed.

Enclosures during the time of Elizabeth I were only a foretaste of what was to come. Between 1760 and 1818 no less than 3,500 Acts of Parliament were responsible for enclosing over 5,000,000 acres of land. The land given to the peasants to compensate for the loss of common land rights was not enough to enable them to make a living, and too expensive to fence, which forced them into selling the little they were left with to land-owners greedy to extend their holdings.

Agricultural wages were pitifully low, and increasingly the peasants were driven off the land and into the burgeoning industrialised urban areas. Denied the traditional system of paid work and common land, the poor became poorer, a fact proved by the grim figure for poor relief in England and Wales that grew from £700,000 in 1750 to £8,000,000 in 1818.

It was against this harsh background that a new method of vegetable and fruit gardening came into being: the Allotment System.

Before the end of the eighteenth century a small number of landowners realised that too much had been taken away from the rural working classes. Men like the Earls of Winchelsea and Chichester, Lord Carrington and the Duke of Ancaster began setting aside land as allotments for their labourers, and in 1845 the General Enclosure Act gave the Enclosure Commissioners special powers to allocate parcels of land for allotments. Before that, an Act in 1782 allowed guardians of the poor to enclose up to ten acres of waste ground near poor houses to be cultivated by the inmates.

Parish wardens were given power by Parliament in 1819 to let up to twenty acres of parish land as allotments, and that limit was raised to fifty acres in 1831, two years later allotment schemes were in operation in forty-two per cent of all parishes in England and Wales.

Even though it might have seemed like too little too late, allotments were not popular with land-owners and farmers who claimed that if their workers were allowed land on which to grow vegetables and fruit for their families this would be a waste of their labour; other people argued that the allotments were merely an excuse for avoiding paying the working classes a proper wage. And there were those who wanted the size of allotments restricted to half an acre or less, because, they said, if more land was given, labourers would subsist on it and refuse to work for agricultural employers.

It was extraordinary that anything so simple and inoffensive as an allotment where a person might grow food should arouse such passions, and in some cases the most ridiculous fears. There was a body of virtuous thinkers who declared that allotments would be a way of diverting the working classes from a life of drunkenness and licentiousness, and tenancy agreements often contained clauses that bound the tenant to being a regular churchgoer who would guarantee to bring up his family in a decent and orderly manner. Clearly it did not always work for there is a popular story of a London allotment plot-holder who kept his mistress in his garden shed!

In the early days of the allotment movement the plots were in the country where it was hoped they would stem the drift from the land, but they were invariably sited well away from villages, which made them impracticable and unpopular. It was among the urban industrial workers that the allotment took root, usually in plots sited on the edge of towns. During the second half of the eighteenth century small plots known as 'Guinea Gardens' from the annual rent, were established in Birmingham, while Southampton had to wait until 1850 for its first allotments.

Artisans and factory workers took to gardening with great enthusiasm. They grew superb vegetables, and became masterly cultivators of prize flowers. The first rose show in England is said to have been held at an inn near allotment gardens in Nottingham.

Towards the end of the nineteenth century allotments became a major issue in national politics. Attempts to have the future of allotments enshrined in an Act of Parliament had met with great resistance. In 1886 an Allotments Bill was introduced, but it was held in abeyance until the outcome of a by-election in Spalding in Lincolnshire where the Conservative candidate was being challenged by an Allotment candidate. When the Allotments candidate won the seat the Bill became an Act which compelled local authorities to provide allotments where there was a need. The Councils resented the new law (Councils traditionally have a predatory eye on allotment land) and they used every means they could to avoid complying with the Act, particularly in Lincolnshire, where the Conservatives had been dealt such a heavy electoral blow. Two years after the Act had been passed there were applications for a total of 1,600 acres, but not a rod, perch or pole was provided. In the 1889 County Council elections the Allotments Party took control in Lincolnshire, but even then it took another four years to increase the available acreage to anything like that demanded.

Between 1873 and 1895 the number of allotment plots in Great Britain nearly doubled from 244,268 to 482,901. Towards the close of the nineteenth century there was some confusion between smallholdings on which people raised stock as well as vegetables, and the true garden allotment. Eventually the distinction was drawn between plots cultivated by the spade and those cultivated by the plough, and in 1900 nearly two-thirds of allotments were garden-sized, thus setting the tone for the urban allotment; a new style of kitchen gardening which was to play a vital role in the coming years.

The First World War gave a tremendous boost to allotment gardening. The 'Every-man-a-Gardener' campaign led to special powers being granted to local authorities under the Defence of the Realm Act to obtain as much land as could be used by amateur gardeners; undeveloped land, playing fields and parts of parks were roped in. Industry and the railway companies let out the unused acres, and between 1914 and 1918 the number of railway plots increased from 27,680 to 93,473. The coal mining companies allowed people to grow vegetables and fruit on land earmarked for slag tips. Before the war in England and Wales there were 600,000 allotments, by 1918 there were 1,500,000 and the kitchen gardening heroes of the war came from the towns.

A Board of Agriculture survey in 1916 found that the urban plots, which were up to a maximum of 600 square yards, were 'Thoroughly cultivated, liberally manured and intelligently cropped on the most intensive lines.'

They yielded, the survey discovered, crops equal to those produced by the best market gardens. But in the rural areas where the allotment movement had been started, it was a dingy picture of plots from a quarter to one acre 'roughly cultivated, scantily manured, and cropped with little method or foresight'.

After the war 50,000 acres of requisitioned land had to be returned to its owners, leaving a demand which outstripped the supply. The demand came from returning servicemen, a renewed interest in gardening created by the war-time campaign, and the high price of fresh vegetables. Between the end of the war and 1926 there were three new Allotment Acts, all designed to safeguard the provision of allotments, but in 1929 the demand for plots began to fall, only to rise again in 1931 because of the effects of the Depression.

By the outbreak of the Second World War there were 110,000 acres of allotment land in Britain. Once again emergency powers were invoked to provide more land, and at the end of 1942 there were over 1,400,000 allotments, as well as other plots and home gardens under cultivation, and allotments alone were credited with producing 1,300,000 tons of food.

The allotment movement was by now so successful that when the Labour Government was formed at the end of the war, the Chancellor of the Exchequer, Sir Stafford Cripps, told the nation that allotment cultivation was vital as a means of solving the nation's economic problems. In 1948 the Minister of Agriculture, Mr. Tom Williams, attended the Annual Conference of the National Allotments and Gardens Society. He told the delegates 'Today, we are digging for our very lives, for food, for dollars and for our self-respect'.

But while the Government wanted kitchen-gardeners to produce more and keep down imports, the planners wanted land for houses and open spaces for recreation. The 'Dig for Plenty' campaign was a sad failure. With peace the urgency had gone out of the appeal, and following the pattern of the past, the demand for allotments began to slide, discouraged by the constant nibbling away of allotment land for development.

In 1949 the Government-sponsored Allotments Advisory Committee said there should be a target of four acres of allotments for every thousand people. That would have meant that by 1960 there would have been 200,000 acres of allotment land available in England and Wales. The real figure was a mere 67,804 acres, and forty per cent of that was shared among the rural population, which was only twenty per cent of the whole. The remainder was shared among the 40,000,000 living in the urban areas, and that was an average of just over one acre for every thousand people.

Between 1950 and 1964 the number of allotments fell from 1,100,000 to 729,013.

Since 1950 there has been precious little attempt by either governments or local councils to stimulate interest in allotment gardening. There is the comfortable belief that should the need ever arise again for a national effort by gardeners, there will always be parks and playing fields to be put to the spade. Town planners loathe allotments. They find them untidy and inconvenient, and some of the tenancy regulations are so pettyfogging that it would seem they are deliberately intended to discourage would-be plot-holders. In one agreement there was a clause that stated: 'Under no circumstances shall the tenant permit seeds to fall on other gardens'.

In the Departmental Committee of Inquiry into Allotments, better known as the *Thorpe Report*, which was published in 1969 and was the last serious attempt by a Government to look at the problems of allotments, a number of Parish Clerks were questioned about their attitude to them. Their replies reveal something of the official mind:

There is a lack of demand; this may be due to the fact that the allotments are some distance from the village and have no amenities.

Today, pensioners want to rest, not work.

There are now no poor people in the parish.

In 1964 in England and Wales there were 5 London Boroughs, 10 Municipal Boroughs, 51 Urban Districts and 1 New Town Authority who provided no allotments at all, and allotment land continues to shrink throughout the country.

While the *Thorpe Report* describes a somewhat depressing picture of the state of the modern allotment movement, it was by no means entirely negative. The Inquiry team, which was based at Birmingham University, decided to redesign an allotment for the second half of the century.

Professor H. Thorpe, chairman of the Inquiry, picked on the Bordesley Green site set in a predominantly working class area of Birmingham, and hemmed in with factories and housing. He and his assistants drew up a set of plans which the plot-holders did not like at all. For one thing they involved cutting down mature trees, and the gardeners feared this would drive away the wildlife that made the site such a charming oasis. A deputation of tenants, whose ages ranged from eighteen to seventy went to see the Professor and as a result of the meeting the plans were redrawn, sixty per cent by the University and forty per cent by the allotment holders.

Now splendidly known as the Bordesley Green Ideal Allotment Holders Association, the site is the largest in Europe, and tenants travel up to ten miles from their homes to cultivate the soil of this former farm and market garden once famous for its rhubarb.

Despite vandalism and pilfering, and the occasional attack on show pumpkins and marrows by jealous rivals, there is no lack of takers for plots, neither is there any let up in the pressure from council and developers for the Association to give up its land. But the plot-holders will not leave. They are the people who, when asked why they wanted plots by the Inquiry, said it was for the love of gardening, and to produce fresh vegetables of a better quality that they could buy in the shops.

Mr. Fred Jex, the Honorary Secretary of the Barnet Federation of Allotments, could have been speaking for them all when he told a *Times* interviewer in June 1983:

I've had an allotment since I came out of the Army in 1946 – I applied to the local council – there were a few available after the 'Dig for Victory' campaign. It was ten poles and I kept it until the powers that be decided to put Brent Cross on top of it. All the manuring and hard work for nothing! I had a lot of strength in those days!

He got a new allotment, and said:

I manure it every autumn ready for brassicas and potatoes. At the moment I've got leeks, beetroot, French beans, potatoes, early and late – we reckon to eat our own from July one year to May the next. Tomato plants, big bed of onions, broad beans, some early cabbage. The gooseberries are just coming and the rhubarb's just finished; strawberries are coming to. In a good year I reckon not to buy any vegetables at all. I give away more than I use – and tell people they can go and pick, but that seems too much effort. When you grow your own you can pick in the morning and eat at lunchtime.

On the site where I am there are one hundred and ninety allotment holders – we all help each other, share. We've got all sorts – doctors, opera singers, bus drivers, labourers. You forget rank on an allotment... you see a lot of people still have their roots in the country, even if they live in high rise flats.

And for those who would see allotments fade into the pages of gardening history, it is worth considering the contemporary experience in America where there has been a huge resurgence in the allotment movement which there is called Community Gardening.

David Zahller, Community Garden Co-Ordinator with the United States Department of the Interior in Washington, D.C., says: 'There are dozens more applications for gardens than available garden plots each year' – and these gardens are specifically for vegetable production.

In 1971, according to The American Community Gardening Association, fewer than 25,000,000 American households (thirty-five per cent of the total) grew some or all of their vegetables. Ten years later over 38,000,000, or nearly half of all households were kitchen gardening. Two years ago 1,500,000 families were involved in community gardening, and a Gallup Poll conducted in the same year indicated that 7,000,000 more families would like to be in the movement if the land was available.

America is a country that is and has been racked by urban social problems; maybe kitchen gardening is one potential balm. Certainly the American experience of the community gardening movement is worth taking into account before more British allotments disappear under concrete.

6
Vegetables at War

Kitchen gardening on a truly national scale, in town and country, came into its own as never before during the Second World War. Certainly the vegetable and fruit growing campaign of the First World War had been a considerable success, helped no doubt by King George V and Queen Mary being photographed digging potatoes, and Princess Mary, the Princess Royal, photographed clambering up a ladder in the orchard at Frogmore. But that campaign came nowhere near the triumph of 'Dig for Victory', which was launched in a Ministry of Agriculture broadcast on 4th October, 1939, which said: 'We want not only the big man with the plough but to get the little man with the spade busy by this autumn . . . Let 'Dig for Victory' be the motto of everyone with a garden.' And Winston Churchill endorsed this in November 1940 when he told the House of Commons: 'Every endeavour must be made to produce the greatest volume of food of which this fertile island is capable.'

In the first 'Dig for Victory' leaflet the Minister of Agriculture and Fisheries addressed this message 'to everyone who has or can get an allotment or garden'.

Owing to the shipping position we shall need every bit of food we can possibly grow at home.

Last summer many gardens had a surplus of perishable vegetables such as lettuce and cabbage. This winter those same gardens are getting short not only of keeping vegetables such as onions, carrots and other root crops, but also of fresh winter vegetables such as late cabbages, savoys and kale.

We *must* try to prevent that happening this year. Next winter is going to be a critical period.

Gardeners responded with tremendous enthusiasm. Schoolchildren dug up the perimeters of sports fields and planted vegetables, railway sidings were cultivated, RAF pilots and air-crew grew radishes beside the runways, and crops were grown in the dry moat around the Tower of London, despite the fact that some of the vegetables were damaged by bombs and shrapnel. Even the bomb sites themselves were used to raise food.

The work of food production went on with the conversion of lawns and public park flower beds into kitchen gardens. Golf courses and even spare ground in cemeteries came under the spade. Potatoes, beetroots and parsnips were planted in the flower beds at Hampton Court and Sandringham, and vegetables were cultivated in the hallowed grounds of Hurlingham Polo Club in London, and in Hyde Park and Kensington Gardens.

A 'Dig for Victory' broadcaster urged the nation to 'turn our gardens into munitions factories, for potatoes, carrots and onions are munitions of war as much as shells and bullets are.' While the gardeners were busy tilling and planting, the Government's propagandists were cheering from the sidelines with slogans like:

We need all the food we can get.

Turn over a new leaf – eat vegetables daily to enjoy good health.

Dig harder to beat the U-boat.

For vitality eat Greens.

Save our seeds.

Potato Pete and Dr. Carrot were invented to encourage the eating of those vegetables, along with slogans like:

Carrots, bright treasures dug from good British Earth and

Potatoes . . . a rich store of all-round nourishment.

The propagandists even got into the hit parade with a patriotic gardener's jingle.

Dig! Dig! Dig! And your muscles will grow big.
Keep on pushing the spade!
Never mind the worms
Just ignore their squirms
And when your back aches, laugh with glee
And keep on diggin'
Till,we give our foes a wiggin'
Dig! Dig! Dig! to victory.

In 1939 it was estimated that an additional 500,000 allotments well worked would feed 1,000,000 adults and 1,500,000 children for eight of the twelve months. The extra allotments were found when the numbers increased from 815,000 in 1939 to 1,450,000 in 1942.

With the basic ration of meat, fats, eggs, milk and sugar so tiny (each commodity was measured in ounces per head per week, not pounds), it was vital for people to get the bulk of their food from vegetables. The problem was that before the war a huge proportion of the nation's supply of fruit and vegetables had been imported. Seventy-four per cent of fruit, including tomatoes, was imported along with six per cent of potatoes, and eight per cent of all other vegetables. It was a big gap to fill in a hurry, and when France and the Channel Islands fell to Germany virtually the entire supply of onions dried up. An onion distribution scheme was introduced in the autumn of 1941 and people had to register with their greengrocer for the three pounds they were allowed during the onion season. A maximum price had to be set to stamp out profiteering. Even an onion substitute was invented, which was nothing more than water with a revolting smell.

One anonymous poet was moved to mourn the scarcity of the onion:

When I was quite a tiny child
My temper was extremely mild;
One thing alone could make me wild;
The evil-smelling onion.

I grew adult, as children do;
My tastes inclined to flavours new,
And steadily upon me grew
A passion for the onion.

Marmalade, butter, eggs and cheese,
I bore it when they rationed these,
But who could guess that they would seize
The sweet and lovely onion?

My cupboard might as well be bare.
Bereft, I wander everywhere
And try, nose in the empty air,
To sniff a whiff of onion.

Margaret Crompton, the biographer of Charlotte Brontë, and George Eliot, kept a private journal throughout the war years, and on 22 February 1941, her entry reads:

As for onions – they have completely disappeared from the market. One wireless speaker the other day told how in the greengrocer's shop he had seen, proudly displayed in a centre position, one large onion, a pink ribbon tied round its middle, and propped against it, a placard with the words 'very rare'.

Gardeners rose to the occasion, and by 1943 the national crop of onions was so large that all restrictions were lifted.

Apples and rhubarb were also in very short supply in the early years of the war, and large queues formed outside greengrocers. Indeed, in the towns there was a constant search for fruit.

Margaret Crompton recorded on 16 March, 1943: 'one watches eagerly other people's shopping baskets – this morning we saw two baskets with a few sticks of rhubarb in them, and finally tracked it to its lair . . . One needs to develop Sherlock Holmes' instincts to do shopping now.'

One of the major problems that faced the country was the inadequate supply of sources of vitamins A and C. The threat of an outbreak of scurvy could not be discounted, and from an early stage of the war gardeners were urged to grow as many carrots and green vegetables as possible. In the event of an invasion they were told to sell their fruit and vegetables to those who could afford to pay, and give them to those who could not.

For the people of the occupied Channel Islands, vegetables prevented them from succumbing to malnutrition, or even death from starvation. One Islander, a Mr. Queree, recorded in his journal that they were allowed a ration of five pounds of potatoes a week. The two ounces of meat, which included the sinew and bone, were simply used to give a little extra flavour to vegetable stews. The daily menu was boiled potatoes for breakfast, vegetable stew for lunch and boiled potatoes for supper. He grew fifty pounds of dried beans a year. In May 1945 potatoes ran out on the islands, and green stuff was scarce. The people survived on swedes.

But on the mainland the majority of people did remarkably well thanks to 'Dig for Victory', in fact some fared better than they did before the war. A survey revealed that there was little difference between middle class and working class diet, although the gap had been enormous in peacetime.

The 'Eat More Vegetables' campaign was backed by a massive barrage of recipes which must have strained the ingenuity of the inventors quite as much as the credulity of the consumers. The BBC put out a programme called 'The Kitchen Front' in which popular broadcasters like Freddie Grisewood and Mabel Constandurous described their favourite war-time recipes; such delights as Location Loaf made from haricot beans, stale bread and sausage meat, or Mock Duck composed of onions or leeks, potatoes, sage and sausage meat, or National Roly-Poly put together with grated potatoes, mixed vegetables, beans and minced beef.

Of all the wartime vegetable recipes the most famous, perhaps notorious would be a better word, was Woolton Pie, devised by the Head Chef of the Savoy, Francois Latry, and named after the Minister for Food, Lord Woolton.

One mother said that she only had to mention the name, Woolton Pie, for her six-year-old son to burst into uncontrollable sobs. And Nurse Katherine Phipps, who kept a diary between 1939 and 1945, made this entry for 13 March 1941, from the hospital where she worked:

A horrible dish has appeared on the dining table and it is to be repeated once a week. It is called Woolton Pie. It is composed entirely of root vegetables in which one feels turnip has far too honoured a place. Evidently the cook is entirely uninterested in it, for it arrived burnt and half raw ... what a combination of errors. There has been an 'Eat more Carrots' Campaign and we are to grow these dull creatures in our flower bed. A girl from the Women's Land Army has arrived to deal with this sort of thing.

Woolton Pie was, in fact, made from potato, swede, cauliflower, carrot, and when available, spring onions. But it was not the only wartime all vegetable dish. There was baked vegetable roll, marrow and walnut cutlets, and the Oslo meal, which was made from shredded cabbage, lettuce, chopped parsley, grated carrot, sliced tomato, grated beetroot, and mixed with a salad dressing made from dried milk, vinegar, water, salt, pepper and mustard.

Even more exotic was Parsley Honey made from five ounces of parsley, stalks and all, one pound of sugar, one and a half pints of water, and half a teaspoonful of vinegar. The liquid was boiled down to a pint, and then the vinegar added. 'Tastes like honey' was the promise, 'but eat in two weeks' was the warning.

Carrots cropped up everywhere. There was a home-made drink, called Carrolade, made from the juice of grated carrots and swedes; carrot marmalade, and toffee carrots.

It was possible for gardeners to produce a varied vegetable diet from a relatively small area of ground. The Ministry of Agriculture drew up a cropping plan for a plot thirty feet by ninety feet which produced broad, dwarf and runner beans, and haricots for drying; beet, sprouting broccoli, Brussels sprouts, spring and winter cabbage, early and maincrop carrots, kale, leeks, lettuce, marrows, onions, parsnips, two crops of peas, and the same of potatoes, radishes, savoy cabbage, shallots, summer and winter spinach, Swiss Chard, swedes, tomatoes and turnips.

The nation was urged to follow the 'Food for Fitness' rules:

Eat more fruits. Eat more vegetables. Take at least one good helping of fresh salad every day as well as cooked vegetables. Plenty of salads, green vegetables, carrots, turnips and swedes will help you resist infection. Cook your green vegetables quickly, or better still, eat them raw.

When you've made sure of your rations and green vegetables, appetite will tell how much more you need. Fill up with potatoes rather than bread – wheat has to be brought here by ships.

Recommended quantities for four people at a meal were one and a half to two pounds of potatoes, and one and a half pounds of cabbage.

The Ministry of Food must have delved back into the old gardening writings for their guide to what the kitchen gardener should grow, for their list of pot-herbs and vegetables for salads could have been written by John Evelyn, or even Master John Gardener.

The herbs suggested to make rationed food more interesting were: balm, borage, bay, celery seed, chervil, chives, fennel, garlic, horseradish, marigold, marjoram, mint, nasturtium, parsley, sage, winter savory, sorrel, tansy and tarragon.

And the vegetables for salads were: cabbage, savory, spinach, Brussels sprouts, kale, turnip tops, watercress, lettuce, endive, beetroot, turnips, parsnips, carrots, kohl rabi, swede, potatoes, radishes, cucumber, onions, leeks, peas, French and runner beans, celery, shallots, chicory, cauliflower, broccoli, and broad beans.

A stream of pamphlets poured out on how to cook cabbage without losing vitamin C; on bottling vegetables and fruit; on drying, pickling, and salting produce, and jam making.

People with gardens or allotments rarely experienced any real shortages. Nurse Katherine Phipps spent much of her spare time with a friend, Ruth, who was clearly a great gardener, and she gives a glimpse of the output from her garden.

Ruth grows with great success all kinds of garden produce and fruit which she sells to greengrocers ... She also bottles enormous quantities for the family.

June 1941: Ruth's potatoes flourish like green bay trees and her lettuce seem incapable of attracting slugs.

On Christmas Eve, 1941 Ruth gave a sackful of onions and cabbages to the crew of the local searchlight camp, and on Christmas day served up a huge meal, finished off with 'damson cheese, home-grown and home-made.'

When Nurse Phipps was travelling through London in March 1942 she recorded seeing neat rows of tomatoes growing on bombsites beside the temporary fire-fighting reservoirs, which had been planted by the firemen.

Mr. A. E. Prior, the headmaster of a council school in Kent, where the staff and children were doing their bit for 'Dig for Victory' was not so fortunate. The school record book has a tight-lipped entry: 'Cattle broke through a hole in the school fence, which had been made by the army, and ate the crops in the school vegetable garden.'

Sidney Chave, a laboratory technician with the Emergency Public Health Laboratory Service, spent what time he could in his garden in Upper Norwood in South London, between working, fire-watching and sheltering from air raids.

On 13 August 1940 he was able to enter in to his *War Diary* that: 'We have a good supply of vegetables in the garden now. There are a few cauliflowers and plenty of cabbages, runner beans, spinach and rhubarb.' And that Christmas he and his family ate cabbage from the garden and stored runner beans.

Cheery slogans, remarkable recipes, and millions of instructional leaflets (10,000,000 alone in 1942) created a vast army of kitchen and fruit gardeners who played a major part in keeping the nation fit and healthy throughout the war.

7
Flower Power

At its most dull, the kitchen garden is a food production area, but there is no reason why it should be purely utilitarian with regimented rows of vegetables, fruit trees and bushes. In the past far greater use was made in the kitchen of plants which are now regarded as ornamental. Flowers were employed extensively in salads, not merely because they made the dishes attractive, but because they were considered as an aid to good health.

The medieval kitchen garden must have been a very colourful place with primroses, violets and roses jostling with onions and leeks, and the fine foliage herbs like fennel, anise and wormwood, many of which were allowed to flower because their seeds were as greatly valued as their leaves, stems and roots.

It was not until the kitchen garden became solely a place for food production that it became somewhat austere. Surrounding the garden with a wall served two purposes; to separate it from the pleasure grounds, and to provide the sheltered environment needed to grow the more tender fruits and vegetables. But now the majority of gardeners do not enjoy the luxury of warm brick and stone walls, and it makes good sense to make the kitchen garden as delightful to look at and be in as the garden of lawns, herbaceous borders, and flowering shrubs.

There are two ways of introducing flowers into the kitchen garden. The first is to grow them as a 'crop' for cutting for the house. I always have a double row of sweet peas, which are charming for their colour, scent and abundance. To have large bowls filled with them in the house is a special luxury of summer, and they do balance nicely with the runner beans with their scarlet, pink and white flowers.

Clearly it is essential to grow annuals for cutting simply because it is vital to keep the kitchen garden soil well tilled and fed, and all the crops rotating.

Iceland poppies are a wonderfully colourful cutting flower, and last over a long season. Larkspur, godetias, foxgloves, such as the Excelsior hybrids, or digitalis 'Apricot', the tall African marigolds, cornflower, sweet william, pyrethrum, rudbeckia, particularly 'Irish Eyes', with its striking green centre, and the spraying Korean Chrysanthemums, will fill vases throughout the summer and autumn.

Without an enormous kitchen garden it is impossible to grow single rows of each variety chosen but with runs of twenty or thirty feet it is a simple matter to plant two or three different cutting flowers in a row.

An ideal way of combining beauty and utility in the kitchen garden is to make a mixed herb and flower border, or edge the vegetable and fruit areas, using those flowers which were as valued in the boudoir as they were in the kitchen. Many of the herbs are as decorative as they are useful: lavender, rosemary and hyssop, with flowers that range through a spectrum of blues; the elegant deep yellow heads of tansy; the pale gold of fennel; the whites, pinks, mauves and reds of thyme; the regal purple of sage, and the shaded pink-mauves of clary. The herb bed that seeks to be an object of pleasure as well as use should be treated exactly like a mixed herbaceous and shrub border.

Roses have always played an important part in medicine and cooking. Rosewater was widely used in sauces and syrups, and candied petals decorated puddings, while fresh petals were mixed into salads. They are also a basic ingredient of pot-pourri. Both for scent, beauty and historical accuracy, choose the old-fashioned roses like the pink cabbage rose, the common pink moss, and *Rosa Gallica officinalis*. The brilliant scarlet Chinese briar, *Rosa Moyesii*, or the sweet briars with their deliciously aromatic leaves, can be included.

Another must among the herb border shrubs is rosemary, from which there are a number of splendid types to choose, from the rugged and familiar *Rosemarinus officinalis*, to the fine-foliaged Sicilian form of

Rosmarinus fastigiatus and the excellent prostrate *Rosmarinus lavandulaceus*. The latter is somewhat on the tender side. One of the glories is the variation in flower colour from a pale slate to a deep Mediterranean blue.

Juniper (*Juniper communis*) grows into a well formed bush, but to get berries for the kitchen it is necessary to have male and a female plants. Bay (*Laurus noblis*) will grow into a sizeable tree unless it is controlled, but within the formality of the kitchen garden it is quite appropriate to clip the bay bush into shape and thus restrict its growth.

Wormwood (*Artemisia absinthium*) which is used in making absinthe, and southernwood (*Artemisia abrotanum*) lend shades of grey and silver to the border. Both are susceptible to frost damage, but produce finer aromatic foliage by being cut back hard. Another sub-shrub which has spicy, scented leaves is the so-called Monk's Pepper, which was grown as a bromide, both for monks and soldiers in years past. No border should be without Verbena (*Verbena tridens*). Once a plant is established it will survive hard winters, and its filmy sprays of rose-lilac flowers are extremely elegant. It also makes a very good pot plant for the house. Rue (*Ruta graveolens*) with its lovely clear gold flowers and blue-green foliage, forms a fine plant with the aid of a little gentle pruning.

The larger shrubs should be generously spaced to allow room for madonna lilies (*Lilium candidum*), paeony, (*Paeonia officinalis*), sage, hyssop, winter savory, and the thymes, both the wiry, mini-shrub types, and the prostrate varieties. Space should also be allowed for bergamot (*Monarda didyma*), which is a splendid bee plant, and has gloriously scented foliage and handsome scarlet and pink flowers. Marjoram is an essential culinary herb, both the green and golden leaved types.

Marigolds (*calendula officinalis*), which used to be known as Golds, can be scattered around for colour. The fresh petals are used in salads, and dried are added to stews and stuffings. Among the other salad flowers are primroses and violets, both of which can be candied, and Indian cress (*Nasturtium majus*). Its leaves add a spicy flavour to salads, and the pickled green seed pods make excellent substitute capers.

Toad flax (*Linaria vulgaris*) and the enchanting little heartsease pansies (*Viola tricolor*) provide additional colour. As well as pinks and carnations, grow some of the gilliflowers of old.

Both the leaves and fruit of strawberries have been valued for centuries, not the lush modern varieties, but the wild native strawberry (*Frugaria vesca*) or the delicious alpine varieties. The fruit has a very special flavour, which is greatly enhanced when it is marinated in white wine for about an hour before eating.

Some of the essential herbs like mint, tansy and costmary can prove a problem where space is at a premium because of their vigorous, spreading habit. One way of coping with them is to confine them within a barrier, such as planks, or metal sheeting sunk to the level of the soil. Apple mint, spearmint and peppermint should not be left out, and it is also well worth growing the scented varieties like Eau-de-Cologne mint, ginger mint and pineapple mint.

Bowers are, alas, rare in modern gardens; scented and secluded they were a place for trysting or just thinking. A corner of the kitchen garden or orchard can be used to make one. A medieval turf seat, seeded with chamomile, can be shaded by honeysuckle, an old-fashioned climbing rose, perhaps hazel nuts, grape vines, or even scarlet runners, which were used for this purpose in Victorian gardens. Another unusual way of growing runner beans is to place a few plants around the apple trees and let them climb into the boughs. They do not interfere with the fruit.

There is no doubt that with imagination the kitchen garden can be a place of beauty and pleasure without any loss of production.

8
The Herbs

Herbs have played a vital part in the history of mankind from the earliest times. We know that the most ancient peoples had a remarkably varied vegetable and fruit diet, and it is perfectly reasonable to suppose that from the start they would have recognised that certain plants improved their health and even cured disease. Historically speaking until very recent times herbs were the primary source of medicine, and even now researchers look to plants for the drugs that will stamp out such horrible afflictions as cancer. The search goes on in herbariums around the world, as well as botanically unmonitored areas of the planet.

In the past finding the right herb was a hit and miss business. In many cases a particular plant acquired a famous reputation simply because eating it produced a sense of well-being, although perhaps it was only because it contained essential vitamins that caused good health. In many cases they were chosen under what became known as the Doctrines of Signatures based on the theory that as God gave disease, so he provided an antidote. For example it was known that marshland produced fever; as the willow grew in marshy land it followed that it was possible willows would cure fever.

But the use of herbs in medicine was not quite so chancy as it might sometimes appear. Every one of the great civilisations developed skill and knowledge in what is now rather slightingly described as folk medicine. In Britain the priestly Druids were said to have been outstanding herbal doctors, as were the Egyptians, Persians, Chinese, Indians, Romans, Greeks and Jews. Today in China herbal medicine is used in conjunction with acupuncture, and in Africa the so-called witch doctors make use of a vast natural *materia medica.*

It was not just for the medicine chest that herbs were cultivated. The Romans used them widely in cooking for sauces, garnishes, stuffings, and in ways that quite transformed the flavour of the basic ingredients, and it is the Romans we have to thank for many of the herbs that we now commonly grow in our kitchen gardens.

After the Romans left Britain, herb growing was kept alive by the monks. Medicinal or physic herbs were the most important, since the monks had to look after the physical as well as the spiritual welfare of the people, but they also cultivated culinary herbs to enliven their otherwise dull diet. The practice spread outside the monasteries, and in castle and manor the herb garden was developed. The poor spread a mixture of butter and herbs on bread, and a late fourteenth-century form of omelette, the *herbolace*, a mixture of eggs and chopped herbs baked on a butterdish, was a favoured delicacy.

The herb garden is considerably older than the kitchen garden, and to many modern eyes would have seemed a somewhat eccentric place; a muddle of flowers, herbs and weeds. Carnations, paeonies, lilies and roses received no better treatment than the chickweed, scarlet pimpernel, and stinking robert which were just as treasured. Pellitory of the wall, which can be invasive and quite a menace, was greatly valued, and the garlic and onions mingled with the wild strawberries and primroses. In fact a well stocked herb garden must have been a joyous thing to see, particularly when an earth seat planted with chamomile, and embowered with wild roses and honeysuckle was set in the midst of this riot of colour and scents. With most people's knowledge of herbs confined to the dried and crumbled product sold in packets, jars and drums, too little is known of them in flower, or of their setting great umbels of seeds.

For a very long time vegetables were included in the herb garden, and since they made people feel fit, those such as the humble cabbage were vested with valuable medicinal properties, but as the variety of vegetables grew eventually they and the herb garden had to part, and the kitchen garden came into being. Sadly there are relatively few herb gardens left, but the revived and growing interest in herbs in cooking, and indeed in medicine, makes them an essential part of any well-stocked kitchen garden:

There is more to herbs than parsley, mint, sage and thyme. Just idle through the pages of Robert Burton's *The Anatomy of Melancholy* to see what was grown in a seventeenth-century herb garden: 'What extraordinary virtues are ascribed unto plants!' he exclaims.

> ... poppy causeth sleep, cabbage resisteth drunkenness etc., and that which is more to be admired, that such and such plants should have a peculiar virtue to such particular parts, as to the head Aniseeds, Foalfoot [coltsfoot], Betony, Calamint, Eye-bright, Lavender, Bays, Roses, Rue, Sage, Campana [Campanula], Hyssop, Horehound, Water Germander, etc., for the heart Borage, Bugloss, Saffron, Balm, Basil, Rosemary, Violet, Centaury, Sorel, Purslane ...

And his list goes on with parsley, mints, pennyroyal, endive, fennel and chicory.

It would be impossible for the average garden to grow all that was considered quite essential three hundred years ago, but there are a large number of herbs which deserve a place, not only to enrich the flavour of food, but also to beautify the kitchen garden.

ANGELICA is one of the most handsome of the herb garden plants, and given the right conditions will grow four feet high, with fine pinnate leaves, large umbels of pale yellow flowers, and a fittingly noble botanical name, *Angelica Archangelica*.

A native of the Alps, and said to grow wild in Germany, Hungary, Lapland and Iceland, and in Scotland, although it could well be an escape there, it has long been valued as a cure and protection against the plague. There is a legend that an emperor and his entire army were stricken with plague. When it seemed that all would be lost an Angel appeared to the emperor and told him to use the plant to treat himself and his army, and they were saved. This story lent the plant a holy quality; it was used as a defence against sorcery and incantations, and earned it its heavenly name, for it was also known as 'The Holy Ghost'. Master John Gardener regarded it highly.

It was used as an antidote to poisonous bites, particularly those from mad dogs. The leaves can also be used in a tisane to ease headaches and tensions. Distilled Angelica water was given to people who suffered from fainting fits, and for heart disorders. Its calming effects were valued by anxious parents who were advised to mix the dried and powdered roots with wine to 'abate the raging lust in young persons'.

In the eighteenth century it was used in the recipe for the truly remarkable Lady Hewet's Water, which was used in cases of severe illness, and was even credited with having snatched patients back from the very jaws of death. It was a decoction which also included: red sage, betony, spearmint, hyssop, setwell, thyme, balm, pennyroyal, celandine, watercress, heartsease, lavender, germander, calamint, tamarisk, colts-foot, avens, valarian, saxifrage, pimpernel, vervain, parsley, rosemary, savory, scabious, agrimony, mother-thyme, wild marjoram, Roman wormwood, Carduus benedictus (the Blessed Thistle), pellitory of the wall, field daisies, rue, yarrow, comfrey, plantain, chamomile, maiden-hair, sweet marjoram, dragons (Antirrhinum), red rose leaves, cowslip flowers, rosemary flowers, juniper berries, china roots, comfrey roots, aniseed, fennel seeds, caraway seeds, nutmeg, ginger, cinnamon, pepper, spikenard, parsley seed, cloves, mace, elecampane roots, melilot flowers, cardamom, rhubarb, veronica (probably bird's eye) and saffron. Clearly Lady Hewet was not running the risk of leaving anything out.

The best known modern use for Angelica is candied as a decoration for cakes and trifles. For this purpose young stem and leaf stalks are gathered in May. The stalks should be boiled until they are tender and peeled, and stood in water over a gentle heat until they adopt a good green colour. Once the right colour is achieved the stalks must be dried, and a candy syrup made – some of the older recipes recommend using rose water for this. Plunge the stalks into the boiling syrup, remove and dry. The leaves can also be candied.

The Laplanders used to, and probably still do, peel and eat the stalks as a raw vegetable, and indeed both the leaves and stalks are eaten occasionally as a vegetable in some parts of Europe. Certainly the peeled and blanched young stalks make an interesting addition to a salad.

ANISE (*Pimpinella anisum*) could well have been introduced by the Romans (although Apicius does not include it in his recipes), nevertheless it is a native of Egypt, Greece and Asia Minor. In *The Retir'd Gardn'r* it comes under the heading of useful herbs, and was certainly valued as a medicinal plant. Henry Lyte in the 1619 edition of his translation of *Dodoen's Herbal* found eleven different uses for it from relieving flatulence, to sweetening the breath, and curing persistent coughs. It was also given to young children developing symptoms of epilepsy, and used in cures for ear and head pains. People who complained of never getting a wink of sleep were told to make up a little bag of seeds and fix it under their nose so that the fumes could waft them into a dreamless sleep. This soporific effect is curiously at odds with its fame as an aphrodisiac. The bruised seeds, made into a tisane, are considered an excellent digestive.

It is a slightly tricky plant to grow, but by no means impossible and well worth the effort. It is best to raise the seedlings under cover, and plant them out in May in a warm border of well worked soil. Although primarily grown for its seed, its somewhat parsley-like leaves can be eaten fresh in salads, to which they lend a most distinctive taste, and they can also be used like fennel and dill as a garnish for fish, or finely chopped and scattered over broad beans.

The seeds have a wide variety of uses, particularly in bread and biscuit baking, and cake making. They give a spicy flavour to apple pie.

BALM (*melissa officinalis*) is one of the most delightful herbs to grow, not simply because it is so easy (I have a large patch which thrives under a very old Brown Turkey fig tree) but because it is a good-looking plant, and its fresh green leaves smell deliciously of lemon. It has always been a favourite bee plant and bee keepers are known to have rubbed the inside of their hives with the herb to prevent the bees deserting.

Medicinally it found its way into a number of remedies. It was an essential ingredient in the highly complicated Great Palsey Water which took months to prepare, but in the end was '... of excellent use in all swoonings, in weakness of heart and decay of spirits; it restores speech in apoplexies and palsies; it helps all pains in the joints coming of cold or bruises, bathing the places outwardly, and dipping cloths and laying on it; it strengthens and comforts all vital and animal spirits, and cleareth the external senses, strengthening the memory; restoreth lost appetite, helpest all weakness of the stomach; both taken inwardly and bathed outwardly it taketh away giddiness of the head, and helpeth hearing; it makes a pleasant breath; it helpeth all cold dispositions of the liver, and beginning of propsies; none can sufficiently express the virtues of this water.' Balm was also an ingredient in the portmanteau recipe for Lady Hewet's Water, and was one of the herbs mixed in butter and pig fat for the green ointment used for treating all kinds of bruises, bumps and wounds. The fresh juice of the herb was also used for treating wounds.

The Arab herbalists regarded it as one of the major herbs, particularly as a pick-me-up and its reputation as a herb that would cheer up even the most pessimistic hypochondriac was recognised by both John Evelyn and Culpeper.

In the early part of the nineteenth century it was made into a tea for disorders of the head and stomach, and for bringing down temperatures. It is also used in cooling summer cups, and is particularly good in a Pimms, and cider and wine cups.

A chicken stuffed with a good handful of balm and roasted takes on a delightful lemony flavour, and it should never be left out of a mint sauce.

BASIL (*Ocymum basilicum*) is a herb which should not be absent from any kitchen garden. It enriches sauces and stuffings; chopped over sliced tomatoes and served with a French dressing it is one of the pleasures of summer, and it is an ideal mate with all kinds of pasta. It is also a useful ingredient in a pot pourri. And yet it is a herb which over the centuries has roused the most extraordinary passions.

It was a herb surrounded by acrimony. The Ancient Greeks claimed that it would not grow if the seeds were not sown to the accompaniment of a barrage of abuse, and in Crete it was linked with the devil. The sobriquet of abuse was carried into France where '*semer le basilic*' (scatter the basil) was a popular expression for slander. It did have some virtues in the west where it was said to be a protection against witches, and even believed to have such power that if a man accepted a shoot of fresh basil from a woman his love for her would be undying. But in India, its native land, it is a plant of great sanctity. It is the herb of Vishnu, Krishna and Siva, and is found planted around Hindu temples, and placed upon the dead.

Culpeper perfectly described its troubled history when he wrote in his herbal:

This is a herb which all authors are together by the ears about, and rail at one another (like lawyers). Galen and Dioscorides held it not fitting to be taken inwardly; and Chrysippus rails at it with downright Billingsgate rhetoric; Pliny and the Arabian physicians defend it... Being applied to the place bitten by venomous beasts, or stung by a wasp or hornet, it speedily draws the poison to it. Every like draws his like. Mizaldus affirms, that being laid to rot on horse-dung, it will breed venomous beasts. Hilarius, a French physician, affirms upon his knowledge, that an acquaintance of his, by common smelling to it, had a scorpion bred in his brain.

Dioscorides claimed that basil actually injured the sight, while Henry Lyte took the opposite view and and recommended a mixture of bruised basil leaves and wine as an eye-wash. But all the arguments didn't prevent people from growing the herb. Philip Miller named no less than seventeen varieties being grown in the eighteenth century while nine were recorded in cultivation in France at the beginning of the twentieth century.

One thing is certain, it does repay the trouble of growing. Being such a tender plant the seeds have to be germinated in heat – the greenhouse or the kitchen window sill or any warm room will do. The plants can then be transplanted into a sunny spot in the open at the end of May or early June, but to be quite certain of a supply of leaves, I think it is better to grow basil under cover. What I have done with considerable success is to grow the plants in a plastic trough used for pre-glued wallpaper (they can be bought very cheaply in any decorating shop) and only need an inch or so of gravel in the bottom for drainage and some decent soil.

BORAGE (*Borago officinalis*) is one of those thoroughly agreeable plants that are invasive, but so attractive that you simply do not mind. A native of Europe and North Africa it has quite large, rather bristly leaves which have the refreshing flavour of cucumbers, and bright blue, star-shaped flowers. Although it is an introduced plant, it is completely at home in Britain, and Philip Miller, who was not a person to mince his words, wrote in his *Gardener's Dictionary*, in which, incidently, he listed five varieties, that borage was 'very common in all parts of England, being often found upon Dunghills, and in public Roads, where the Seeds have been scattered from Gardens...'

In the thirteenth century it was grown as a medicinal herb, but by the fifteenth century it was more widely used in cooking, particularly for sauces.

The sixteenth-century herbalists considered it a cheerful herb, and if the leaves and flowers were allowed to soak in wine for a while before drinking, they would, according to Henry Lyte: ' . . . cause men to be glad and merry, and driveth away all heavy sadness, and dull Melancholy'.

Wet nurses drank herb soups that included borage, as well as lettuce, sorrel, parsley, buglos and chicory in the belief that it encouraged milk. The leaves were boiled with other pot-herbs to ease sore throats, and it was used as a laxative. Fresh leaves were laid on new wounds.

But its most attractive use is in summer cups (no Pimms is complete without its sprig of borage) and its flowers are colourful in salads. The flowers can also be candied like violets or rose petals. Young leaves are a refreshing ingredient in salads, but they should be chopped fairly small as the whole leaves are sometimes too coarse for comfort.

The Elizabethans cooked borage with mutton, along with the roots of buglos and parsley.

BURNET (*Sanguisorba officinalis*) is now largely regarded as a salad plant, but its rightful place is in the herb garden or border. It is a pretty thing with fine, almost ferny leaves, and pine-cone shaped heads of pale pink flowers. It does not need to be grown in great quantities, but a few of its cucumber-flavoured leaves are an asset to any herby salad. It is also another good addition to wine and cider cups.

A native plant of Britain, it is also widely distributed throughout Europe, and extensively used as a medicinal herb. In Hungary there is a story that after a particularly bloody battle, the king at that time, King Chaba, cured the wounds of fifteen thousand of his men with the juice of the plant, and Middle Eastern magicians advised steeping the blades of swords in burnet juice and moles blood. The purpose seems a little obscure, unless it was to make the swords more effective and heal the wounds they inflicted at the same time.

Using the French name *pimprenelle*, John Gardener spells it pimpinell, which makes one wonder whether the pimpernel in his fifteenth-century list of essential plants is not burnet, which he does not mention.

The Elizabethans used it with mugwort, comfrey, betony, agrimony, Dyers weed, plantain, sage, bramble leaves, parsley, stinging nettle, marigold, sanicle, bugle, mouse-ear, dandelion, hemp, female fern, buglos, gentian, vervain, hinds-tongue, ground ivy, water germander, catmint, herb robert, cinquefoil, tansy, stoned raisins, liquorice, flowers and seeds of St. John's Wort, and the seeds of the blessed thistle, all steeped in white wine to heal internal wounds.

Apart from its use in curing internal and external wounds, it also had a reputation as a merry herb when mixed with wine, particularly claret. By merry the herbalists meant that it gave one a lift, and for this reason was given to people suffering from heart trouble. In the early nineteenth century it was still used to make a cordial to bring people out of a fever.

Burnet is quite simple to grow, although it does appreciate a bit of chalk in the soil, and a dry, sunny spot. With me it has done best when it has self-sowed: My original bought plant died without doing particularly well, while the succeeding generations which sprang up around it have done infinitely better.

The small leaves should be stripped from the stalks and chopped to release their flavour into salads. Bruise them before adding to a cup.

CHAMOMILE (*Anthemis noblis*) is perhaps one of the best known, but least understood herbs. It is too bitter for flavouring (although it was a fifteenth-century pot-herb), and in the household sense it is no longer used medicinally, although chamomile tea crops up regularly in historical novels. In more recent years it has been promoted quite ruthlessly as the ideal plant to make a labour saving lawn; a lawn that hardly ever needs cutting, and indeed those who have fallen for blandishments of advertisers have discovered why: it hardly ever survives for more than a year. The plants die out quite easily, do not take all that kindly to being trampled over all the time, and rot off if the lawn becomes water-logged. Despite its poor showing as a lawn plant, it certainly deserves a place in the herb garden, if only for its fine-cut foliage, and bright white flowers, and above all its distinctive scent. It is perfect for turf seats.

Its medicinal use is of great antiquity, and it was employed to treat fevers, jaundice, and a whole variety of aches and pains. Chamomile baths, have long been used to soak away aches and pains while chamomile tea is a great help in settling stomach disorders. In the late nineteenth century it was a substitute for quinine in treating malaria, and was included in the famous green ointment. The flowers were an ingredient in a plaster for aching joints made from red coleworts, danewort, bean flowers and roses.

CARAWAY (*Carum carvi*) is an excellent culinary herb. It is mainly grown for its seeds, but the fresh, feathery green leaves are good chopped into a salad, with fish, or added to stuffings, stews and soups. Some of the older writers believed it to be a native of Britain, and while it does grow wild throughout many parts of Europe, and in Siberia, northern Iran and the Himalayas, it was almost certainly introduced to this country by the Romans, who would not have left it behind when they colonised these islands, since it played a most prominent part in their cuisine. One method of cooking cabbage, described by Apicius, included chopped leeks, caraway seed and fresh coriander; and with lovage, coriander, onion and mint it was used in a sauce that went with pigeons. It was also an essential ingredient for a sauce with flamingo, which was stewed with leeks and coriander. The sauce included pepper, coriander, mint, rue and dates.

Caraway featured in most of the sauces for Roman gourmet dishes, particularly those served with venison and with crayfish and prawns. The shellfish sauce was made with spring onions, lovage, caraway, cumin, dates, honey, vinegar wine, oil, mustard, *liquamen* and *defrutum*. The original *liquamen* would have been left to marinate for two months but a more instant form can be made by boiling fish bits in a strong brine with oregano until it reduces somewhat; strain until clear and bottle for use.

Defrutum was wine much reduced into a semi-concentrate. Tinned grapefruit juice reduced to a third is an easy substitute. This can be added to *liquamen* in the concocting of sauces.

Over the centuries caraway seems to have slipped in and out of favour, but it certainly had a place in fifteenth century gardens where it was grown for its roots, which were boiled and considered better than parsnips, and highly recommended for old people because they are easily digested. John Parkinson was such an enthusiast that he proclaimed caraway should be planted in every garden.

The use of a caraway as a root vegetable seems to have entirely disappeared. Little or no mention of this use is made in authoritive eighteenth- or nineteenth-century gardening books beyond saying that the roots could be eaten.

The best known use of caraway seeds is in seedy cakes, loved by men and mice. I once recall having tea with an elderly lady in a London flat. A beautiful seed cake was sitting on the lower shelf of the tea trolley when, to my astonishment, I saw a sleek, untroubled mouse stroll over to the cake, climb on top, and squatting comfortably begin to pick off the seeds and eat them. Since my hostess did not notice, and it seemed impolite to suggest that her flat was infested with vermin, the mouse took tea undisturbed.

Candied caraway seeds used to be served with fresh fruit at the end of dinner, and the eighteenth-century housewife used them with coriander and dill seeds when she pickled walnuts. The seeds are a flavouring for cheeses and bread.

CHERVIL (*Anthriscus cerefolium*) is a native of the Caucasus, Western Asia, and South and Central Russia, and was almost certainly brought to this country by the Romans, and while it has been grown in British gardens for centuries, it is not a herb which has the automatic place in every kitchen it should have. In France it is the base of *fines herbes*, and is quite invaluable as a flavouring in soups and stews where it very readily takes the place of parsley. Throughout history its first use was in cooking, and for hundreds of years was an essential ingredient in making Loblolly, a thick, meaty gruel.

The seventeenth-century herbalists employed the roots as protection against the plague, and in the treatment of blood complaints, including breaking up blood clots. Henry Lyte believed that it had an uplifting character and declared that 'It is good for people that be dull, old, and without courage, for it rejoyceth and comforteth them, and increaseth their strength.'

He also recognised its culinary value and wrote that it greatly improved the flavour of meat, to such an extent, indeed, that it '... stirreth up meat lust'. It was and still is popular in salads. Sometimes the green seeds were eaten with oil, vinegar and pepper, or the young leaves were mixed with mustard and cress as a refreshing green side-salad.

Many of the authorities of the past refer to eating the boiled roots of chervil, but these were unlikely to have been the roots of the herb chervil, but of the turnip-rooted variety which is dealt with later as a vegetable.

There is an intriguing eighteenth-century recipe for chervil tart (spinach can be used as a substitute):

> Shred a gallon of chervil very small; put to it half a pound of melted butter, the meat of three lemons picked from the skins and seeds; the rind of two lemons grated, a pound of sugar; put this in a dish or patti-pan with puff-paste (pastry) on the bottom and top, and so bake it; when it is bak'd, cut off the lid, and put cream or custard over it, as you do codlin-tarts (apple tarts); scrape sugar over it; serve it cold; this is good among other tarts in the winter for variety.

Like so many herbs, chervil can be disappointing on the first attempt to grow. If it gets too dry, or is over exposed to the sun, it tends to bolt, and you end up with a lot of seed and not much leaf. Rather like burnet, it has a perverse tendency to do better when left to its own devices. Plant your first lot of seed somewhere where it need not be disturbed. Do not give up in despair when it bolts, just let it scatter its seed and you will have the delightful surprise of fresh young plants with lots of leaf coming up in the late summer and early autumn. These will stand happily through the winter, which is hardly surprising since the plant flourishes in the woods of the Crimea.

CLARY (*Salvia Sclarea*), sometimes called Clary Sage, is an extremely handsome plant, and gives height and dignity to a herb garden or border. The large grey-green leafs, which sometimes appear almost blue, perfectly set off the tall spikes of pinky-purple flowers. A native of the south of Europe, it is perfectly hardy, and useful as well as beautiful. There are now some rather highly coloured varieties which have been bred for herbaceous borders, but I think they are garish and best avoided.

Some of the older writers claim that it was introduced into this country in 1562, but it must have been here a good deal earlier as it is mentioned in the fifteenth century as a culinary herb. It could very well have been brought by the Romans, or introduced by monks, who called it *Oculus Christi*.

Originally its use was almost entirely medicinal, particularly for eye complaints, thus its alternative name Clear-eye, which came from the practice of placing clary seeds in the corner of an eye to attract foreign bodies. The leaves were made into a plaster to draw out thorns. It also had a great reputation as a treatment for weak backs.

In the seventeenth century the leaves were dipped in batter and fried and 'accepted by many, unpleasant to none'. One herbalist insisted that the fritters were good for bad backs, but does not make clear whether they should be eaten or worn. He scorned the popular use of clary for treating kidney complaints, a source of back pains, declaring that even if sufferers were to eat '... as much clary as will grow upon an acre of ground, their backs are as much better as though they had pissed in their shoes; nay, perhaps much worse.'

Clary was esteemed as an aphrodisiac, and was included in a brew used to induce fertility. After a week's course of a syrup made from orris-root, the would-be mother had a nightly wine-glass of a brew which contained three pints of good ale which was brought to the boil with marrow from the backbones of cattle, half a handful of clary, a handful of nep or cat bos (catmint), a quarter of a pound of stoned and sliced dates, a handful of raisins, and three whole nutmegs which had been pricked all over. The whole mixture was reduced to half its volume and strained, and a wine-glass was drunk at bedtime. Until the ghastly mixture was finished the husband was banned from the bedroom.

Clary was also supposed to make people drunk, and some brewers mixed it with their brew instead of hops to make it more powerful.

Now its place is in the kitchen, and the fresh leaves, used with reasonable moderation, are a pleasant addition to stews and soups, and to stuffings. The very young leaves can be chopped into salads, and also into omelettes. In the past, apart from being made into fritters, the tender leaves were beaten into cream and fried in butter, and served with orange- or lemon-flavoured sugar.

Clary wine was valued as an aid to sleep, and according to a seventeenth-century recipe is not complicated to make:

To ten gallons of water, put thirteen pounds of sugar, and the well-beaten white of sixteen eggs. Boil slowly for an hour, skimming the whole time, and allow to get cold. Place a pint of Clary flowers, complete with small leaves and stalks, into a barrel with a pint of brewers yeast, add the liquid, and stir twice a day until it had stopped working. Seal the barrel and keep for four months before bottling.

CORIANDER (*Coriandrum sativum*) is native to the Mediterranean region, and was one of the most favoured and widely used of the Roman herbs. Its presence in Britain is undoubtedly a legacy of the occupation. It is surprising that it has survived so successfully because its popularity declined almost to the point of extinction, although it has now made a considerable come-back largely thanks to the Indian immigrants who have settled in Britain since the war, and who have popularised their cooking through their many restaurants. I met a Sikh gardener working on his plot on an allotment at Birmingham who was growing coriander like mustard and cress.

The Romans used coriander in sauces, vegetable cookery and with meats and poultry; with marrows, beets, and globe artichokes, and in salads; in fricassees and soups, with pigeons, flamingoes and fungi.

Alexander Neckham, a St. Albans schoolmaster, who eventually became Abbot of Cirencester and wrote on gardening during the latter half of the twelfth century, insisted on its cultivation. It was in Saxon gardens, grew among the vegetables in medieval olitories, and was an important fifteenth-century pot-herb.

The seeds were crystalised and served as a sweetmeat by the Elizabethans, and the leaves were eaten as a salad with oil and salt, and considered to be a defence against infection, despite the fact that most of the herbalists believed that the fresh leaves induced fits.

By the eighteenth century it was cultivated almost exclusively as a medicinal herb, not only in Britain, but also in France and Germany. This change of use must have contributed to its unpopularity in the kitchen. Another problem seems to have been the pungent odour of the leaves, which was compared with the smell of ticks, but it is not noticeable when it is used in sauces, or sparingly in salads. However, the seeds are the most useful part of the plant, and when dried they have a slight scent of tangerines. They are superb in a stuffing for boned lamb, and give a most distinctive flavour if they are crushed with lovage seeds and scattered on a pork joint before roasting.

I have found that the most successful method of culture is in a row in the kitchen garden, just like any other vegetable crop. About fifteen feet will produce a good harvest of seeds, but care must be taken to make sure that they are thoroughly dried. The capsules will often seem to be bone dry, but when they are put into a sealed container the slightest moisture will cause mildew.

COSTMARY or Alecost, or even Mace, Little Balsam or just Cost (*Chrysanthemum balsamita*), is one of those ancient herbs which is too much neglected in modern gardens, when its use in the kitchen is well worth its mint-like invasiveness. Introduced to Europe from Western Asia where it grows wild, it was cultivated by the Romans, who used it in sauces, and doubtless brought it to Britain. It certainly featured in Saxon gardens, and with sage, parsley, dittander, wild thyme and garlic, produced a popular fish sauce in Norman times.

Elizabethan herb gardens always featured costmary, where it was grown for both culinary and medicinal purposes. Also known then as Balsamint or Mawdelin (Maudlin), the leaves were boiled in wine with parsnip seeds to treat stomach upsets, and a conserve, made of the leaves with sugar, was taken for catarrh. It was also used to purge worms, for urinary complaints, agues and sores. In the kitchen it was used with meat, and in sauces and salads.

At the beginning of the sixteenth century costmary was still planted among the sweet and pot-herbs, but by the middle of the seventeenth century its use had seriously declined. Philip Miller only included it in his *Gardener's Dictionary* because 'as it hath been an old Garden-herb, I thought proper to mention it in this place.' In the past, he said 'many people were fond of it in soups'. Fifty years later it was largely neglected.

In fact it is a rewarding plant to grow. Its flowers are not spectacular, but they do produce an appealing drift of pale yellow against the slightly blue-green foliage. The leaves tend to remain during the winter, and when mint has died down they make an excellent sauce for roast lamb, prepared in the same way as mint sauce. In fact I always add costmary leaves to fresh mint sauce; along with balm it enriches the flavour.

A most aromatic, spicy herb, CUMIN (*Cumin cyminum*) is a Mediterranean native which has travelled all over Europe, to China, and to India where it is used in curry powders. It must have been brought to this country by the Romans, because it was used very extensively in Roman cuisine.

One of the more unattractive sounding, but nevertheless popular, Roman delicacies was the stuffed wombs of animals, and an essential ingredient of the various stuffings was cumin, along with leeks and rue. It was also widely used in sauces for vegetables, notably marrows and cucumbers. One of the most usual methods of serving up cabbage was with a sauce made from cumin, salt, old wine and oil, and it was also in a sauce for beets made from chopped leeks, coriander and raisins, thickened with flour. This sauce was also served with carrots and parsnips. Cumin, honey, vinegar, *liquamen*, *defrutum* and oil was poured over turnips.

Boiled ostrich, one of the most flaboyant dishes served at Roman feasts, was garnished with a sauce made from grilled cumin, celery seed and dates. Cumin was also used in a sauce for roast boar; with mutton, lamb, beef, veal and shell fish, and almost all the gourmet dishes.

It was one of the herbs which survived the departure of the Romans from their British colony, and was grown in Saxon gardens, particularly in the physic gardens of convents and monasteries. Certainly its use seems to have been very largely confined to medicine; it was prescribed for flatulence and 'gnawings and frettings of the belly', and the seeds pounded and mixed with vinegar, and sniffed, were supposed to stem nose bleeding. But if it was eaten to excess it produced a pale and sickly complexion. The seeds were included in broth for sufferers from chest complaints. And in the eighteenth century it was still being grown for home-made medicines, although Philip Miller hardly considered it worth the trouble of cultivation. When he grew it in the Chelsea Physic Garden he found his plants tended to damp off when they reached a height of four or five inches.

There is no doubt that cumin is somewhat tricky to raise, but worth it nevertheless. The seeds need to be germinated in the greenhouse or on the window sill, and the hardened plants put into a dry, warm spot. With all herbs grown primarily for their seeds, there is no need to cultivate huge quantities. Half a dozen plants will produce a fair quantity of seed; it is not as though they are being used every day, but they are an excellent flavouring for soups and pastries.

DILL (*Anethum graveolens*) grows wild throughout many parts of Europe, but had to be brought across the Channel, probably by the Romans, and certainly by the monks. Its scent and flavour must be among the most familiar, for dill water has been used by generations of mothers to calm colic in their babies, and dill pickles are sold across the counter in most fish and chip shops.

The use of dill as a carminative is very ancient. The Romans put it in aromatic salts which were taken to aid digestion, as well as in their very rich gourmet dishes. The name is derived from the Saxon word, *dillan*, which means to lull or soothe, and they made it into draughts to make babies sleep. In medieval gardens it was grown for its beauty, as well as its flavour.

Seeds were bruised and boiled in wine as a cure for flatulence, while the leaf tips and seeds were boiled in water to increase milk in nursing mothers and wet nurses. If the water was exchanged for oil the mixture became an aphrodisiac. The seeds were also chewed to stop hiccoughs, and although this was a popular remedy, many herbalists considered it a complete waste of time.

But where dill is successful is in the kitchen, particularly in pickling cucumbers, using the plants when the seeds begin to form. The seeds were also used in pickling walnuts in the eighteenth century.

It goes beautifully with fish, either laying the fresh green fronds on the fish during cooking, or made up into an aromatic and attractive green sauce. Stews, particularly lamb stews, benefit greatly from the herb, and from the earliest time it has been used in soups. In the fifteenth century it was grown specifically as a pottage herb. The Romans used dill in making a thick soup which had a basis of barley, chick peas, lentils and peas. To this was added dill, coriander, fresh leeks, fennel and fennel seed, beets, mallow leaves, young cabbages, oregano and lovage. It goes particularly well with bean soups, and a sprig or two with broad beans makes a refreshing change.

In addition to making dill pickles with cucumbers, John Evelyn was particularly partial to dill pickles made with cauliflowers instead of cucumbers. He said you should boil the cauliflowers 'till they fall to Pieces: Then with some of the Stalk, and worst of the Flower, boil it in a part of the Liquor till pretty strong: Then being taken off, strain it; and when settled, clear it from the Bottom. Then with Dill, Gross Pepper (whole pepper corns), a pretty Quantity of Salt, when cold, add as much Vinegar as will make it sharp, and pour all upon the Collyflower.'

A tisane made from dill is said to have a calming effect and induces sleep.

ELECAMPANE (*Inula helenium*) does not really belong in a kitchen garden, since it is entirely a medicinal herb, but it deserves a place in the modern kitchen and herb garden on two counts. The first is that it has earned it by being one of the oldest herbs brought in from the wild, and the second is that it is a plant of beauty with its huge pale green leaves and large, bright yellow flowers borne on powerful stems that can rise to five feet.

I first came across this plant growing in the grass verge of a narrow lane in County Cork in Ireland. The small group of plants had obviously been hacked down in their prime by a roadman, but despite this set-back they had produced another set of their great leaves, and it was their magnificence that decided me to get out a couple of pieces of root, which have grown into fine plants in my garden. While I was admiring the Irish plants a farmer stopped and told me that a man used to come down every year from Dublin to harvest the leaves, which he used in a poultice for racehorses, so its old country name of horseheal is not an idle one. That is the name used in the fifteenth century and probably before, as well as Ploughman's Spikenyard (which is inaccurate), and Little Helen, the latter no doubt from the legend that Helen of Troy's hands were full of the herb when she was captured by Paris. Another legend says that the first plants grew from her tears.

The main reason for its culture in Saxon gardens was as a treatment for coughs and lung complaints. The root was used, either dried and powdered, and taken with honey, or made into a drink, or candied and made into a kind of cough sweet. Sir John Hill in his *Family Herbal* writes:

> Its greatest virtue is against coughs, and for this purpose it is best taken candied, provided that be well done. A little of it may in this way be held almost continually in the mouth, and swallowed gently, so that it will take effect much better than by a larger dose swallowed at once.

A sixteenth-century recipe describes the really quite simple method of candying. The roots must be thoroughly scraped and cleaned, cut up and boiled until soft. Then they must be beaten to a fine mush in a mortar (use a food processor now). The pulp is mixed with two or three times its own weight in sugar or honey and allowed to set. The roots should be candied in October.

They can also be made into a tonic. Slice them finely and add three pints of boiling water to every quarter of a pound. Boil for a few minutes, cool and strain. Take one wineglass four times a day.

FENNEL (*Foeniculum vulgare*) is a native of the Mediterranean region, and has adopted many other European countries, but it might just as well be a native of Britain from the way it romps off into the wild, particularly around the coast.

The Romans used it extensively in sauces, particularly one in which globe artichokes were cooked, which was made of oil and *liquamen*, fennel, rue, mint, coriander, pepper, lovage and honey. Fennel seed was used in sauces for chickens and boar.

In Ancient Greece garlands of fennel were presented to victorious warriors, as Longfellow wrote in his otherwise rather gloomy poem *The Goblet of Life*:

Above the lowly plants it towers,
The fennel, with its yellow flowers,
And in an earlier age than ours
Was gifted with the wondrous powers,
Lost vision to restore.

It gave new strength and fearless mood;
And gladiators, fierce and rude,
Mingled it in their daily food;
And he who battled and subdued,
A wreath of fennel wore.

It was almost the top of the list of what every good twelfth-century garden should have and a combination of being the most difficult of plants to destroy, and a marvellous companion to so many dishes, particularly fish and soups, has ensured that it has held its position in the herb and kitchen garden regardless of the effects of vast social change, wars, famine and fever.

It was grown for a variety of medicinal uses including kidney complaints, the stingings and bitings of 'wicked and venomous beasts', and the bites of mad dogs. It eased ague, and the whole plant, root, stem, leaf and seeds were taken for lung infections, ear troubles and eyesight problems. The green leaves were given to nursing mothers to ensure an abundance of milk.

John Parkinson in 1629 recorded that apart from fish cookery, fennel was used in pickles, including pickled fruit, and the seeds were used to flavour pippin pies, baked fruit and bread, and the shepherds, he said, used to roast the flower heads and eat them with pepper and salt. This practice may well have been to damp down the appetite, for it was a common practice among the hungry poor to eat fennel to reduce hunger pains, and it has been used for centuries as a slimming aid.

John Evelyn included it in his salads, peeling the young stalks and treating them like celery. He also served the leaves, chopped, and dressed with vinegar, or oil, and pepper, as a dish on its own.

Fennel, either the green or bronze type, is a fine decorative plant, as well as being useful, but it can demonstrate its success in an alarming way. Take heed of Philip Miller's warning: '. . . do not suffer their Seeds to shed upon the Ground: for the Plants will come up, and over-run everything that grows near them, and they are with much more Difficulty extirpated.' No truer words were written or spoken. Once the flowers are over, and they are decorative, cut off the seed-heads, except for a few which you can allow to mature for keeping, but remove those and dry them before the seeds drop.

A small spot should be found among the herbs for FEVERFEW (*Chrysanthemum parthenium*), which is also known as Bachelor's Buttons. It is a pretty little plant with yellow-green, sometimes completely golden foliage, which it holds through the winter, and bright white daisy flowers. As its name suggests it is an ancient physic garden herb, and has long been used, powdered or fresh, to treat headaches. I know of one person who suffered badly from migraine, but has been able to keep it in check by eating two or three leaves of feverfew every day. A soothing tisane is made from the leaves and flowers.

WHITE HOREHOUND (*Marrubium vulgare*) is another small medicinal herb which earns a place in the herb garden because its woolly grey-green leaves covered with soft white hairs, are a good winter colour. It has a reputation for easing colds, and at least one modern authority on herbs claims that if a few of the very bitter leaves are chewed every day, it will protect the eater from catching colds. Although it grows wild it is sometimes difficult to start, and it is best to let a bought plant self-seed, because its young will invariably be a lot more robust. The leaves can be used to make a tisane, which needs sweetening.

HYSSOP (*Hyssopus officinalis*) is one of the most beautiful of the herbs, as well as being among the oldest. It forms an almost shrubby little bush, which will become straggly if it is not clipped, and produces heads of intense, bright blue flowers. It originates in southern Europe, but is completely hardy in Britain, coming easily from seeds, with only the tips of the wiry branches being pruned back by the frost. Although it was primarily grown as a medicinal herb, it is useful in the kitchen, and should be grown for that use as well as for its attractiveness.

The Romans, who would certainly have introduced it in the first place, mixed it with other herbs for making the aromatic salts which they used as a digestive. It was to be found in Saxon gardens, and was grown as a distilling herb, and for inclusion in pottages and sauces.

Medicinally it was widely used to treat throat infections and chest complaints, and the leaves well soaked in vinegar were held against a tooth to relieve toothache; boiled in wine it was employed as a shampoo to get rid of head lice. The green leaves, bruised and mixed with sugar were included in a plaster for wounds and cuts; a tisane relieved catarrh.

John Gerarde, in the sixteenth century, listed four varieties – hyssop with blue flowers, with reddish flowers, white flowered and thin-leaved. But nearly two hundred years later, Philip Miller was able to describe no less than thirteen varieties; they included, red-, white- and blue-flowered types, two with hairy leaves, and a most attractive sounding form with gold-striped leaves.

Miller's advice was not to make too much of a fuss of hyssop. He wrote that they '... are very hardy Plants, which will endure the Cold of our Winters in the open Air, provided they are planted in a dry undunged Soil; for when they are planted in a rich Soil, they grow very luxuriant in Summer, and are less able to resist the Cold in Winter: so that when any of these Plants grow out of the Joints of Old Walls (as they frequently do), they will resist the most severe Frost; and will be much more aromatic, than those that live in a rich Soil.'

In the seventeenth century it was put to an interesting use to save fish that was getting close to going off. The fish was covered with fresh hyssop and winter savory and laid on a bed of rushes.

In the eighteenth century it is listed among the sweet herbs, although medically it remained in favour until relatively recent times for the relief of coughs.

Hyssop is a bitter herb, but used in moderation it is quite excellent in stews, stuffings, soups, and even chopped very fine, in a salad. In the past in cooking it was normally used in broths but the flowers and top leaves were ground down to a powder to enliven dull food.

LOVAGE (*Levisticum officinale*), which is sometimes known as lovache in the old writings, is an ancient herb, which like so many was brought to this country by the Romans, who used it extremely widely in their cooking. Its kitchen use in this country had almost completely tailed away by the mid-seventeenth century, but now, happily it is again being recognised as a useful and delicious flavouring. But it is doubtful if it will ever again get quite the same attention as was paid to it by the Romans. They used lovage in all kinds of sauces, and it was an important ingredient in the smoked Lucanian sausage, which was made from meat and fat, pepper, cumin, savory, rue, parsley, lovage, leeks, mixed herbs, laurel berries, pine kernels and *liquamen*.

Fried marrows were garnished with a mixture, which included lovage, as well as cumin, oregano and onions, and it was also used in cooking cabbage, and in a dressing for artichoke hearts. The herb went into patinas, fricassees and soups, and vegetable and fruit stews.

Lovage was extensively employed in cooking all kinds of birds. A sauce for ostrich was made from it mixed with cumin and savory, and it went into sauces for crane, duck, chicken and pigeons, as well as for fungies, venison, mutton, lamb, veal, and shell fish. They dressed oyster with lovage, pepper, egg yolk, vinegar, *liquamen*, oil and wine. It was the kind of distinctive flavour that the Romans particularly liked.

Lovage survived the departure of the Romans to become a common plant in Saxon gardens; it was adopted as a physic herb by the monks and nuns and was used for a whole range of internal disorders as well as jaundice, and for sweating out fevers. A more pleasant cosmetic use was as a skin cleanser.

By the mid-seventeenth century lovage was virtually banished from the kitchen garden being grown almost exclusively for the dispensary. It kept a tenuous hold on culinary use with the seeds being ground as a kind of pepper substitute. The young stems, leaves and seeds were included in salads, or rather rarely cooked as a vegetable.

Lovage is an extremely useful herb, well-worthy of a place in the kitchen garden. It is a handsome plant from the moment its purple-tinged young growth appears in the spring, right through the development of its strong celery-like foliage to the pale yellow flowers set on top of stalks that grow to four feet high. The leaves are delicious in soups, stews and stuffings, and finely chopped and raw in salads. The stems are extremely handy in those many recipes that ask for a stick of celery, and its strong celery flavour is also contained in the seeds, a few heads of which should be harvested and dried. The seeds are an excellent vinegar flavouring.

Of all the herbs brought to this country, none is sweeter, or more useful, than MARJORAM. Two kinds are grown, Pot, or Perennial marjoram (*Origanum vulgare*), which is extremely hardy and can be picked right round the year; and Sweet, or Annual marjoram, sometimes called Knotted marjoram (*Origanum majorana*), which some authorities say originates from the east, but according to the *Oxford Book of Food Plants*, is native to the Mediterranean. It is a tender plant, and will hardly ever survive a winter in Britain, but it is an easy annual.

Curiously it does not seem to have been as widely used as many other herbs by the Romans, although it was included in a sauce that went with cooked bulbs, which were regarded as an aphrodisiac. It was one of the herbs that Alexander Neckham considered to be essential in all gardens in the twelfth century, and it was being grown as a pottage herb in the fifteenth century. Medieval gardeners listed it as a plant that should be grown for its flavour and beauty, and it has always been one of the ingredients of a bouquet garni.

Marjoram was also highly thought of in the physic garden, and the Elizabethans used it with sage and rosemary boiled in wine to treat black teeth. It was one of those compendium herbs that could be used for a wide range of illnesses and injuries: dropsy, bruises, scorpion stings, dislocated joints, head complaints, and for making sweet smelling ointments. It was said to be 'very profitable against all cold griefs and maladies', as well as toothache and singing in the ears, and was put into perfumed baths.

In the kitchen, winter marjoram (Pot marjoram) was a 'farcing herb', used in forced meats, as well as being dried, powdered and scattered over salads.

The sweetness of its scent is what is so appealing, and legend says that originally marjoram was the name of a serving boy in the court of King Cinyras of Cyprus who, when he dropped and broke a jar of rare perfumed, collapsed in terror and was transformed into the sweet herb. Apart from its use in the kitchen and by the apothecaries, it was a strewing herb, and was put among linen. One herbalist declared that just to smell it was enough to put a man or woman into good health, and in the past it was the ingredient for a tisane known as 'Spring Tea', which was considered to be a stimulating tonic.

Marjoram pudding is a dish that was ancient even when this seventeenth-century recipe was written:

Take the curd of a quart of milk finely broken, a good handful or more of sweet marjoram chopped as small as dust, and mingle with the curd five eggs, but three whites, beaten with rose-water; some nutmeg and sugar, and half a pint of cream; beat all these well together, and put in three quarters of a pound of melted butter; put a thin sheet of paste (pastry) at the bottom of your dish; then pour in your pudding, and with a spur cut out little slips of paste the breadth of a little finger, and lay them over cross and cross in large diamonds; but some small bits of butter on the top, and bake it.

By the early nineteenth century the herb was slipping out of fashion, and the decline worsened during the century. A contemporary writer dismissed it as 'a common garden plant, of no great beauty', although it was still grown to make an infusion for headaches and dizziness.

The description of its appearance is unjust for marjoram is a pretty little plant, with its neat leaves and pinky-white flowers that seem to powder the tips of the branches. And the golden forms are a delight, particularly when they produce their new growth. They can be used for edging, or just tucked into odd corners in the herb bed or border. Although Pot marjoram does not have quite the intense flavour of Sweet marjoram, both are superb in all kinds of stuffing. I use them in turkey stuffing at Christmas, and grow a pot of Sweet marjoram under cover just for that purpose.

Neither wars, revolutions, invasions, fads or fashions have been able to diminish the popularity of MINT (*Mentha*). It is one of the few cultivated plants that always manages to survive in the totally neglected garden, and it is the one that the least adventurous cook insists on having in the kitchen garden.

From the earliest times a variety of mints and, in the opinion of the users at least, mint relatives were used, not only in cooking, but in medicine, beauty preparations, and as strewing herbs to perfume rooms. The mints are very widely distributed, and many grow wild in Britain, so it is hard to say with any kind of certainty whether or not they were introduced by the Romans. What is quite certain is that the Romans used them in their cuisine. Dried mint was an ingredient in sauces. Pennyroyal, the neat, prostrate and strongly perfumed mint, was used with cucumbers, and as a dressing for melons, and garden mint was used along with pepper, lovage, rue and coriander in cooking cabbage. It was also cooked with globe artichokes, and in sauces for flamingo, wild boar, mutton and lamb, and both it and pennyroyal were ingredients in salads.

Mints were important in seventeenth-century salads. Spearmint was 'dry and warm, very fragrant, a little press'd, is friendly to the weak Stomach, and powerful against all Nervous Crudities: The gentler Tops of the Orange-Mint, enter well into our Composition, or are grateful alone (as are also the other sorts) with the Juice of Orange, and a little sugar', according to John Evelyn.

Although in these times it is common to chop fresh mint over a potato salad, the Elizabethans used it in considerably more complicated salads which also included parsley, sage, garlic, small onions, leeks, borage, fennel, cresses, rue and rosemary. Earlier still in the twelfth-century garden, and in the fifteenth century, Calamint, the so-called mountain mint (*Calamintha ascendens*), and catmint were grown for the pot. Calamint and red mint were the varieties especially valued for salads, and the former was also used in cups.

As the years passed the varieties of mint being cultivated increased. In Saxon times pennyroyal and peppermint were to be found in monastic physic gardens. By the end of the sixteenth century, red garden mint, curled mint and spearmint (good for stomachs, watering eyes and treating the bites of mad dogs), as well as catmint (pains in head and stomach) and calamint (agues and fits), were common garden plants.

The seventeenth century saw eight varieties being cultivated to treat a wide range of complaints. It was considered to be such a powerful aphrodisiac (Aristotle started the belief) that people were warned to take it in moderation. It was mixed with the juice of a sour pomegranate to relieve stomach complaints, and boiled with wine to help a woman through a difficult labour.

In the kitchen it was used in a sauce to serve with mackerel, and although this is not a sauce much used, if used at all, these days, it was still quite common in some parts of the country in the 1830s. George Lindley observed that 'there have been formerly one or two other sorts of Mint grown in gardens, particularly in and near Norwich, and used in sauce for mackerel; but they are nauseous, rather than otherwise, and therefore are now rarely to be found in a cultivated state.' Since he only mentions two varieties, spearmint and peppermint, it is interesting to speculate on what mint was used in the sauce.

Before Lindley's time, in the mid-eighteenth century, apart from some types only grown as botanical curiosities, there were ten varieties in common garden cultivation; spearmint, peppermint, long-leaved horsemint, water-calamint, water-mint, orange mint, spearmint with a variegated leaf, great round-leaved water-mint with a variegated leaf, spearmint with a rugged leaf and strong scent, and narrow-leafed Allepo mint.

While so many herbs have disappeared from gardens, the mints have increased in number, and now it is possible to buy the roots of quite a number of exotically scented varieties, such as Eau de Cologne, ginger, lemon, and pineapple. My own favourite for mint sauce is apple mint, with its good looking velvety leaves and deliciously fresh flavour, which really does have a touch of apples about it. It is a sound plan to grow a selection, including spearmint and peppermint, so that they can be blended together for mint sauce; I also add leaves of verbena and balm. There are few more delicious meals than lamb roasted with rosemary and garlic and served with young summer cabbages, new potatoes, and a carefully made mint sauce. Collect a selection of mints, balm and verbena, and chop very fine, mix with white wine or cider vinegar (if you make your own herb flavoured vinegars it will add a new dimension) sugar, salt and pepper. You can also add crushed garlic, but that is strictly a matter of choice.

While it is the most tenacious plant, mint is all the better for being split up and re-planted every three years.

Although its use in the kitchen is extremely limited, MUGWORT (*Artemisia vulgaris*) is an attractive addition to the herb garden, and its bitter, aromatic leaves can be used very sparingly as a seasoning. A tisane made from the leaves is supposed to bring relief to rheumatism sufferers. It is a plant surrounded by superstition, and on the Continent is called the Herb of St. John the Baptist, and was regarded as a protection against the plague. It was also credited with being able to forecast if a very ill person would recover, the test being that if the patient slept after the herb was placed under their pillow they would recover; if they did not sleep they would die. People who were on their feet for long hours would line their shoes with the leaves of mugwort, and according to one old authority, could walk forty miles before noon and not feel tired. It was also used in a multi-herb draught to treat internal wounds.

It would be hard to imagine a garden, or a kitchen, without PARSLEY (*Petroselinum crispum*), which is not only one of the very few fresh herbs offered for sale by greengrocers, but one that has remained firmly in use throughout all the vicissitudes of culinary fashions, even remaining popular in the so-called good plain English cooking of more recent years.

A native of southern Europe, parsley occupied a most noble place in the lives and culture of the ancients. The leaves were woven into the garlands of heroes, indeed Hercules immortalised it by selecting it for his own use. It was used in the crowns of victors in the Grecian games, and was grown in great quantities in Greek gardens, and upon the graves of their ancestors.

Because the seeds are quite often slow and eccentric in germinating, seed planting has attracted some strange rituals and beliefs, one, at least, which is enough to put a macho gardener off growing the herb at all. It is said that if a man is successful in growing parsley, he is disappointing in bed.

Eleanor Sinclair Rohde in her book *A Garden of Herbs* quotes the most elaborate advice on getting the seeds to germinate swiftly: 'To make the seedes appear more quickly steep them in vinegar and strew the bed with the ashes of bean-water with the best aqua vitae, and then cover the beds with a piece of woollen cloth, and the plants will begin to appear within an hour.' Many people do soak the soil with boiling water before planting.

Anyone who transplants parsley will, it was once widely accepted, bring misfortune and disaster on his house and family. Altogether parsley would seem to be a tricky plant to cope with, but for all that an essential one in every kitchen garden.

Alphonse de Candolle in his *Origin of Cultivated Plants* says that Dioscorides and Pliny only regarded parsley as a medicinal plant, but that in the Middle Ages, Charlemagne ordered it to be grown in his garden. He was particularly fond of a cheese flavoured with parsley seeds. He contends that it first appeared in English gardens in 1548, a date also accepted by George Lindley. But William Rhind was less sure. He wrote in his *History of the Vegetable Kingdom*: 'It is said to be a native of Sardinia, whence it was brought into England about the middle of the sixteenth century: but the plant is of so ancient culture in this country, that the period of its introduction cannot, perhaps, be accurately assigned, and though supposed not to be indigenous to Britain, it is now completely naturalized in various parts of England and Scotland.'

Rhind's suspicions that it was of much older cultivation in Britain than the middle of the sixteenth century were correct. William Longland, who lived between 1330 and 1400, wrote in *Piers the Plowman* of peasants growing parsley and leeks in their gardens, and certainly the herb was used in pottages, and in a popular Norman fish sauce composed of parsley, sage, costmary, dittander, thyme and garlic. It was recorded in twelfth-century gardens, and if this was not sufficient evidence to place parsley in our gardens well before the mid-sixteenth century, consider the fact that it was employed in Roman cookery, and it is doubtful if it was left at home when Roman invaders settled in Britain.

The seeds were used in the aromatic salts made by the Romans, and the fresh leaves in sauces, and in the spicy smoked Lucanian sausage, with chicken and in gourmet dishes.

In Elizabethan times meat balls were cooked with parsley, and the roots boiled with mutton. From an early stage it was found to go beautifully with any kind of salad, either mixed or individual, particularly potato salads, cucumber salads and tomato salads. One mixed sixteenth-century recipe included parsley, sage, garlic, small onions, leeks, borage, mint, fennel, cresses, rue and rosemary, but curiously the great master of the salad, John Evelyn, does not appear to have greatly relished parsley, which he considered more useful in the sick room than the salad bowl, allowing only that 'some few tops of the tender Leaves may yet be admitted; tho' it was of old, we read, never brought to the Table at all, as sacred to Oblivium and the Defunct.' Perhaps its ancient association with death lingered on but despite this three varieties Common, Curled, and Virginian were grown. Smallage was incorrectly included as a parsley, although it was too bitter for most tastes.

Medicinally it was used for liver and kidney complaints, and mixed with breadcrumbs or flour to make poultices. It was also given to epileptics.

By the eighteenth century the botanists had got into a muddle over parsley, adding celery and celeriac to the family. In fact they listed thirteen varieties, while in reality there were only four true parsleys among them; the Common, Curled, Broad-leaved and Round-leaved.

For a time parsley was highly regarded by farmers who believed, with some justification, that it was a defence against footrot in sheep. They were fed on the herb for two or three hours twice a week, and their flesh was said to be most delicately flavoured. The practice was continued in Hampshire and Buckinghamshire into the nineteenth century. Parsley was also planted in fields to attract hares.

The varieties grown in kitchen gardens increased by four at the turn of this century; Double-curled, Champion moss-curled, Double-curled dwarf, and Fern-leaved.

Apart from its use as a flavouring, parsley, which contains vitamin C, iron and iodine, can be made into a tisane and used as a diuretic. The smell of garlic can be removed from the breath by chewing a few leaves of the herb.

In the Christian culture, ROSEMARY (*Rosmarinus officinalis*) is among the holiest of flowers, seen as a defence against evil and only growing successfully for the most virtuous. For the old Arab herbalists it was the plant that restored strength, memory and speech, and it was its reputation as a powerful aid to memory that inspired Shakespeare to have Ophelia to say: 'There's rosemary, that's for remembrance; pray, love, remember...' And it was also for remembrance that it was carried at funerals, and the sprigs cast on to coffins.

Because it was under the social protection of Mary, legend has it in Spain that the lovely blue flowers were transformed from white when Mary placed her robe on a rosemary bush. It was widely believed that if you slept with it under your pillow you would not suffer from disturbing dreams.

In medieval and Tudor gardens it was grown extensively as much for its appearance as its use, and walls were often smothered with the shrubby herb, presumably growing ten or twelve feet high, despite the traditional assertion that it never grows above the height of Christ when he was on earth. The modern gardener is fortunate in having a fairly wide choice of rosemarys, all of which can be used in the kitchen, from *officinalis*, the old herb garden form, to those with deep blue flowers, and the prostrate form, *lavandulaceus*.

Since it is a native of the Mediterranean region and Asia Minor, it is probable that the Romans brought it to Britain, although they did not seem over-enthusiastic in using it in cookery. But it certainly was to be found in Saxon gardens, especially in monastic physic gardens, and was valued as a distilling herb.

Its attraction to bees, placed it among the most important bee plants and herbs, and still is a favourite with bee-keepers. However, its major use was in cephalic medicine, from curing headaches and brain disorders to restoring hair and curing toothache. The Elizabethans used the wood to manufacure toothpicks, and the ashes for tooth-powder. For toothache they mixed figs with rosemary and sage in wine until the wine was absorbed, and then the hot figs were placed against the offending tooth, and it was used in a wine decoction for black teeth. Of course it was in Lady Hewet's Water, which included both flowers and leaves.

Many people still use the liquid from boiling rosemary in water as a hair rinse, and it is also claimed to prevent hair uncurling in the rain. For many years it was credited with the ability to restore hair, and indeed put the green colour into most popular pomatums. It is the main ingredient of Hungary Water, which was invented by a holy man for Queen Elizabeth of Hungary, and was used to cure her of paralysis.

Despite its prominent place in the physic garden, rosemary should not be ignored in the kitchen. It can be used in salads (but sparingly – more a hint than a mouthful), and the flowers used to be used in vinegar. They were also candied. In the seventeenth century a stock for cooking pike and carp was made from rosemary, parsley and thyme, and sometimes gooseberries and barberries were added.

It also goes very well in most stuffings, and with olive oil and garlic makes a marvellous marinade for chicken pieces, which should then be grilled or cooked in the oven in a very high heat.

But undoubtedly lamb sprigged with rosemary and slivers of garlic, is the use of the herb at its finest.

RUE (*Ruta graveolens*), the Herb of Grace, is among the most ancient inhabitants of the kitchen garden. Revered and valued by Greeks and Romans, and by the Druid priests, its branches of lovely grey-blue leaves were later used by the Christian church to sprinkle holy water. Grown in the herb border it forms, providing it is kept in order, a neat bush whose foliage lends colour throughout the year; it is particularly beautiful when starred with its clear, pale yellow flowers.

Its widest use was in medicine, in counteracting poison, but faith in its curative powers went far beyond mere poison. Henry Lyte stated that the leaves eaten with ordinary meals, or mixed with dried figs and walnuts, was 'good against all evil aires, and against the pestilence, and all poyson, and against the bitings of vipers and serpents.' It was to be steeped in wine and drunk to ease the effects of scorpions, bees, wasps, hornets and mad dogs, and its virtues did not end there. Rue was used in treating women after childbirth; taken by men as a contraceptive; for poor eyesight (great artists like Leonardo da Vinci, and Michelangelo, bathed their eyes daily in rue water to improve the sharpness of their vision); rue juice heated in the dried skin of a pomegranate was used to relieve earache, and mixed with roses and vinegar it was a sovereign cure for headache. It was employed as a skin cleanser, as an embrocation to relieve painful joints, and made a medicine for stomach disorders; even nose bleeding was treated by laying the leaves on the nose.

The most distinctive aroma of rue leaves was considered to be a defence against the plague, and it was included in the bouquets carried in court by judges anxious not to contract jail fever, and bunches of rue were scattered on the court-room floor. It was commonly planted in window boxes and on balconies in the town and cities, and in London there was a brisk trade in plants in the spring. No doubt they were regarded as a pretty screen against the disease that hatched in the streets and open sewers. Certainly the fresh and dried foliage was used to repel insects, including fleas. The Elizabethans would scatter bunches of rue at the entrance to chicken runs and houses to keep away predators, particularly cats and fulmars. It was planted around buildings housing cattle and sheep, as it was supposed to ward off adders and lizards (the latter were thought to be poisonous), this practice stemming from the belief that weazels ate rue before hunting snakes. The growing of rue in Elizabethan gardens involved some special practices. It should be planted in the shade of a fig tree, or grafted to fig bark, to sweeten its taste and smell. It was believed to grow better if set in a bean or an onion, and that strong plants would control garden pests, as well as defending the household against sorcery and incantations. It was also used in veterinary medicine. Head pains in animals were treated by pouring beaten garlic in wine down the creature's nostrils. This was followed by bathing the head with a decoction of rue, sage, marjoram, lavender, bay and walnut leaves.

John Gerarde quoted a number of verses extolling the virtues of rue in his *Herbal*. One claims:

> It stays the cough if it be drunk,
> It cleanseth monthly flowers,
> If you seeth in water, and
> Thereto put wine that scours (vinegar);
> Such broth doth stay the belly gripes.
> It helpeth breast and lung;
> It cures the sickness of the sides,
> Called plurisy in Greeks tongue.
> The gout and the sciatica,
> And agues it doth cure,
> If it be drunke: and other things,
> As writers do assure.

Parkinson recommended it for chest and lung complaints, and said that chewing the leaves takes away the smell of garlic. He added that it was pickled and eaten to strengthen the sight.

It is scarcely surprising that such a versatile herb has been grown in gardens without a break for centuries. In the early nineteenth century it was still being prescribed to treat fevers, headaches and nervous complaints. A conserve of fresh rue leaves beaten up in three times their weight of sugar was taken for stomach pains and 'hysteric disorders'.

As a culinary herb, rue has very largely fallen out of use, despite being most variedly used by Romans, who made it into a sauce for flamingoes, and for vegetables; used it in stuffings, and ate it with oil and salt as a salad. In fact it is delicious in salads, and nobody should be put off by the strong aroma of the freshly cut leaves. A little, and I do emphasise little, of the young growth chopped very finely over a salad, gives it a unique and delightful flavour. But one caution; rue can produce a rash on some sensitive skins.

SAFFRON (*Crocus sativus*) has been used in cooking, at least the dried style has, for centuries, and until the end of the eighteenth century was grown commercially in England, and so for its historical associations, as well as for the beauty of its large, purple flowers, it deserves a place among the herbs. It is said that saffron was introduced during the reign of Edward III, and first grown at Walden in Essex by one Sir Thomas Smith thus giving it the name of Saffron Walden. Later it was cultivated extensively in Herefordshire, Hampshire and Cambridgeshire, and seems to have been a tricky crop to raise. As Brian Matthew, the Kew botanist and leading authority on crocuses, says in his book *Dwarf Bulbs*: 'It seems, from historical accounts of the industry, that very rich well-manured ground is needed, as is division and replanting each year into fresh ground.'

Saffron was cropped for two years, and the land left fallow the third, and ideally the corms were planted in soil that had carried a crop of barley the year before. The saffron fields, which were rarely over three acres, were manured with twenty or thirty loads of well rotted dung per acre, and were ploughed three times before the planting. Finally a man armed with a narrow-bladed spit-shovel made a shallow trench into which women set the corms; 392,040 to an acre. The flowers had to be gathered before they opened in the early morning, and the long scarlet style picked out and dried over a fire.

As it is one of the autumn flowering crocuses, it does bring a welcome spot of colour to the garden, and also attracts the late bees, which was one of the reasons it was valued by the Elizabethans. It was used to revive those close to death, and 'is with good success given to procure bodilie lust'. Earlier, in the fifteenth century, it would seem that the corm was also eaten, since it is listed among root vegetables such as turnips and radishes.

The Romans used the seeds of *Crocus Sativus* as a vegetable rennet in cheese making. While it was an important ingredient in cooking, and still is, the Tudors valued it with meat balls, it was treated with some suspicion in this country. Not so in Germany where it was made into little balls with honey, thoroughly dried, powdered and sprinkled over salads. In Spain and France it was used extensively with a wide variety of dishes, but in Britain it was always added very sparingly to food.

In medicine it was highly regarded for breast, lung, liver and bladder complaints, and was mixed with food as an aid to digestion. Some botanists warned that it should be used with great caution, and that large doses were poisonous, although Sir John Hill in the early nineteenth century called it 'A noble cordial'. Clearly it does have an enlivening effect, and Sir Francis Bacon insisted that what made the English a sprightly race was 'the liberal use of saffron in their broths and sweetmeats.'

SAGE (*Salvia officinalis*) is another of the southern European herbs which have become as familiar as buttercups in our gardens. It is a plant valued equally in cooking and medicine, but above all its popularity for centuries was largely due to its reputation for aiding people to grow to a healthy old age. Sage ale, sage wine and sage tea were all taken as a regular tonic drink.

Quite how sage came to Britain is uncertain. It could well have been brought by the Romans, although Apicius did not appear to make use of it in his recipes, but it was employed extensively by the ancient Greeks and Arabs, and it was certainly grown by the Saxons, who derived all their knowledge of herbs from the writings of the ancients. In medieval households it was particularly valued as a distilling herb, and the

Elizabethans used it in medicine, especially for treating toothache. They saw it as a defence against venomous beasts, and as a medicine to calm trembling hands, soothe aching muscles, to stimulate the appetite, cure headaches, sweeten breath and act as a purgative. They also treated their sick animals with it, and planted it for their bees.

It was regarded as an effective gargle for sore throats, and recommended for baths to ease the aches and pains of old age, and to strengthen the bodies of the young. It was steeped in beer to make Sage Ale, which was a tonic especially used by pregnant women, particularly if they threatened to miscarry.

During the fast periods laid down by the Church, it was mixed with parsley and butter and spread on bread.

In cooking, apart from its use in stuffings, it was put in with boiling calves heads, and also mixed with the brains, vinegar and pepper to serve with the boiled head, and well bruised and mixed with currants it made a sauce for a dish of roast pigs brains.

Of the various sages, and no less than fifteen were listed in the eighteenth century, red sage was regarded as the most virtuous and was the one sought for salads. John Evelyn wrote that: 'The tops of the Red, well pick'd and wash'd (being often defil'd with Venomous Slime, and almost imperceptible Insects) with the Flowers, retain all the noble Properties of the other hot Plants; more especially for the Head, Memory, Eyes, and all the Paralytical Affections. In short, 'tis a Plant endu'd with so many and wonderful Properties, as that the assiduous use of it is said to render Men immortal: We cannot therefore but allow the tender Summities of the young leaves; but principally the flowers in our cold Sallet; yet so as not to domineer.' How right he was in that final remark, for over done, sage, makes a salad unpleasant.

Walter Bayley, who was one of the doctors who looked after Elizabeth I, condemned sage as a cause of flatulence, which was a condition which aroused a great deal of concern. The Normans, however, valued it as an ingredient in a popular fish sauce, which was made from sage, parsley, costmary, dittany, thyme and garlic. Often mint was also added. In the mid-eighteenth century it had become an essential ingredient in forced meat which was stored in earthenware pots.

Take part of a leg of mutton, veal or beef and pick off the skin and fat, and to every pound of meat put two pounds of beef suet; shred them together very fine, then season with pepper, salt, cloves, mace, nutmeg and sage; then put all into a stone mortar, and to every two pounds of meat put half a pound of oysters, and six eggs well beaten, then mix them all together, and beat it very well; then keep it in an earthen pot for your use; put a little flour on the top, and when you roll them up flour your hands.

Red sage was used at that time to make a distilled water for improving eyesight, which also included betony, rue and chicory, and was included in a medicine for curing rickets.

Sage wine, which as the following traditional recipe shows, was a simply-made tonic credited with almost magical powers.

Take four handfuls of red Sage, beat it in a stone mortar like a green sauce, then put it into a quart of red wine, and let it stand three or four days close stopt, shaking it twice or thrice, then let it stand and settle, and the next day take of the sage wine three spoonfuls, and of running water one spoonful, then fast after it one hour or better; use this from Michaelmas to the end of March: It will cure any aches or humours in the joints, dry rheums, keep from all diseases to the 4th degree; it will help the dead palsy, and convulsions in the sinews, sharpens the memory, and from the beginning of taking it will keep the body mild, strengthen nature, til the fulness of your days be finished; nothing will be changed in your strength, except the change of your hair; it will keep your teeth sound that were not corrupted before; it will keep you from the gout, the dropsy, of any swellings of the joints or body.

And with an endorsement like that it is hardly surprising that sage has always been grown in good gardens.

SAVORY, both Summer savory (*Satureja hortensis*), an annual, and Winter savory (*Satureja montana*), a twiggy little perennial, is at last becoming more familiar in kitchen gardens after a long period of neglect. Indeed Philip Miller, writing in the mid-eighteenth century, remarked: 'These Plants were Anciently more cultivated in England than at present, they being very little in Use to what they were formerly, when they enter'd most Dishes of Soups etc., but at present they are very little used in the Kitchen, being chiefly cultivated for medicinal Use.'

W. Hooker del. 1817

The Queen Pine

The Queen Pine was one of the most successful of the pineapples grown in English gardens. Enormous skill and ingenuity were employed to produce the fruits. They were raised in special pine pits in carefully mixed hot-beds of tanner's bark.

The Bigarreau Cherry

From very early gardening days cherries were greatly valued, and varieties like the Bigarreau Cherry were carefully nurtured in orchards or grown against walls. Apart from being essential to any well-kept table, they also inspired poets like Robert Herrick.

The Violette hâtive Nectarine

Like their better known cousins, peaches, nectarines have been cultivated for centuries. The rich, luscious appearance of varieties like the Violette Hative inspired John Milton with the idea that they were among the fruits gathered by Adam and Eve in the Garden of Eden.

The Algiers Apricot

At one time apricots were grown in every garden, from those of the squire to the cottager. The Chinese grew them 3000 years ago, and the Romans stewed them with mint, honey and pepper. John Tradescant the Elder fought pirates to collect the Algiers Apricot for English orchards.

No herb bed or garden should be without sage, an essential ingredient for flavouring stuffings.

Rue, the Herb of Grace, first a medicinal herb, is delicious used sparingly in salads.

Lovage, a magnificent plant loved by the Romans, and superb in soups and stews.

Hyssop is as ancient as it is beautiful. Tea made from its leaves relieves catarrh.

A rare naive painting of the 19th century portrays those vegetables to be found in every cottage garden: cabbages, turnips, radishes and vegetable marrows.

At first wild strawberries were collected from the woods, but it was not until the Chile Strawberry was introduced and crossed with the rather tasteless Virginia Strawberry that hybridizers began to breed the familiar, richly flavoured modern varieties.

The Golden Pippin is one of the oldest of the English apples. It was raised from a seed in Sussex during the reign of Henry VIII, and later became popular throughout Europe.

Plate XXV

1. Ribston Pippin

The Ribston Pippin was the only one to germinate out of three seeds sent from Normandy in 1709 to Sir Henry Goodricke in Yorkshire. It was an instant success and is the parent of Cox's Orange Pippin.

Allotments grew out of the iniquitous Enclosure Acts which robbed peasants of their Common Land. In wartime they played a vital role in helping to feed the nation.

This carefully planned kitchen garden at the Royal Horticultural Society's garden at Wisley in Surrey shows how a considerable variety and quantity of vegetables can be produced from a small modern garden.

Marigolds and phlox mingle with potatoes and other vegetables in this cottage garden. Such gardens as these have kept alive the riotously colourful tradition of mixing the practical and decorative.

Few modern gardens have the room for large displays of vegetables, flowers or shrubs. This garden shows how the massing plants of the herbacous border live happily with vegetables.

A tiny town house courtyard has room for a herb collection. This circular bed, surrounded by pots, holds a large selection which includes bay, fennel, marigolds, chives, sage, basil and thyme.

Always extremely formal, the potager can still be made delightfully decorative. The potager originally was intended to produce the pulses, roots and cabbages which were the basic ingredients of potage, the staple diet of working people of the past.

Rosemary, chives and borage in beds set in brick and cobbles at Newington House, Oxford.

Lavender, silvery Stachys lanata, and red hollyhocks enrich Cogges Farm Museum kitchen garden, Witney, Oxford.

Celery repays care. The trench must be well based with manure, and always kept moist.

Grapes thrive and crop outside against a warm wall. Black Hamburg is a sound variety.

Jerusalem artichokes can easily grow six feet tall and make a useful windbreak, especially on open allotments. They will stand any weather and are dug in winter as needed.

A well stocked kitchen garden with healthy rows of carrots, spinach, turnips, beetroot, parsnips, onions and shallots, backed by a screen of asparagus fern. The fine foliage which appears after the tender spears have been cut mixes well with flower arrangements.

Sweet peas and potatoes line a grass path leading to the arbour at Barton Abbey kitchen garden. Cluster roses, vines, wisteria, honeysuckle, golden hops or jasmine can be trained over such frames.

Grace and elegance is achieved at Cogges Farm, where the gravel paths are edged with lavender. The arch supports 'Wedding Day' and 'The Garland' rambling roses. Lavender and roses are backed by espaliers of Cox's Orange Pippin and Worcester Pearmain.

A simple pole and plastic netting cage protects brassicas from marauders. Pigeons, in particular, can destroy a season's work in a few hours. It is easy and cheap to erect.

Soft fruit is relished by most garden birds. An hour or two of work will guarantee an unmolested crop. With all cages enough height must be allowed for free movement for weeding, watering and harvesting.

(Top) Bright beads of red and white currants.

(Above) The statuesque globe artichoke.

Cherries, particularly Morellos, which make a rich jam, thrive when sheltered and trained against walls.

Walls not only provide valuable protection, well planted they bring a Mediterranean touch to the garden, with grape vines and in figs trained against them. Here peas and runner beans are cropped front of them in the wall borders.

Originally scarlet runner beans were grown for the vivid beauty of their flowers. None of that is lost when they are cultivated in the kitchen garden for their luscious pods.

A warm brick wall is a perfect shelter for bee-hives, and the broad bean flowers provide a feast for the bees.

Both come from the Mediterranean region of Europe (Winter savory is also found in North Africa), but of the two, Summer savory has the most marked flavour, while Winter savory has the practical advantage of being a source of flavouring the year round. The Romans used them extensively in sauces, particularly with ostrich, and in making the spicy Lucanian sausages, and undoubtedly they brought the plant to Britain, for it featured in Saxon gardens.

Although savory fell out of favour in the nation's kitchens, it did not disappear altogether, and in Elizabethan times was cooked as a flavouring and anti-flatulent with beans, peas, rice and wheat. It also went into stuffings, puddings and sausages. It was valued for its use in drink made from rue and vinegar which was given to prevent people falling into comas, and at the beginning of the nineteenth century a tisane made from it was a cure for colic.

Savory, particularly Winter savory, is so easy to grow, and such an attractive plant for the herb bed, that it is surprising that it is not as familiar as thyme and sage, because it is the most delicious flavouring for all the pulses, and excellent in stuffings. A few sprigs are essential in a dish of broad beans.

TANSY (*Tanacetum vulgare*) used to be as common as mint in kitchen gardens and herb beds. In fact it was employed to make a sauce for lamb before mint sauce became virtually obligatory. Although its somewhat bitter flavour might be found off-putting, it is a most versatile herb, and anyway is worth growing just for its appearance, with its ferny leaves and large round flat heads of bright yellow flowers. A native of Britain, and common throughout Europe, even flourishing in Siberia, it is a very hardy plant, and the only problem of cultivation is curbing it from taking over the entire herb border.

Tansy does not seem to have featured in Roman cookery, but it was certainly grown in medieval gardens, and in the physic gardens of monasteries and convents. The Elizabethans used it for treating internal wounds. Its widest medicinal use, however, was to destroy worms, although counted among its virtues was the prevention of ague, and treatment of rheumatism, urinary complaints and gout.

Culpeper declares tansy to be a herb that will help women to conceive, and '. . . is their best companion, the husband excepted.'

He also launches into an extraordinary diatribe against 'the pope and his imps' and doctors, and accuses the latter of limiting the amount of tansy eaten in the spring, so that people would be sickly in the summer and need their services. It is a typical Culpeper outburst, but it does help to underline the value put on the herb as a pick-me-up after the long winter of increasingly poor food.

In the eighteenth century tansy was still a popular plant, and eight varieties were grown. It has lent its name to tansies, a kind of cross between an omelette and a cake. The young leaves, according to John Parkinson, were shredded with other herbs and beaten into eggs and fried. Tansy pudding was a more elaborate recipe.

Boil a quart of cream or milk with a stick of cinnamon, quartered nutmeg, and large mace; when half cold, mix it with twenty yolks of eggs; and ten whites; strain it, then put to it four grated biscuits, half a pound of butter, a pint of spinach juice, and a little tansy, sack and orange flower water, sugar, and a little salt; then gather it to a body over the fire, and pour it into your dish, being well buttered; when it is baked, turn it on a pie dish; squeeze on it an orange, grate on sugar, and garnish it with sliced orange and a little tansy.

In another recipe, still with the same large number of eggs, the tansy appeared as more of a custard.

To make a tansy to bake: Take twenty eggs, but eight whites, beat the eggs very well, and strain them into a quart of thick cream, one nutmeg, and three Naples biscuits grated, as much juice of spinach, with a sprig or two of tansy, as will make as green as grass; sweeten it to your taste; then butter your dish very well, and set it into an oven, no hotter than for custards; watch it, as soon as 'tis done, take it out of the oven, and turn it on a pie plate; scrape sugar, and squeeze orange upon it. Garnish the dish with orange and lemon, and serve it up.

Another variation was a gooseberry tansy: 'Put some fresh butter in a frying pan, and when 'tis melted put into a quart of gooseberries, and fry them until they are tender, and break them all to mash; then beat seven eggs, but four whites, a pound of sugar, three spoonfuls of sack (sherry), as much cream, a penny loaf grated, and three spoonfuls of flour, mix all these together, then put the gooseberries out of the pan to them, and stir all well together, and put them into a sauce pan to thicken; then put butter into the frying-pan and fry them brown: Strew sugar on the top.'

In County Cork in Ireland there is a unique blood pudding called Drisheen, which is displayed in butcher's windows immersed in a tray of water, which traditionally is served with tansy butter.

The tansy tonic was made from the dried leaves and flowers, while the crushed dried leaves were also used to discourage ants and clear fleas from pets. And for a very long time it formed the essential ingredient in a facial treatment, usually steeped in buttermilk.

TARRAGON (*Artemisia dracunculus*) is one of those herbs which is definitely better used green since its penetrating spicy flavour fades with drying. It is an ingredient of sauce tartare, and is always a good accompaniment with fish. Chicken roasted with a bunch of the fresh herb in its cavity assumes a delicious flavour. Despite this, however, it is not a herb very widely grown, and perhaps this lack of popularity can be traced back to the old belief that it was a cause of flatulence.

In spite of this it was for a considerable time listed as a salad herb. John Parkinson approved this use, while at the same time dismissing as an 'absurd and idle opinion' the strange notion that the plant had been created by inserting a flax seed into an onion.

Long known as the Biting Dragon, it was chopped into salads to add a sharpness to the bland flavours of lettuce and the less spicy salad herbs and vegetables. In fact it was used as a substitute for salt and vinegar.

At the same time it was considered an effective tonic that would clear the head and tone up the heart and liver.

Russian tarragon (*Artemisia dracunculoides*) is a very robust form, but its inferior flavour, and huge demands on space, do not make it worth growing, although it is certainly a good deal easier than the True or French tarragon, which is a native of southern Europe. The main problem is that it hates excessive damp, and that combined with the cold of a British winter often proves fatal. There are people who are able to establish large, thriving colonies of the plant, but I find that the safest measure is to grow it in a big pot which can be brought under cover during the winter.

THYME (*Thymus vulgaris*) is a herb that must have been created for the kitchen. Every time the leaves are crushed in the hand or underfoot, the lovely scent cries out to be added to a dish. It is, of course, essential for a bouquet garni, but over the centuries cooks have put it to a variety of uses, none more so than the Romans. It featured in their sauces, including that for boiled ostrich, boar, chicken, mutton, lamb and the other various bulbs that the Romans consumed in their relentless search for aphrodisiacs.

In Norman times it was used in fish sauce, and in Elizabethan gardens it was grown both for the pot and for the bees. From the earliest times it was essential in all kinds of stuffings, to make sauces for both meat and fish, and was a favourite stuffing for goose. It was also mixed with breadcrumbs to coat meat and fish before roasting or frying. It must have been grown in very considerable quantities, for it was strewn on floors, and added to baths to sweeten the water.

Inevitably a herb which was so popular around the house and in the kitchen, was also in demand in medicine. Herbalists and doctors used it to comfort head, stomach and spleen pains, as well as treating shortness of breath, worms, tumours, swellings, warts, failing sight, and a variety of gynaecological problems. While the familiar garden thyme was used in medicine, wild thyme, rather delightfully called Mother of Thyme, was considered the most effective. Apart from recommending it for sciatica and rheumatic pains, the medical profession used it to treat people suffering from depression.

There are a large number of thymes, apart from the common garden forms, such as lemon-scented thyme, and caraway-scented thyme, and they also come in all sizes and shapes from the shrubby form to the prostrate, and with flowers ranging from scarlet to white. In a kitchen garden with paved or brick paths the tough, creeping forms can be grown in cracks to bring an added touch of colour and scent, and they do not mind being trodden on. There is no reason either why they should not be planted in grass paths.

9
The Vegetables

In terms of the whole history of food gathering, the universal growing and eating of vegetables in any great variety is comparatively new. Until quite recent times the small private garden, cottage garden or allotment was used to grow much the same crops year after year: cabbages and other greens, peas and beans, carrots, turnips, onions and leeks. It was the great houses with their large walled kitchen gardens who were left to produce the delicacies, often at great expense and effort, and some of that quite needless.

William Robinson, arguably the greatest gardener of modern times, wrote in the preface of the 1920 third and last English language edition of *The Vegetable Garden* by Vilmorin-Andrieux: '...all agree that the greater use of the best vegetables in our food would be a gain. The reason why the more delicate vegetable foods are neglected is because the cooks of Europe have served an apprenticeship of a thousand years on the carcases of ox, pig, sheep, and we are meat-eaters because our fathers had little else to eat. The plains and hills of the cold north were dotted with wild grazing animals, as an English park is with deer, or a Western prairie with antelope, and men killed and cooked the only food they had.'

He urged people to pick and eat their vegetables when they are young and tender, and at their most delicious, and it is advice that serves a small garden well because in that way one can achieve a swift turnover and release the land for other crops. He also pleaded for more care in the cooking. In Britain we certainly do have a long tradition of destroying vegetables in the kitchen, and what he wrote more than sixty years ago is sadly still true in many cases, although the standards of cooking in the home have undoubtedly improved and are doing so all the time. But William Robinson did find that: 'In places of public resort where the best meat, game, and fish are to be had, the cooking of even the commonest vegetables is disgraceful.'

The kitchen garden is not merely a patch for growing vegetables to go with meat and fish; it is a place for herbs, the many delicious salad vegetables, and also a place for experiments with unfamiliar crops. In my own kitchen garden, which is only fifty-eight feet by thirty-six, I am able to grow up to thirty different types and varieties of vegetables.

It would be unfair to dismiss all our forefathers as cheerfully accepting ruined vegetables to go with huge hunks of meat. The Romans greatly valued vegetables and went to remarkable lengths in preparing them for the table, and during the Middle Ages and the Tudor period salads were greatly valued, and often extremely elaborate.

John Evelyn, who devoted so much of his talent and genius to gardening, believed that no day should pass without a dish of salad of some kind on the table, and of course it was a very sound and healthy principle. In *Acetaria: A Discourse of Sallets* he quotes the great botanist Ray on the place of plants in our lives:

The Use of Plants [says he] is all our Life long that of universal Importance and Concern; that we can neither live nor subsist in any Plenty with Decency, or Conveniency or be said to live indeed at all without them: whatsoever Food is necessary to sustain us, whatsoever contributes to delight and refresh us, are supply'd and brought forth out of that plentiful and abundant store: and ah, how much more innocent, sweet and healthful, is a Table cover'd with these, than with the reeking Flesh of butcher'd slaughter'd Animals! Certainly Man by Nature was never made to be a Carnivorous Creature; nor is he arm'd at all for Prey and Rapin, with gag'd and pointed Teeth and crooked Claws, sharpened to rend and tear: But with gentle Hands to gather Fruit and Vegetables, and with Teeth to chew and eat them: Nor do we so much as read the Use of Flesh for Food, was at all permitted him, till after the Universal Deluge.

Ray's seventeenth-century readers must have thought him quite demented, for vegetarianism had yet to arise, and where it was practised it was the consequence of poverty and shortage of meat, not choice.

On the continent there was a greater use made of vegetables, and John Evelyn remarks that the 'more frugal Italians and French, to this Day, Accept and gather Ogni Verdura, any thing almost that's Green and Tender, to the very Tops of Nettles; so as every Hedge affords a Sallet (not unagreeable)...'

When Evelyn gets into full cry on the subject of vegetables it is hard to imagine why we ever eat meat. In the plants in his kitchen garden he finds '...such fiery Heat in some to warm and cherish, such Coolness in others to temper and refresh, such pinguid Juice to nourish and feed the Body, such quickening Acids to compel the Appetite, and grateful Vehicles to court the Obedience of the Palate, such Vigour to renew and support our natural Strength, such ravishing Flavour and Perfumes to recreate and delight us: In short, such spirituous and active Force to animate and revive every Faculty and Part, to all kinds of Humans, and, I had almost said Heavenly Capacity too. What shall we add more? Our Gardens present us with them all; and whilst the Shambles are cover'd with Gore and Stench, our Sallets scape the Insults of the Summer Fly, purifies and warms the Blood against Winter Rage: Nor wants their Variety in more abundance, than any of the former Ages could show.'

Gardeners, he declared, could share the same food as the greatest potentate on earth.

> Vitellius his Table, to which every Day
> All Courtiers did a constant Tribute pay,
> Could nothing more delicious afford
> Than Nature's Liberality.
> Help'd with a little Art and Industry,
> Allows the meanest Gard'ners Board,
> The wanton Taste no Fish or Fowl can chuse,
> For which the Grape or Melon she would lose.
> Tho all th' Inhabitants of Sea and Air
> Be lifted in the Glutton's Bill of Fare;
> Yet still the Sallet, and the Fruit we see
> Plac'd the third Story high in all her Luxury.

Although kitchen gardening never really did reach such Olympian heights as Evelyn would have wished, increasingly vegetables have

119

played an important part in diet, particularly that of the poor and less well off.

Flora Thompson, writing of her childhood in the countryside of Oxford at the turn of the century recalled that the villagers 'Then ate plenty of green food, all home-grown and freshly pulled; lettuces and radishes and young onions with pearly heads and leaves like fine grass. A few slices of bread and home-made lard, flavoured with rosemary, and plenty of green food, "went down good" as they used to say.' When autumn came to the villages the gardens were harvested '... the plums on the front wall of the house were ripe, and the warm, fruity smell of boiling jam drew all the wasps in the neighbourhood. Other jams, jellies, and pickles already stood on the pantry shelves. Big yellow vegetable marrows dangled from hooks, and ropes of onions and bunches of drying thyme and sage.'

The freezer has now largely taken over from the bottling jar and the salting crock, and certainly there is not the same pride in preserving, or the same care and labour needed as in the past. There is also a dangerous obsession with uniformity which has resulted from growing for the freezer. But, as you will discover in the following pages, the kitchen gardener still has the opportunity to feast from 'Nature's Liberality'.

GLOBE or FRENCH ARTICHOKES (*Cynara scolymus*), quite apart from being one of the most handsome plants, is also one of the most delicious of vegetables. Its disadvantage from the point of view of the small modern garden is its size; up to five feet tall and three feet across. This problem can be overcome by having two or three plants growing among shrubs or in the herbaceous border. Its foliage is a fine background and foil for other plants, its purple thistle-like flowers are magnificent, and while it is the flower heads which are eaten a few should be allowed to mature for the sake of appearance.

Easily propagated by seed or off-shoots, the artichoke has been treasured for its flavour for many hundreds of years. It was a delicacy of the Greeks and Romans, and being a native of the Mediterranean region grew to great perfection for them.

Apicius served them with a dressing of *liquamen*, oil and chopped hard-boiled eggs. Alternatively the Romans cooked them in a mixture of rue, mint, coriander, fennel, pepper, lovage, honey, *liquamen* and oil.

120

No doubt the Romans brought Globe artichokes with them to Britain, although whether they survived their departure or not is a matter for speculation. They were a feature of the royal gardens at Hampton Court, and in fact a sixteenth-century writer claims they were introduced during the reign of Henry VIII. It was grown so well in this country that the globes were exported to France, Italy and the Low Countries, and on the English market were an expensive luxury.

Some herbalists rather oddly contended that the heads of artichokes were unwholesome to eat, particularly raw, as they were, not surprisingly, difficult to digest in that condition. Their advice was to boil them in a beef broth and serve with a sauce of butter, or oil, salt and vinegar.

While they were more commonly boiled in broth, they were also eaten raw with pepper and salt, and also the middle ribs of the leaves. A number of varieties, including the White artichoke, the French artichoke and the Thistle artichoke, the latter virtually a wild plant, were grown in the sixteenth century, usually being boiled and served with melted butter, and a little vinegar and salt.

By the eighteenth century they were firmly established favourites in all good kitchen gardens, and because they occupied so much space other vegetables were grown between them, such as radishes, spinach, cauliflowers, cabbages and cucumbers. To make space for these the gardener left a gap of ten feet between the rows of artichokes.

The reason for growing such quantities of the vegetable was that it was employed in a wide variety of dishes. Artichoke bottoms were used along with currants, raisins, potatoes, damsons and gooseberries in lamb pie. They were also used as a side dish, first being boiled when the bottom was removed, dipped in beaten eggs and coated with flour, salt and grated nutmeg, rolled in breadcrumbs, fried, and served with a thick butter sauce. But clearly a rich and favourite method of serving them in the eighteenth century was as artichoke pie:

Boil the bottoms of eight or ten Artichokes, scrape and make them clean from the core; cut each of them into six parts; season them with cinnamon, nutmeg, sugar, and a little salt; then lay your Artichokes in your Pye. Take the marrow of four or five bones, dip your marrow in yolks of eggs and grated bread, and season it

121

as you did your Artichokes, and lay it on top and between your Artichokes; then lay on sliced lemon, barberries and large mace; put butter on the top, and close up your pye; then make your lear [a thickened sauce] of white-wine, sack, and sugar; thicken it with yolks of eggs, and a bit of butter; when your Pye is drawn, pour it in, shake it together, and serve it hot.

An earlier recipe was for the bottoms to be fried, garnished with chopped parsley, and served with slices of bone marrow and a sauce of butter, sugar and fresh orange juice. In Italy, the globes were boiled and as the scales opened they were basted with fresh olive oil, and similarly were served with orange juice and sugar.

To preserve the artichokes for use in winter, the bottoms were pickled or parboiled and dried in the oven for two days. They were also parboiled and preserved in butter like potted meats, or they were strung on thread and dried. Globe artichokes were such a luxury that every well-ordered household wished to be able to serve them in one form or another the year round.

At the end of the seventeenth century the vegetable was still a considerable luxury and the globes commanded high prices. But a hundred years later the process of improvement and culture had produced a wide choice of varieties: the Paris artichoke, the Green Provence artichoke, the Flat-headed Brittany, the Copper-coloured Brittany, Perpetual artichoke [which in the South of France produced masses of small heads as early as January which were eaten raw with oil and vinegar], Early Purple artichoke, Grey artichoke, Black English, Roscoff artichoke, Oblong St. Laud, Sweet Green artichoke of Genoa, Purple Provence, Violet Quarantain artichoke of Carmargue, Florence artichoke and Purple Venice. Six major seed merchants now offer precisely one type, the Green Globe.

It is sad that increasing uniformity has reduced the choice of varieties, which is also reflected in the way Globe artichokes are cooked, usually just boiled and served with melted butter, or cold with a vinaigrette sauce. But they can be served as croquettes, and elaborately and expensively with foie gras or fresh truffles.

A simple but delicious recipe is for Artichoke bottoms Au Gratin. For this the artichokes are boiled and the scales and choke removed from the fleshy base, which is the only part used. These are placed in a well buttered dish and covered with the yolks of two eggs beaten together with milk and a little cream. The dish is baked slowly in the oven and topped with cheese.

The JERUSALEM ARTICHOKE (*Helianthus tuberosus*) is not an artichoke at all, and not even remotely related to the Globe artichoke, but the knobbly tubers do have something of the same flavour. Neither do they come from Jerusalem, but are a close relative of the sunflower, and are natives of North America, not South America, as some of the older authorities insist. This confusion could have arisen from the fact that they were introduced to British gardens at roughly the same time as the potato, which does come from South America. The earliest botanical mention of it was in 1616.

John Parkinson had their origin more or less right when he called them the Potatoes of Canada, and indeed they were also known as Battatas of Canada, French Battatas or Hierrusalem artichoke, the latter being a corruption of the Italian, Girasole (sunflower), while the French called it, and still do, Topinambour, which was believed to be a fair representation of the native Indian name.

Redcliffe N. Salaman produced an interesting, and probably correct, interpretation of the origin of the English name Jerusalem artichoke, which is the more convincing since they were originally known as the Potatoes of Canada.

Writing in the *Journal of the Royal Horticultural Society* in 1940, he argued that the name is not derived from the Italian 'Girasole', but from the fact that the vegetables were grown commercially at Ter Neusen in Holland and that they were known as 'Artichokes van Ter Neusen'. The tubers were landed at Custom House Wharf in London and 'here they would be bought by the hawkers of the town, who, after an initial effort to cry their wares as Artichokes van Ter Neusen, quickly metamorphosed it into Artichokes of Jerusalem – Jerusalem Artichokes.'

Whatever the origin of its name, the Jerusalem artichoke was an immediate hit in Britain, far more so than its contemporary introduction, the potato.

At first they were regarded as a great delicacy. They were boiled until tender, then peeled and sliced and stewed in butter and wine and considered a dish for a Queen, being as 'pleasant as the bottom of an artichoke'. But because they were so extremely easy to grow they became very common, particularly around London, and cheap to buy, which, brought them into contempt, even loathing. Towards the end of the eighteenthcentury,theyweregrownasanimalfeedinthenorthofEngland.

One problem with them is that they do cause extreme windiness in some people, and this consequently led to a decline in popularity, not helped by such great authorities as Philip Miller writing in his *Gardener's Dictionary* that while some esteemed them as much as potatoes: 'they are more watery and flashy, and are very subject to trouble the Belly by their windy Quality, which hath brought them almost into Disuse'. The eighteenth-century gardener was advised to find some remote corner of the kitchen garden for them as they were viewed as no more appealing than a weed.

It is true that they can be invasive if they are allowed to run wild, but in reality they are extremely easy to keep under control, and as they grow five or six feet high, they can be used as a very useful wind-break on an open site, such as an allotment. The secret is not to grow too many; fifteen or twenty tubers will provide a ready supply, and enough over to plant the next year's crop. I disagree with Philip Miller that they are unsightly, but it is certainly a good idea to put them in some not very productive corner, since they seem to prosper in even the most unpromising spot.

The most common use for Jerusalem artichokes is as a soup, but they are also quite delicious roasted round a joint with potatoes, and treated in exactly the same way. They can also be fried like chips. As a dish on their own they should be boiled in milk, drained and put in a dish and covered with a cheese sauce made from the milk they were boiled in, and baked in the oven. They can also be made into a souffle.

Another so-called artichoke, the CHINESE ARTICHOKE (*Stachys tuberifera*), again quite unrelated to the other two, is not very widely grown, but is ideally suited to small gardens which cannot spare any space for the towering Jerusalem artichoke. The plants only grow about fifteen inches high, and the tubers are quite a lot smaller, but of a similar delicate flavour. Like the Jerusalem artichoke, the tubers are left in the ground until they are wanted.

In some books they are called Japanese artichokes, and claimed as native of Japan, in others, and more generally, Chinese artichokes. Clearly they come from the East, although they reached Europe in 1890 through a doctor in the Imperial Russian diplomatic service, who gave some tubers to a Monsieur Pailleux of Crosnes. At first they were a popular curiosity, but now they are offered by seed merchants who stock unusual, as well as common vegetable seeds.

While they can be treated in the kitchen in the same way as Jerusalem artichokes, a particularly pleasant way of cooking and serving is to parboil them, dip them in egg and breadcrumbs, and fry. They should be cooked for ten, rather than the full twenty minutes they need to become tender, drained and sauteed in butter. Cream is added before serving and the whole dish is sprinkled with chopped ham.

ASPARAGUS (*Asparagus officinalis*) is one of the most ancient and valued of vegetables. It was eaten by the Greeks, and the Romans often started their feasts with a dish of cooked or raw spears, and preserved them for out of season eating by plunging them into boiling water and drying in the sun. It is impossible to know with certainty whether they brought the vegetable with them to Britain. If they did it was a casualty of their departure, for most authorities agree that the first recorded mention of asparagus in Britain is in 1535.

There is a native form, *Asparagus officinalis Subsp. prostatus*, that is to be found in coastal areas, but is has, as the name suggests, a creeping habit, unlike the garden form with its stout, errect spikes. Those who have grown the wild form claim that it is sweeter, and produced spikes early without the aid of forcing in any way.

Asparagus acquired a number of names: Sperage, Sparagus, even Sparrowgrass, but whatever it was called its popularity has been universal since it first appeared on the tables of the rich. It was credited with some medicinal properties, and was claimed to be good for urinary problems, and mixed with wine was supposed to relieve aches and pains, but John Parkinson held that it should be boiled and eaten with butter, vinegar and pepper, or oil and vinegar. Some thought it a gentle laxative, and also recommended eating the spears boiled in broth. A recipe of the sixteenth century had it chopped with onions, or Welsh onions, and mixed with toasted cheese.

The Elizabethans made a drink from the plant which they believed produced a good complexion, and acted as a deodorant.

By the eighteenth century it was an essential vegetable in all good gardens, and asparagus spears were among those vegetables, fruits and buds pickled for a winter relish. The Rev. James Woodforde, the country parson who faithfully recorded his meals in his diary wrote with pleasure on 18th June 1782: 'We had for Dinner, three Fowls boiled, a bit of Pork boiled, a Leg of Mutton boiled and Capers, a green Goose roasted and Asparagus . . .'

At the beginning of this century a London nurseryman sold crowns at ten shillings (50p) per hundred. Now the same quantity costs over £20.

In the nineteenth century there were two popular varieties, Battersea and Gravesend, but they seem to have been the same, the only distinction being probably merely the growing area. By the turn of the century there were five varieties.

No vegetable should be over-cooked, and this is particularly true of asparagus. The trick is to plunge the base of the bundle of spears in boiling water with the green tops out of the water so that they are cooked in the steam. Generally the tendency is to cook and serve with melted butter, rather like Globe artichokes, or cold with an oil and vinegar dressing; or at cocktail parties and wedding receptions in the most repelling form of all, wrapped in brown bread and butter, a combination which ruins both the bread and butter, and the asparagus.

There is no reason at all why asparagus should not be served quite simply as a vegetable on its own or mixed with peas in a creamy white sauce. The spears can be cooked in veal stock. Part of the liquid is used to make a sauce thickened with egg yolks and cream. Surplus stock can be kept for making soup. Chopped asparagus is delicious in an omelette.

It is one of those vegetables surrounded by a great deal of gardening mystique. Many of the older books describe the need to excavate special beds, and make them up with sand and seaweed, and a good deal else besides. Like most plants it needs to be well fed, well-watered, and kept free of weeds. An asparagus bed does take up space particularly as it really is necessary to have crowns coming along over a three year cycle.

For sheer antiquity the BROAD BEAN (*Vicia Faba*) has few rivals. Evidence of its cultivation has been found on prehistoric sites in Europe and the Near East, although the earliest proof of its culture in Britain comes from the Iron Age sites at Glastonbury, and on pre-Christian sites on Dartmoor and the Cleveland Hills. The early forms would have been tiny, wretched things compared to their modern cousins, and were probably grown as a cereal crop to be dried and kept for the winter when they would have been ground down to a flour. Indeed the Romans, who on the whole despised beans as fit only for animals and the very poor, used bean flour in bread and porridge. Its reputation as a poor man's food lived with the broad bean for centuries, and it was an ingredient in the thick pottages which formed the basis of the peasant's diet. Certainly it was among the vegetables sold in the early markets, and was to be found on the carts and stalls of the fourteenth-century traders in Gracechurch Street and Cheapside, and when market gardening became more established they were grown in considerable quantities at Lewisham and Blackheath.

The distinctive, and to some people unpleasant, flavour of broad beans must have been much more pronounced before the vegetable was improved by selection and breeding. John Parkinson describes how the flavour was tinkered with by cooking them in salt water, followed by stewing in butter, and finally adding salt and vinegar. As for John Gerarde he simply dismissed them as 'windy meat', and recommended that they should be used for making poultices.

Despite, or perhaps because of, its down-market image, broad beans were grown in very considerable quantities. In the eighteenth century it was estimated that four million bushels of beans were consumed each year, and a survey of 1774 stated the dried beans were 'exported for the food of the negroes in our plantations, and are employed in feeding horses at home.'

In its garden form the Mazagan was almost certainly the earliest cultivated. It produced numerous short pods containing three or four beans, and was clearly not too far removed from the horsebean. The Windsor bean, which is still widely grown, was said to have been introduced by refugee Dutch families who established market gardens in the Windsor area.

By the first half of the nineteenth century there were ten varieties: Dwarf Fan, Early Lisbon, Early Mazagan, Green Genoa, Green Nonpareil,

Long-pod, Sandwich, Toker, White-blossomed and Windsor. Lindley mentions another which was known as the Mumford bean, but says it was merely a small Windsor which was selected by a grading sieve. Eleven were being grown at the turn of the century, two of which, Aquadulce and Green Windsor, are still offered by seed merchants.

Perhaps because it freezes so well, the broad bean is an increasingly popular vegetable, and I think that one of the great pleasures of the kitchen garden year is the delicious scent of the bean flowers on a warm, early summer evening. As a general rule the beans should be picked when they are young, tender and sweet. Some people claim that the best way of treating them is to pick the pods when they are only two or three inches long and cook them, pod, immature bean and all, like French beans. But old beans, and you are bound to be left with some, should not be discarded. They can be served hot with a parsley sauce, or cold with a French dressing, and for those who find the husks too chewy, these are easily slipped off after cooking. The husked beans can also be pureed. Always include a sprig or two of Winter or Summer savory, as this greatly enhances the flavour.

Broad Bean Mousse is a dish on its own. Take a pound of cooked beans, some artichoke bottoms, green peas, the heart of a lettuce and a small onion. When cooled they should all be put in a blender, and the puree returned to a saucepan and stirred over a heat until it thickens. Add butter and seasoning, and a little sugar, and just before serving whisk in two tablespoons of cream.

FRENCH or KIDNEY BEANS (*Phaseolus vulgaris*) have never had to put up with the scorn and derision handed out to broad beans. Almost certainly a native of South America, they arrived in Britain in the sixteenth century, and took little time to become a popular vegetable, when they were boiled green, buttered and eaten whole. By the middle of the seventeenth century there were four varieties being grown for food, and they also had acquired a reputation as an effective treatment for horse bites.

The popular types were the Large and Small, White and Speckled kidney beans which good housewives pickled and salted for winter use.

Their popularity was not due to their ease of culture judging by the experiences of 1759 of the Rev. Gilbert White, who was having a hard time with his French beans during a difficult season. On May 20 he was able to remark 'The Dwarf french-beans are come-up pretty well', but eleven days later gloomily recorded 'Continued picking vast quantities of slugs from the french-beans, which are in a poor way.' On June 5 a violent storm all but destroyed what was left of the crop and three days later he had to re-sow. In the end he noted the observation that his bean crop was 'extraordinary', which one can only hope meant that it was good.

The varieties of French beans multiplied rapidly. Philip Miller wrote in the *Gardener's Dictionary* that 'It would be to little Purpose to enumerate all the Varieties of this Plant which have come to Knowledge, in this Place (Chelsea Physic Garden); since America does annually furnish us with new Sorts, so that there is no knowing what Varieties there may be produc'd in England'. Apart from the climbing beans, which in his time were grown for their flowers, he listed only six varieties which he considered worth growing for the kitchen; the Common White or Dutch kidney-bean, The Lesser Garden kidney-bean, the Upright or Tree kidney-bean, the Dwarf White kidney-bean, which was mainly culti- vated for forcing on hot-beds, the Canterbury kidney-bean and the Spotted Tree kidney-bean.

The White, Dutch and the Canterbury were still being cultivated when George Lindley drew up his list of fourteen varieties in the 1830s and by the early years of this century there were no less than 175 varieties of dwarf and climbing kidney beans with such heroic names as Wonder of France, King of the Green Beans, The Shah, The Monster, The Imperial kidney bean, and the Emperor William.

Now the good seed lists can only muster nine or ten varieties.

There is probably no better way to cook French beans than to pick them when they are young, and cook them until they are barely tender, drain them and toss them in melted butter and ground black pepper in a frying pan. This makes a delicious hot hors d'oeuvres.

A Polish variation is to cook the bean as above, and add a wineglass of sour cream and a squeeze of lemon juice, and top off the dish with chopped parsley.

The SCARLET RUNNER BEAN (*Phaseolus coccineus*) came to Britain from South America as an ornamental annual climber, and it was a well deserved place for it since its trusses of bright flowers are among the beauties of the summer. Breeding and development has produced white and pink flowers. But it was the scarlet form that first attracted attention, and was commonly grown. Mrs. C. W. Earle in *Pot Pourri from a Surrey Garden* combined utility with beauty. She wrote: 'I grow Scarlet Runners singly, or two or three together, between the Apple-trees; and it is a good plan, as they bear much better than when planted in rows in the open, and look much prettier. They creep up into the branches of the Apple-trees; the growth is so light it does not harm while it protects the late pods from frost.'

William Cobbett, who felt more at home producing food than flowers, was an enthusiast for the Scarlet Runner as a vegetable. He called them rough runners because the pods were coarser than kidney beans. Writing in *The English Gardener*, he declared:

These are most admirable plants: they bear prodigiously; their product is, perhaps, the most delicate of all; and form the latter end of July, until the actual coming of the frosts, they continue to blow and to bear without the least relaxation, let the weather be as hot or as dry as it may . . . . the rough runners will grow in the shade, will climb up hedges and trees, will suffer their stems to be smothered with weeds, and will continue to ornament whatever they cling to, and to produce in abundance at the same time.

In the past it was common practice to lay down runner beans in large crocks between layers of salt. Now, in the age of the deep freeze, they are even more invaluable as a crop to see families through the winter. Whether for freezing or cooking fresh they are best picked young, and the temptation to grow massive pods should be resisted, but those that do grow large and tough can still be put to a good use. They need to be well boiled and served with a little of the cooking water and butter.

Runner beans can be treated as a perennial. After the plants have cropped the vines should be cut off at the roots, lifted and stored like dahlia tubers. As soon as the danger of frost has passed they can be planted out and will produce an early crop. In a nineteenth-century account of this technique the roots were planted on April 7th, and in just over a month produced new growth of about nine inches. The roots had been stored in sand. In Southern Ireland I have seen runner beans flourishing after being left in the open all the winter.

There are a number of other attractive and unusual beans to be grown, and worth trying if you have the space, or want to make the space. One of the most striking is the climbing purple-podded kidney bean, and 'Blue Coco'; the asparagus bean, with very long, slender pods, which needs a warm spot; haricot beans, grown for their seeds; lima beans, which certainly need a good deal of warmth; and soya beans. The problem is that in a good many cases it is extremely difficult, if not impossible, to obtain seeds of these unusual varieties, unless you know an enthusiast who saves seed, or have friends in the countries where they are readily available.

A few years ago there was a considerable promotion for a variety of soya bean which was said to be able to thrive in our uncertain climate. It really was not a success. I grew a thirty-foot row, which germinated and developed well, but only produced one large dish of beans, which were certainly quite delicious.

At one time a wide variety of BEETS (*Beta vulgaris*) were grown in gardens, but over the centuries they have been refined down in the kitchen garden to beetroot, Spinach beet and Seakale beet, all of which spring from the common parent, Beta vulgaris.

Beetroot, with its deep red roots, and green and red foliage (the yellow rooted form has never been particularly popular), has been an enduring favourite over the centuries, although today too often it is served so horribly drowned in vinegar that it is difficult to detect its delicate, sweet flavour. The Romans used to make a broth containing beetroot and leeks which served as a mild laxative, but they also used them in *patinas*, which were mixtures of herbs, vegetables, and such things as eggs, brains and small birds, baked in shallow dishes.

Since *Beta vulgaris* is widely distributed throughout Europe, including Britain, it is reasonable to assume that it was an article of food, in some form, before the Romans invaded and brought their kitchen garden plants with them, but it is equally possible that they did introduce the finer forms, such as beetroot. Certainly good Saxon gardens grew beets, and they have endured ever since. The sixteenth century saw green, white, yellow and red beets being grown for pottages, and in France they were being boiled whole and served with various meats. The stalk of what was called Italian beet, which sounds identical to Swiss chard, was boiled and eaten separately from the leaf in salads with oil, vinegar and pepper, and was considered to be something of a delicacy. Beetroot was often cut into fantastic shapes and used to decorate dishes of meat and fish. There was also White and Streaked beet, and Red or Roman beet.

Three types, red, black and white, were used by John Evelyn, the white form being chard, of which he said that the rib 'being boil'd melts and eats like Marrow'. The beetroot he recommended as 'a grateful Winter Sallet'.

By the eighteenth century beets were widely grown as animal feed, although in the early part of the century red, white and Roman beets were still recommended for the kitchen garden, while beets were included in a stew-like pea soup which was made in a broth produced from a leg of beef, a sheep's head and a piece of bacon.

Towards the end of the century seven varieties were grown in gardens, of which beetroot was the most popular, although chard was highly esteemed. It was quite a common practice to sow a mixture of beetroot and carrot seed, with the carrots being pulled first to make room for the beets to mature. By the nineteenth century there were sixteen varieties of beet grown in European gardens, although only three of beetroot, and three of leaf beet were grown in British gardens.

Great care should always be taken to prevent damage to beetroots before they are cooked. The leaves must be screwed off, not cut, because if the root bleeds it will lose its rich red colour. The simplest way of dealing with them is to wash the root thoroughly and bake them slowly. If they are to be used for a salad they should be served separately. One of the most grisly sights is a salad of lettuce, potatoes, hard boiled eggs and beetroot all stained and smeared with red.

A delicious hot dish is beetroot cut into small cubes after being baked or boiled, and lightly fried in oil with crushed garlic and chopped parsley.

Swiss chard is one of the most valuable vegetables in the kitchen garden. Its leaves are a year round substitute for spinach, and in many ways a preferable alternative as it does not have the slightly mouth-drying irony taste. The broad, white centre ribs are served as a separate dish, boiled until tender and dressed with a white sauce, flavoured with nutmeg. It can also be served up cold with a French dressing as a winter salad.

BORECOLE or KALE is a member of the highly variable cabbage family (*Brassica oleracea*) and is closest, in looks at least, to the wild cabbage, wortys, and coleworts of old. It was certainly grown in Saxon and medieval gardens, and doubtless went further back still, particularly as cabbage was greatly approved of by the Romans.

Sixteenth-century gardeners grew the Ruffed or Curled Cole, the Smooth Cole, the Curled Garden Cole, Parsley Cole, and Fine Cut Colewort, all of which, along with cabbages and cauliflowers were not only excellent food, but supposed to be good for the eyesight, the spleen, poisoned bites, ulcers, deafness and worms, and if eaten raw before meals would prevent drunkenness.

John Parkinson's description is of a kale-type of cabbage, loose-leaved and very hardy, and he said they were widely used by 'the poorer sort of people'. He recommended boiling the leaves until tender, and removing the middle rib to eat cold with oil and vingegar.

Borecole, Curled Colewort, Common Colewort, and Perennial Alpine Colewort were to be found in eighteenth-century gardens, but were never eaten until exposed to heavy frosts. The most highly recommended was curly kale, which came in after Christmas and lasted until April.

William Cobbett disapproved of Borecole, declaring that as Savoy cabbages stood the winter as well 'there really seems to be very little reason for troubling one's self with this very coarse vegetable; for it is ridiculous to seek a variety in getting bad things to take their turn with good.' Cobbett's attitude became widespread, and for a considerable time Borecole or Kale was considered more fitting as a feed for animals. Now that dwarf forms of curly kale have been bred they fit into a small modern garden very easily, and will take whatever the weather throws at them. It certainly is important to wait until the leaves have been well frosted before cutting for the kitchen.

It is advisable to trim off the stouter parts of the leaf stalks, particularly towards the end of the season. The leaves should be steamed or boiled until tender, but not allowed to become a soggy dark green mass. Serve with a few knobs of butter and a sprinkling of coarse-ground pepper.

BROCCOLI must now be amongst the most popular vegetables,

more through the efforts of commercial growers and food freezers than pure garden culture. Compared with cabbages, their brassica cousins, broccoli is a relative new-comer. It was long believed to have originally been imported from Cyprus about the middle of the sixteenth century, but this was more of a traveller's tale than absolute reality. It is much more probable that it reached Britain from Italy, where it has been grown for a very long time.

The Italian broccoli and the Green broccoli became widely grown in the eighteenth century. Italian broccoli was divided into two varieties, Roman and Naples, with the Roman broccoli being particularly recommended. It was allowed to develop large heads before cutting with about four inches of stem, which was peeled before the whole head was tied up in a linen cloth and boiled, rather like a plum pudding. It was served with butter.

Clearly broccoli became increasingly popular, for by the early nineteenth century there were no less than thirteen varieties in cultivation: Purple Cape, Green Cape, Grange's Early Cauliflower, Green's Close-headed Winter, Early Purple, Early White, Dwarf Brown Close-headed, Tall Large-headed Purple, Cream coloured Portsmouth broccoli, Sulphur-coloured, Spring White Cauliflower broccoli, Late Dwarf Close-headed Purple, Late Green Danish and Siberian broccoli.

The varieties increased to over thirty by the 1920s, but in the average garden today the Purple and White Sprouting broccoli, and the green headed Calabrese, are the most satisfactory. Calabrese should be grown as an autumn vegetable, with the freezer in mind, while the sprouting varieties, particularly Purple Sprouting, stand through the winter, and produce their delicious shoots once more delightfully called Asparagus broccoli.

The simplest way of cooking this vegetable is to boil it until tender, drain and toss it in butter over the heat for a few minutes.

CAULIFLOWER is one of the finest off-shoots of *Brassica oleracea*. Its origin is quite obscure, although there are some who believe that it was first cultivated in Cyprus, and eventually reached Britain from that source, where it was not grown seriously until the arrival of Dutch gardeners in the seventeenth century. Early in that century it was still a great rarity, and as much as three shillings, an enormous sum for the time, was paid for a pair of cauliflower heads. Once their culture became established, Britain was famous for them, and they were exported to Holland, Germany and France, and British seed was much sought after.

John Gerarde in the sixteenth century mentions the Cole Florie among the coleworts, and at an even earlier date there are references to the Caul. They were slow to become popular and did not do well in gardens due to poor seed. However, by the early eighteenth century they were listed among the vegetables that should be grown in a gentleman's garden.

Although it is often eaten raw these days, in the past it tended to be boiled, steeped in milk and then seethed in beef broth, which would seem to have been a good way of reducing it to some kind of soup.

Dr. Sam Johnson, unless he was being facetious, had a fondness for them, for he once remarked: 'Of all flowers I like the cauliflower best', and Sir Joseph Banks used them to demonstrate the principles of botany to children, as George Colman the Younger recalled from a holiday he spent with Sir Joseph. Every day he and a young companion were sent out to botanise in the meadows and woods.

We were prepared over-night for these morning excursions by Sir Joseph. He explained to us the rudiments of the Linnaean system, in a series of nightly lectures, which were very short, clear and familiar; the first of which he illustrated by cutting up a cauliflower . . . . I can still distinguish a moss-rose from a Jerusalem artichoke; and never see a boiled cauliflower, without recollecting the raw specimen, and the dissecting knife in the hands of Sir Joseph; and thinking of the fructification, sexual system, pericarpium, calynx, corolla, petals etc., etc., etc.

Even by the early nineteenth century there were only two listed cauliflowers; Early and Late, although eighteen were being grown early in the present century.

Like all the cabbage tribe, cauliflower must not be over cooked, and should arrive on the table still firm and crisp. Apart form serving it simply as a boiled vegetable, the classic method is to cook it with cheese; either a cheese sauce, or lightly browned in butter, dipped in seasoned breadcrumbs, and finished in the oven with a good covering of grated cheese.

BRUSSELS SPROUTS are one of those vegetables with which the British seem to have a love-hate relationship. Well grown and well cooked, they are excellent, but so often they seem to be the victim of the barbaric treatment of slow drowning in hot water. Of all the cabbage tribe they do have the strongest smell while cooking which hangs around and reminds one of the more tired type of boarding house. In *The Magic Army*, Leslie Thomas's very funny book about the disastrous preparations and practice for the D-Day Landings carried out in the West Country, he describes an American General's first meeting with sprouts in the dining room of a small hotel.

'Sprouts?' asked General Georgeton. 'I am about to display my ignorance. What is a sprout?'

Scarlett and Schorner looked towards Bryant. The young Englishman said: 'Sprouts, sir? They're green and sort of oval.'

'Like small cabbages', put in the waitress quite briskly. 'Boiled.'

Later after eating them: The general said quietly: 'When we start to bomb this area, let's make sure we hit the sprout fields, okay?'

It is all very unfair on Brussels Sprouts, but as a popular vegetable they did take a considerable time to get a foothold in Britain. Although the Belgians have been eating them since the beginning of the thirteenth century, they were not a common kitchen garden crop in this country until well into the nineteenth century. The Belgians claim they received them from their Roman invaders, but the evidence that the Romans actually grew sprouts is purely speculative. It does seem possible, however, that the Brussels Sprout sported from one of the small-headed cabbages.

Despite being much maligned, it is an invaluable vegetable, and goes well with all the meats, particularly the Christmas turkey. Now that there are good dwarf forms on the market (the record height for a Brussels Sprout plant was nine feet) they will fit into small gardens. A frost does seem to improve them. They should be picked when they are hard and a clean, fresh green colour, but even when they begin to break open in the early spring they need not be ignored. Pureed with a little butter, cream and nutmeg they make a delicious dish. Even the leafy tops are useful, particularly at a time of year when fresh vegetables are becoming a little scarce.

CABBAGES are the most familiar of the family, and in terms of culinary use, among the most ancient of vegetables. Cabbage seeds have been found in late Bronze Age settlements at Itford Hill in Sussex. The Romans, both rich and poor, were prodigious eaters of cabbage, which they believed kept them in good health. Some optimists even considered it to be an aphrodisiac. They went to a great deal of trouble to produce fine plants, carefully fertilising them with seaweed, and prepared them elaborately for the table. A common method of cooking was to seethe them in cumin, salt, old wine and oil, or to use the sauce as a dressing after boiling. Sometimes pepper, lovage, mint, rue and coriander were added. Another method was to serve cabbage with chopped leeks, caraway seed and fresh coriander leaves.

Probably they brought their favourite varieties to Britain, but since cabbage grows wild in this country, it is a large plant of loose grey-green glaucus leaves which still thrives around the coast of Britain and Ireland, it is unlikely that the modern strains we grow actually originate from any Roman imports.

The Anglo-Saxons cultivated the vegetable, and it was described as a food essential for people of all classes.

Elizabethan gardens were stocked with White Cabbage Cole, Red Cabbage Cole, the Open Cabbage Cole, the Savoy Cole, and the Sugar Loaf cabbage. In those times, they were boiled with powdered beef and eaten with quantities of fat poured over them. Cabbage seed was added to broth as a treatment for colic, while the pulped stalks were mixed with honey and almond milk for shortness of breath and consumption. The juice was also supposed to be an antidote for fungi poisoning.

Eight varieties of cabbage, which included the addition to the older varieties of the Russian cabbage, the Flat-sided cabbage, and the Early Battersea cabbage, in the eighteenth century rose to fifteen main types for garden cultivation a hundred years later.

One variety, the Vanack cabbage, was becoming scarce by the mid-1800s and has probably disappeared. But from contemporary descriptions it seems to have been an ideal plant for the small garden.

In 1831 George Lindley recorded: 'It has been cultivated in the garden of the Earl of Egremont, at Petworth (West Sussex), so long since as the year 1776. Seeds of it have been presented to the Horticultural

Society of London by Mr. Torbron, gardener to the Countess of Bridgewater, at Ashridge, in Hertfordshire. It was cultivated some time ago by the gardeners in Sussex and Hampshire. By timely sowings the Vanack Cabbage is always in season; it makes excellent spring Coleworts, becomes a white-hearted Cabbage very early, and pushes fine sprouts from the stump after the Cabbages are cut. In quality it is inferior to none of the best Cabbages.'

Some authorities considered the Vanack Cabbage as a synonym with Battersea, Enfield Market, and The Fulham cabbage. So its sap is probably coursing through some of our modern varieties.

During the eighteenth century many thought that cabbage was only fit for cattle feed, a fate dealt out to many other vegetables. It is as well for us that it remained such an important crop in cottage gardens as a vital companion for boiled bacon and potatoes, which was the basic diet of country working people. Neither was it altogether banished from the tables of the wealthy, where it would appear quite elaborately dressed. An old recipe for boiled fowls and cabbage, was not quite so ordinary as it sounded:

Take a well-shaped cabbage, peel off some of the outside leaves, and cut a piece out of the top; then scoop out the inside, and fill the whole with savoury forced meat beat up with two eggs; let it be tied up as a pudding in a cloth, but first put on the top of the cabbage. When the outside is tender, lay it between two boned fowls, and on them all some melted butter and slices of dried bacon. Cook together.

An extraordinary Cabbage Pudding was also popular for which you had to take 'two pounds of the lean part of a leg of veal; take of beef suet the like quantity, chop them together, then beat them together in a stone mortar, adding to it half a little cabbage scalded, and beat them with your meat; then season it with mace and nutmeg, a little pepper and salt, some green gooseberries, grapes or barberries in the time of year; in the winter put in a little verjuice [presumably a substitute for the fruit], then mix all well together, with the yolks of four or five eggs well beaten, then wrap it up in green cabbage leaves, tie a cloth over it, boil it an hour; melt butter for sauce.'

By the end of the nineteenth century the cabbage was well and truly rehabilitated, and now, for all practical purposes it has ceased to be fed to stock at all; one still sees fields of kale, but rarely the great Drumhead cabbages the size of coffee tables that used to be grown by farmers.

The end of the nineteenth century saw ninety-one varieties, of which the Sugar loaf and the York were long-established favourites. One of the very few to have survived is the pointed Ox-Heart Summer cabbage, Winnigstadt.

Apart from the spring, summer, winter, Red and Savoy cabbages which should be in every kitchen garden, there are the less usual such as the Portugal cabbage, Couve Tronchuda, whose leaves are shredded as fine as grass for the classic Portuguese green soup, Caldo Verde, and the giant Jersey cabbage which can, over three seasons, grow six to eight feet tall, and whose slender stems are dried and made into walking sticks.

Chinese cabbage, which is genuinely oriental and a cabbage, and not just a name of convenience, has become familiar through commercial exploitation as Chinese leaves. It is deservedly popular because it is equally good raw as a salad, or cooked, preferably stir-fried as it really does only need the minimum of cooking. As a garden plant it can be off-puttingly disappointing. The problem is that many people find that while the seeds germinate readily the plants bolt before forming any worthwhile leaves. The fault is in planting too early. Chinese cabbage should not be sown before the end of July, then it will grow and mature very quickly. The two varieties to grow are Pak-Choi (*Brassica chinensis*), a loose-leaved plant with broad, chard-like leaf stalks, and Pe-Tsai (*Brassica pekinensis*), the more familiar Cos-like Chinese leaves.

When it is plainly cooked in water, cabbage must never be over done. Over-cooked cabbage is that ghastly soggy mass wallowing in arsenic-green liquid, which has haunted most of us through the school dining-room, canteen and café, and even in hotels regarding themselves as rather grand. The secret is to cook it in little more than an inch of boiling water just until it is tender, drain and toss in butter and pepper.

Another excellent treatment is to shred the cabbage, heat some olive oil, add crushed garlic and bruised juniper berries, toss in the shredded cabbage and stir fry.

A simple cabbage-based meal is made by cooking the leaves in the normal way, with a little olive oil and vinegar added, plus grilled sausages put in half way through the cooking.

Red Cabbage is a warming winter vegetable in butter and broth, and stands being well cooked with salt, pepper and a little flour, for about an hour and a half over a low heat, stirring from time to time. During the last half hour pour in a glass of red wine.

Another Red cabbage recipe is: melt butter in a saucepan, add vinegar and brown sugar, when dissolved add shredded cabbage, stir thoroughly, and cook very slowly for an hour or more (the longer the better), making sure that at all times there is just enough liquid to cover the bottom of the saucepan. Add water as necessary. About half an hour before serving, add one diced cooking apple.

Cabbage leaves can be stuffed as a substitute for vine leaves. My father used to cook a marvellous stuffed pike, which he packed with a mixture of breadcrumbs, onions, sage, and thyme moistened with a little wine or brandy. The fish was smeared with butter, wrapped tightly in cabbage leaves and baked slowly.

Those who like to take strenuous exercise with their cooking should try their hand, and feet, at making real sauerkraut, according to nineteenth-century instructions. For this you need a large cask and a good supply of hard white cabbages. Shred the cabbages and lay them in the cask in four-inch layers, with salt, whole pepper and a little oil between each layer. Then, wearing a pair of clean wooden shoes you climb into the cask and tread down the cabbage. This is repeated until the cask is packed tight. Weights are placed on top until the mixture ferments, then the cask is closed.

THE CARDOON (*Cynara cardunculus*), or Chardon, as it is sometimes called by the old writers, is a close cousin of the globe artichoke, but has never achieved the same level of popularity in this country. Unlike the globe artichoke it is not grown for its flower-heads, which in its case are small and spiny, but for its leaf stalks which are earthed-up and blanched like celery.

It arrived in this country considerably later than the globe artichoke, and although it must have been fairly common knowledge that it was a prized vegetable in France, it appears to have been grown more as a curiosity than anything else. Henry Lyte in the sixteenth century referred to it as the Thistle, or Prickly Artichoke, and merely remarked that it had long leaves and sharp prickles.

Gradually they became more widely grown, but chiefly in the kitchen gardens of large houses and great estates. In the eighteenth century cardoons were on the list of recommended vegetables to grace a gentleman's table. They were served either as a salad with oil, pepper and vinegar, or cooked and topped off with melted cheese.

By the nineteenth century cardoons had obviously gained in popularity, and there were four types in cultivation; the Common cardoon, the Spanish cardoon, the cardoon de Tours, and the Red cardoon. French gardeners grew the Spanish and Tours types, but in Britain the most successful was the Spanish cardoon because there was a preference for the larger and more solid ribs.

Raised from seed, the plants needed well-rotted manure laid in the trenches in which the seedlings were planted, and plenty of water, particularly in dry weather; a process very similar to that of growing celery. When nearly full grown they were bandaged with matting. These days it is simpler and cheaper to use corrugated paper tubes, or simply newspaper tied round the plants, which are then earthed up.

Only the inside stalks should be used, as even with blanching those on the outside tend to be tough. When they are cut into pieces they should be put in water with lemon juice to prevent discolouring. Although originally they seem to have been used mainly in salads, in more recent times the vegetable has been cooked slowly for about two hours in stock, and served with a creamy sauce.

After being well scraped and cleaned the stalks should be boiled in water with herbs, salt and pepper, and a decent piece of bacon. They should be served with a brown sauce flavoured with sherry, and marrow on slices of toast.

THE CARROT (*Daucus carota*) is a vegetable of great antiquity and enduring popularity. Crisp, sweet and attractive, even the most reluctant vegetable eaters find it hard to resist. It can be ruined in the preparation, but to destroy it in that way takes a special kind of dedication to the dubious art of bad vegetable cookery. Despite at one time being grown extensively as animal feed for both cattle and pigs, it has remained a dish fit for the best tables.

Both the Greeks and Romans grew carrots in their kitchen gardens, and according to Apicius they were eaten raw dressed with oil, salt and vinegar, or cooked and served with a sauce made from cumin, salt, old wine and oil, the same sauce used with cabbage.

Wild carrots, which have a tough, white, strongly-flavoured root, were part of the diet of prehistoric people, and it is probable that the carrots grown in Britain in medieval times were selected from the wild, especially as the older writers do describe a white-rooted variety. The finer types with which we are familiar most likely came from the Continent (where vegetable culture was a good deal more sophisticated), with the refugees from religious persecution who fled to Britain, and did so much to improve gardening.

In the late sixteenth century carrots were boiled with fat meat, which suggests that they were used as a flavouring rather than as a vegetable accompaniment. This changed in the seventeenth century, no doubt as a result of the introduction of better strains, and they were served up with cabbage and turnips as separate vegetables to go with boiled beef. There were then three types: red, yellow and deep gold and the plant's fine feathery foliage was used as a decoration in women's hats, but the fashion was short-lived as the foliage wilts rapidly, so that what would have started out as a brave show, ended up looking very tired and limp.

The roots were also considered to be an aphrodisiac, but one must suspect that this had more to do with the Doctrine of Signatures than any kind of reliable proof, although at least one herbalist was satisfied with their performance, claiming that carrots 'provoke ... the worke of venery'. He did not think them particularly nourishing, and eaten to excess 'engendereth evill bloud'.

Such discouraging regard for carrots was not shared by John Evelyn, who thought that the yellow type was the best, and 'very nourishing'. By the eighteenth century the vegetable was so important that serious scientific work was carried out to improve the existing strains, particularly for agricultural use; cattle fed on carrots were said to produce especially fine milk. The development work must have been successful, because by the early years of the nineteenth century growers were producing roots two feet long, twelve to fourteen inches in circumference at their thickest, and weighing in at four pounds each. Sandy in

Bedfordshire became famous for the fineness of its carrots, and nearly half the local population was engaged in their culture. According to Sir Joseph Banks, writing in the last decade of the eighteenth century: 'The carrots of Sandy, a village in Bedfordshire, are carried on asses all round the neighbourhood, which in general is a stiff soil, and purchased with alacrity by the very persons who have in their gardens large crops possibly from the same seed that produced those growing on a more clayey soil . . .'

In the same century, while it was being fed to farm stock, the carrot was a favourite in the kitchen, not only as a vegetable, but for making a rich Carrot Pudding:

Take raw carrots, and scrape them clean, grate them. To half a pound of carrot, take a pound of grated bread, a nutmeg, a little cinnamon, a very little salt, half a pound of sugar, and half a pint of sack, eight eggs, a pound of butter melted, and as much cream as will mix it well together; stir it and beat it up well, and put it in a dish to bake; put puff pastry at the bottom of your dish.

Another was Carrot Puffs which could also be made with parsnips or a mixture of the two:

Scrape and boil your carrots tender; then scrape or mash them very fine, add to a pint of the pulp the crumb of a penny-loaf grated, or some stale biskit, if you have any of it, some eggs, but four whites, a nutmeg grated, some orange-flower water, sugar to your taste, a little sack, and mix it up with thick cream; they must be fried in rendered suet, and the liquor very hot when you put them in; put in a spoonful in a place.

In a modern kitchen garden with all the demands on space I doubt whether it is really worth while growing large carrots for keeping, since they tend to be cheap to buy, but growing carrots to crop when they are young (at this stage they freeze well) is essential. A deliciously simple way of cooking baby carrots is to boil them until just tender, and then toss them in butter and sugar. The tiny ones are also marvellous raw in a salad.

CELERY (*Apium graveolens*) has been in gardens in one form or another from the earliest times. It is one of those vegetables which was

143

invited into the kitchen garden, since it grows wild in most parts of the world, including Britain. Early gardeners went out to the hills and cliffs where it grew and selected the best looking plants, and from them harvested seed that eventually led to the big crisp heads of celery that we now enjoy. Until quite recently it was common to grow a loose-branched variety for soups which was very similar to the wild plant. Because it tends to grow near the coast, seafarers would seek and harvest it when they made landfall, not merely to freshen up the ship's dull rations, but because it was a useful anti-scorbutic. It was also used in cooking in close association with alexanders (*Smyrnium olustrum*), another coastal celery-like plant, which is no longer cultivated in gardens.

Both celery, or smallage, as it was sometimes called, and alexanders were used in Roman cookery, in vegetable purees, which included lettuce and onions, and patinas; and the seed was an ingredient in a hot, peppery sauce served with wild boar.

Although celery was grown in medieval gardens, it is very unlikely that it was cultivated in the same manner as today. It was not until the late seventeenth century that it was regularly listed along with endive, cardoons and chicory as a vegetable for blanching.

Botanists in the eighteenth century tended to lump celery together with parsley, and knew it as *Apium dulce, Celeri Italorum*. A century before it was simply called *Apium Italicum*, revealing that the most popular garden form came from Italy, the source of so many good vegetables.

Celery was blanched as it is today, and served as a salad with oil and vinegar. It was so highly thought of that no great banquet was considered complete without a celery salad.

By the nineteenth century there were three varieties: Italian, Red Solid and White Solid, as well as celeriac, the so-called Turnip-rooted celery. This increased to twenty-four celeries, and seven celeriacs. Methods of cultivation greatly improved by 1815 when a single head of celery weighing nine pounds after being washed was recorded.

Both celery and celeriac are rather too rarely grown in modern kitchen gardens, probably because they do need a good deal of care at the seedling stage, and if they are not well manured and watered, can be disappointingly tough when mature. But they are both quite splendid vegetables, either raw in salads or with cheese, or cooked as a vegetable in their own right, and not simply as a flavouring.

Celeriac is probably the easier of the two, since it needs no special blanching and takes up less room. Grated or sliced, and served with a French dressing, it is delicious as a winter salad. It can be sliced and fried, or cooked along with other root vegetables in a good stew.

A particularly delicious way of preparing celeriac is to cut the vegetable into quarter to half inch cubes. Melt two ounces of butter in a heavy saucepan. Put in the cubes, stir and cook slowly, covered, until soft, stirring from time to time with a wooden spoon. Take care not to over-cook, otherwise the celeriac will become mushy. Season when cooked and add a generous quantity of chopped parsley. For a variation on this dish add a finely chopped onion to the celeriac before cooking, and cook all together.

Celery served raw with cheese and biscuits, or stuffed with a soft cheese, is a refreshing snack. As a cooked vegetable the nicest method is to braise it. A good head of celery should be cut long ways into manageable pieces; small, firm heads can simply be halved. Blanch in boiling water for ten minutes and drain. Put bacon rashers in the bottom of a dish with finely sliced carrots and onions, and lay on the celery with a large lump of butter. Cover with stock, place buttered paper over all, and cook slowly; about an hour in a medium oven. Serve the stock it was cooked in reduced to half its volume.

CHICORY (*Cichorium intybus*) is one of those vegetables more frequently bought from the greengrocer (often at remarkably high cost), than grown in the kitchen garden, when in fact it is an extremely easily cultivated plant. So easy that it has cheerfully escaped into the wild, and before the days of powerful selective herbicides, was a common corn field weed.

The Roman's used it quite extensively. Chicory, or succory, as it was more generally named, no doubt survived the Roman departure by taking to the open, particularly in chalky areas, and was not introduced by Arthur Young from France in 1788, as the eighteenth-century botanist, Thomas Martyn, asserted. However, Arthur Young did recommend its use as cattle feed. The Elizabethans used it cosmetically, making up a drink which was taken to clear spotty skins and it was prescribed for jaundice, and liver and spleen complaints.

As well as medicinal uses it was from early times blanched and eaten in salads, just as it is today, although oddly the champion of salads, John Evelyn does not make any reference to blanching, but simply says of succory '... for being very bitter, a little edulcorated with Sugar and Vinegar, is by some eaten in the Summer, and more grateful to the Stomach than the Palate.'

Despite being an ancient kitchen garden plant, it did not acquire the popularity of its close relative, endive. Philip Miller puts it at the end of his list of five endives and declares that it is '... seldom propagated in Gardens; it growing wild in infrequented Lanes, and Dunghills in divers parts of England, where the herb-women gather it, and supply the Markets for medicinal Use.'

On the Continent it was widely grown as a vegetable, which maybe accounts for the fact that it is still regarded as a somewhat exotic foreign import. It is a very hardy plant, and will stand the winter well. In the past it was quite common to earth them up in order to blanch the new growth, but the simplest method is to sow the seed in May or June, and thin the seedlings to eight or nine inches apart. Lift them when wanted, trim the leaves to about half an inch from the crown, and blanch indoors. I have two metal oil drums with the tops cut out, well cleaned before use, and filled with peat to within two or three inches of the rim. The roots are 'planted' in the damp peat, the drums are closed with a cardboard box, and the whole lot kept in a cupboard under the stairs. Most books recommend the Witloof or Brussels Chicory, but I have always grown the best chicons from the variety, Normanto.

While its greatest value is as a winter salad (try to have it ready to eat with cold turkey after Christmas) chicory is also excellent wrapped in bacon and served with a cheese sauce as a supper dish. It can also be blanched in boiling water, laid on a bed of chopped bacon, carrots, onions and herbs; after a few minutes cooking all should be covered with a chicken stock and braised for an hour in a low oven. A sauce should be made from the remaining stock.

The roasted and ground root has long been used as a coffee substitute, or as an additive to coffee.

Another salad from the wild is CORN SALAD or LAMB'S LETTUCE (*Valerianella locusta*); the older books give it as *Valerianella olitoria*.

146

Not too often grown, and yet extremely easy, it is an excellent winter salad. Sown about mid-summer, or a little later, it produces neat rosettes of succulent, distinctively flavoured leaves, which are picked off individually.

Since it is a native of this country there is no problem with it standing the winter, and as its attractive name, Lamb's lettuce, suggests, it comes into its best at lambing time from late winter into early spring, making it extremely useful at a time when there is little that is fresh to be had from the garden.

From the earliest times it was an essential winter salading, and by the seventeenth century no less than twelve types were being sown. A hundred years later gardening writers declared no gentleman's garden was complete without it.

Most seed catalogues now offer it, and it can be slotted into a space vacated by an early season crop, such as peas. Many references describe it as being used in a mixed salad, but it is hard to fault served on its own with a good French dressing. It also makes an excellent winter salad when mixed with the outer stalks of celery.

CRESS, or more accurately, GARDEN CRESS (*Lepidium sativum*) is no longer grown as it used to be for many centuries, when it was allowed to mature for salads, and was valued for its sharp, spicy foliage, as was MUSTARD (*Sinapis alba*), which was also an anti-scorbutic. Now mustard and cress are best known as the seeds that introduce very young children to growing plants, when they raise them on wet blotting paper, or an old flannel, and harvest them as tiny seedlings. They are also stuffed into sandwiches, scattered over steaks, and generally used to bring a bit of freshness to the more tired types of mass produced food.

Unless a gardener has the good fortune to have a source of fresh water such as a stream or a pond, it is difficult to grow water cress with any success, but the ideal alternative is American Land Cress, or Bells Isle Cress (*Barbarea verna*). It is quite as good as watercress, although perhaps not as succulent.

A native of Europe, it is extremely easy to grow, and a dozen plants or even less will supply the average family with salading throughout the winter, as well as the principal ingredient for cress soup.

Cress, mustard and rape have been grown as salad vegetables from earliest times, and mustard seeds have been found at prehistoric sites. Mustard was extensively used in Roman cookery, and was a regular crop in Saxon and medieval gardens, as was cress.

Sixteenth-century gardeners mention Winter cress (probably American Land Cress), Garden cress and Garden mustard as saladings, and at that time the Dutch ate Garden cress on bread and butter. Mustard was not normally grown as a green vegetable, but was cultivated for its seeds and the manufacture of mustard powder to be used in a very liquid sauce with fish and meat. Mustard fluid was also poured down the throats of epileptics, and smeared on their bodies to bring them out of fits, as well as being used to treat coughs and shortness of breath. The effect can only be imagined!

The value placed on cresses and mustard can be judged from the fact that six mustards and ten cresses were recommended for eighteenth-century kitchen gardens.

Few cultivated vegetables and fruits can claim the antiquity of the CUCUMBER (*Cucumis sativus*), which has been grown in its native India for at least three thousand years. It was introduced into Chinese gardens two hundred years before the birth of Christ, and had reached Greece at an even earlier date, and doubtless it was from there that it moved to Italy to become a favourite of the Romans.

During a Roman feast cucumbers would appear in several different guises. In the first course it was normally served raw; as a cooked vegetable it was seasoned with cumin, celery seed and pennyroyal, and it was one of the ingredients in patinas.

There is little doubt that the Romans brought cucumbers to Britain, although it certainly had to be reintroduced. They were grown in bourgeois gardens of the thirteenth century, and in Tudor kitchen gardens. But it took a considerable time for it to gain wide culinary popularity, because the medical men regarded it with some suspicion, even suggesting that it was potentially poisonous.

One wrote: 'Cucumber taken in meats, is good for the stomacke and bowels that are troubled with heat; but it yieldest small nourishment and evill, insomuch that the immeasurable use thereof, filleth the veynes with cold naughty humors, the which (because they may not be converted into good bloud) doe at the length bring forth long and great agues and other diseases . . . . ' Not a very good recommendation. Its table use was hardly enhanced either by its vulgar name, cowcumber.

The Tudors had a choice of five varieties: Common cucumber, Turkey cucumber, Adders cucumber, Pear Fashion cucumber and Spanish cucumber, and declared that eaten with meat they were not only good for the stomach, but also for the complexion, liver and blood. John Gerarde the herbalist had a recipe for good health and good looks:

> The fruit cut in pieces, or chopped into pottage with oatmeal, even as herb pottage are made, whereof a mess eaten to breakfast, as much to dinner, and the like in supper; taken in this manner for the space of three weeks together without any intermission; doth perfectly cure all manner of Saucefleme [swelling and inflammation of the face] and copper faces, red and shining firy noses (as red as red Roses) with pimples, pumples, rubies and such like precious faces.

Cucumbers were also eaten peeled and raw like an apple, or pickled and used in sauces in the winter.

By the turn of the seventeenth century the poison slur had worn off, but only just, as John Evelyn remarked in *Acetaria*: 'The Cucumber it self, now so universally eaten, being accounted little better than Poyson, even within our Memory . . . .' he, of course, was an enthusiast, insisting that cucumbers were 'the most approved Sallet alone, or in Composition, of all the Vinaigrets, to sharpen the Appetite, and cool the Liver.'

He complained that people drained the liquid off the fruits before serving, and used too much oil. They should, he said, be sliced and mixed with chopped onions, and dressed with lemon or orange juice, or vinegar, salt and pepper. Old cucumbers, should be boiled, skinned, and eaten with oil, vinegar and honey. Young fruits could be boiled in white wine, and cucumbers of all ages were added to pottage.

Little wonder that by the eighteenth century they occupied an important place in the kitchen garden, and like melons employed all the efforts and skill of the gardener.

The Rev. Gilbert White, a famous melon grower, also devoted much of his energy to his cucumbers, raising the young plants on a nursery hot-bed. In 1754 he was raising considerable numbers of plants, and experimenting with Dutch seed never before tried in England. It failed to germinate. He had pots plunged in hot-beds, and pots at his fireside. Often foul weather and late frosts wrecked his plants, but more often than not his efforts paid off. On 9 April 1759, he was able to record in his *Garden Kalender* that he had cut his first cucumber of the year: '. . . it had a good flavour & smell. Several more set. The seeds were put into the Ground 10 weeks, & two days ago.' A week later he cut two more. On one day in July he gathered thirty-six ripe cucumbers. By this time he was having great success with White Dutch Cucumbers, and on August 27 cut 'a vast quantity . . . One that was young & eatable weighted 2 pounds 5 ounces'.

Arthur Young during his tour of the North of England from London saw whole fields of cucumbers being grown in Bedfordshire.

Its use as a cooked vegetable was more general in the eighteenth century than it is now, being served in a white sauce with chicken, rabbit and veal. They were also fried to go with mutton. According to one recipe

You must brown some butter in a pan, and cut the cucumbers in thin slices; drain them from the water (that is their juice) then fling them into the pan, and when they are fried brown, put in a little pepper and salt, and a bit of onion and gravy, and let them stew together, and squeeze in some juice of lemon; shake them well, and put them under your mutton.

Another way was to flour and fry sliced cucumbers in butter until brown, and then simmer in stock, a little claret, pepper, cloves and mace.

Pickled cucumbers known as Mango cucumbers were a great eighteenth-century favourite, even if a little time consuming to make.

Cut a little slip out of the side of the cucumber, and take out the seeds, but as little of the meat as you can; then put in the inside mustard seed bruised, a clove of garlic, some slices of ginger, and some bits of horseradish; tie the piece in again, and make a pickle of vinegar, salt, whole pepper, cloves, mace, and boil it and pour it on the mangoes; and so do for nine days together; when cold cover them with leather.' [Modern seals would be better, unless you want to be a purist.]

Cucumbers can be glazed, sautéed, or stuffed with a mixture of ham and veal mixed with onion, parsley and cucumber pulp. The stuffed cucumbers are cooked slowly in stock and butter in the oven. They can also be stewed in stock and served as a separate vegetable.

The most common pickling cucumber is the gherkin (*cucumis anguria*) a native of the West Indies and tropical America, but small ridge cucumbers will do just as well.

By the turn of the nineteenth century there were fifty-two varieties while modern seedsmen offer an average of a dozen for both greenhouse and outside culture.

During the Second World War, DANDELION (*Taraxacum officinale*) was one of the plants of hedgerow, roadside and field that people were urged to gather and eat as salad. This was no new idea, since the plant has been cultivated in kitchen gardens, as well as harvested from the wild, for centuries. However, its place in the garden as a salad plant has largely disappeared, although seeds are offered by seedsmen. Its reputation as a pernicious weed, and for causing children to wet their beds (thus its French name *Pissenlit*), and its ancient English name 'piss-a-beds', has done nothing to help its popularity.

Nevertheless, it is a useful early spring salad. It does not need to be said that it is easy to grow, but to eat it at its best it should be blanched, either by covering the plants with a good layer of sand, or by tying the leaves together and placing a flower pot over them.

For those who wish to produce a caffeine-free coffee substitute, the roots should be roasted and ground.

ENDIVE (*Chichorium endiva*) is a native of northern China and southern Asia, and has been used as a vegetable over many centuries, although it has tended to be more popular on the Continent than in Britain. It is, however, a very useful winter salading. Like its European cousin, chicory, it is a bitter herb in the green state and needs blanching, which is normally achieved either by placing a flower pot over the plant or by a covering of hay. But it is vital to keep a close watch on the blanching process since the plants pass rapidly from a good crisp condition to becoming rotten. In the past the leaves were boiled to remove some of the bitterness.

Only two varieties, Curled and Broad-leaved (*Batavian*), are grown in British gardens, while the French cultivated some twenty different types.

Unblanched leaves can be used in moderation mixed with other saladings, but it is also a good cooked vegetable, being first plunged into salted boiling water for ten minutes then drained and the moisture pressed out. Because they cook down so much, allow one head per person.

Another delicious method is to simmer a pound of endive in a hot roux for five minutes, add a little less than half a pint of veal stock and seasoning, and cook covered gently for an hour in the oven. Excess liquor is strained off after cooking, and two tablespoons of cream added before serving.

A soup can also be made from endive cooked in veal stock, liquidised, with milk added to achieve the desired consistency. A well beaten egg is added before serving.

FINOCCHIO, or FLORENCE FENNEL (*Foeniculum vulgare* var. *dulce*) is a relative new-comer to British gardens. After it made its appearance in the eighteenth century, Philip Miller in his *Gardener's Dictionary* wrote: 'The Finochia is a Plant which of late years has been introduced into the English Gardens; where it is cultivated as a Sallad-herb, and is by some People very much esteemed, though the Generality of English Palates do not at present relish it.'

It is still not very widely grown, largely because of relatively inexpensive imports. In fact it is not at all difficult, although the globular base has a tendency to become very woody unless it is well watered. It needs a light fertile soil.

The raw 'bulbs' are delicious in a salad, or as a salad on its own. They are first rate boiled and served with a fresh tomato sauce as an accompaniment to fish.

It is a mystery to me why anyone with a kitchen garden or an allotment ever buys GARLIC (*Allium sativum*). Not only is it one of the most ancient of all vegetables, it is also ludicrously easy to grow, and if you remember to keep a few bulbs back, it is a free, self-perpetuating vegetable.

The ancient Egyptians loved it, the Roman's steeped their dishes in it. It has survived every known man-made and natural disaster. Its distinctive and dominent odour has destroyed friendships and love affairs, and presumably bonded others. It is said that to eat one or two cloves a day ensures good health.

A good French salad dressing would be nothing without garlic. It can be used in a multitude of sauces, and is excellent crushed on steak, and combined with rosemary on roast lamb.

I have been growing the plant for a garlic-loving family for many years. Between January and March, depending on the weather, draw out a two- to four-inch deep trench and fill it with well-rotted manure or compost. Split up the bulbs and plant the individual cloves nine inches apart pressed well into the manure or compost. Cover with soil and firm down. The garlic is ready for harvesting when the leaves and stalk wither towards the end of the summer. The bulbs must be well ripened, preferably in the sun, if there is any. I hang them in loose bundles from the washing line, or if the weather is foul, in an open or partly open window. My experience is that home-grown garlic lasts longer than imported bulbs, and has a better flavour.

GOOD KING HENRY (*Chenopodium bonus-henricus*) was once as familiar as cabbages in the kitchen garden, but now it is hardly seen at all, except as a curiosity, although seed is readily available. Being such an antique vegetable it has acquired a confusing catalogue of names such as Good Henry, Bonus Henricus (not too much trouble there), and then Perennial Goosefoot, Wild Orache, Herb Mercury and English Mercury.

A native of Europe, it is to be found growing wild in Britain, particularly in Lincolnshire, and according to one of Culpeper's somewhat sweeping statements 'in waste places, and among rubbish'. It could well be a naturally British wild plant.

Until quite recent times it was grown for the market by Lincolnshire farmers who always had a bed of the plants in their gardens. The bed should be sited in a warm corner of the kitchen garden, and if well manured will produce a plentiful supply of tender shoots about two weeks before asparagus and continue for a number of weeks.

Although its traditional use was as a kind of spinach, indeed many people thought it preferable to spinach, the shoots can be treated like asparagus.

William Robinson, who edited *The Vegetable Garden* wrote:

In preparing it for use, if the outer skin or bark have become tough, strip it off from the bottom upwards, and then wash and tie it up in bunches like Asparagus. It is best boiled in plenty of water. When tender, strain and serve simply, or upon toast. Some have melted butter with it, others eat it simply with the gravy and meat'.

It is a perennial plant so a patch can be established for a number of years. After bringing on seedlings, plant them in deeply dug and manured soil. The patch must be well fed if it is to perform well each year, and a thick top-dressing of loam, compost and manure will keep it in good heart as well as ensuring tender new shoots.

KOHL RABI (*Brassica olearacea*) is a member of the cabbage family, but eccentric in that it is grown for its swollen stem, which gave it the name of the Turnip Cabbage, not to be confused with the Turnip-Rooted cabbage, which we now know as the Swede.

It is a vegetable with a limited following, despite the fact that it is trouble free to grow, and delicious to eat. Part of its unpopularity in this country could be the result of having at one time been grown as cattle feed in France. Nevertheless it has been around for a considerable time in Britain, but not as Kohl Rabi. It is almost certainly the Swollen Colewort of the sixteenth century.

In the seventeenth century Philip Miller gives the 'Turnip-cabbage' the botanical name, *Brassica gongylodes* (the approved modern botanical name is *Brassica olearacea* var. *gongylodes*) and said it was more popular in former times than in his day. In Germany and Italy it has been long established as a valued vegetable, at one time in those countries there were eight types in cultivation. Now normally two are offered; White and Purple Vienna.

Although some authorities say you should raise the seedlings in a seedbed, and transplant them to their growing position, the simplest method is to sow a row in the kitchen garden, and thin to nine inches apart. They should be cut for use when they are the size of a tangerine, and can be eaten raw, sliced or grated in a salad, or cooked. It is important to peel them carefully as they have a thick fibrous rind. They are very good boiled or steamed, and finished in a glaze of butter and sugar.

There cannot have been a time in the history of man the cultivator when the LEEK (*Allium ampeloprasum* var. *porrum*) was not grown in his gardens. For many years it was thought to have originated in Switzerland, but now botanists believe that it is a native of the Near East and Eastern Mediterranean. But the wild form does crop up in the islands of the Azores, and in parts of England and Scotland. It is said that the famous Musselburgh leek is a cross between the wild form and a type brought to Scotland by immigrant Dutch gardeners.

It was grown in Jewish gardens in ancient times and when the Tribes of Israel were wandering in the wilderness, leeks were one of the things they sorely missed from their years of captivity in Egypt, where raw and finely chopped leeks are still a popular dish.

The Romans, with their passion for strong flavours, made very wide use of leeks. They were baked in cabbage leaves, or served with a bean sauce, and included in patinas, fricassees, soups and vegetable stews. Leeks were served with flamingo, as well as with chickens, beef and veal, and with mussels.

Being such an important Roman vegetable no doubt they brought it to Britain, where it stayed put. It was on the plant list for the good twelfth-century kitchen garden; confirmed a hundred years later by the authorities of the day, not least Thomas Tusser who wrote about leeks in his *Five Hundred Points of Good Husbandry*.

While they were to be found growing in gardens at all levels of society, it was essentially a vegetable of the poor, being used to enliven their thick pottages of dried peas and beans, and sometimes the entrails of animals. Working class gardeners have achieved a rare skill in its culture, which is seen as its most monumental and magnificent in the leek contests of the North-East and the North-West in which huge leeks compete for large prizes. It is not unknown for competition specimens to be sabotaged by jealous rivals. Champion leeks are exhibited weighing only a few ounces under ten pounds.

The Tudors favoured a variety called the French or Vine leek, which was an important part of the Lent diet. Leeks also had their place in medicine and were used to relieve bronchial complaints, while the leaves were boiled and made into a poultice for treating haemorrhoids.

While he recommended the plant for treating a number of ailments, such as using the green leaves for stopping nose bleeding, Henry Lyte thought it a dangerous vegetable unless boiled two or three times. 'Leeks ingender evill humors, and windinesse: they cause heavy and terrible dreames, they darken the eye-sight, and are very hurtfull for them that have any exulcerations or going off of the skin of the bladder, or reynes.' Roasted leeks, however, were regarded as an antidote to drunkenness.

Interestingly they were also used in veterinary medicine, and the leaves and those of garden cress were finely chopped, mixed with wine and fed to chicks as a defence against Pip, an unpleasant disease of poultry. Leeks and garlic were stuffed into mole runs to drive the animals away from the kitchen garden.

By the eighteenth century there were two widely grown varieties; the Common leek and the London leek, which were probably the same, the only variation being that the London leek had a broader leaf. These were the only types mentioned in the first half of the nineteenth century, but by the turn of the century, there were thirteen.

Leeks were considered to be an aid to fertility, based quite unscientifically on the observation that the Welsh who ate them in great quantities had large families. Indeed, an early traveller in Wales recorded: 'I have seen the greater part of a garden there stored with Leeks, and sometimes the leaves were chopped into salads, otherwise commonly the whole vegetable was boiled in milk.'

It is an agreeable vegetable simply boiled, but not until it is soggy and falling to pieces, and it is particularly good cooked in stock, which is then thickened and enriched with cream and butter, and poured over the dish before serving.

As a supper recipe it is hard to beat leeks wrapped in bacon or ham. First they must be boiled until tender, but still crisp, then covered with grated cheese and finished off under the grill.

If, when all the new spring and early summer vegetables are coming in, you still have some Leeks left, leave them in the ground and small bulbs will form at the roots which can be detached and used in soups and stews.

LETTUCE (*Lactuca sativa*) is a companion in antiquity with leeks in the kitchen garden, and valued over the centuries even more. Its country of origin is by no means established beyond doubt, although there are claims of wild forms growing in Siberia, and in the North of India, as well as the Near East and the Mediterranean region. What is certain is that lettuces have been cosseted and cultivated in gardens for an extremely long time, although the early forms were loose rangy plants compared with the crisp, dense-headed modern varieties. The Ancient Egyptians grew them; so did the Greeks, and the Romans served them as an hors d'oeuvre, after blanching them under a flat stone.

Some of the older authorities insist that the lettuce was not introduced into Britain until Tudor times, and quote as proof that a reward was paid for providing Henry VIII with them. This must have been for some refined variety from the Continent, because lettuces had become common in gardens for a considerable time before. They were certainly grown in Saxon gardens. It seems likely that the Romans brought their variety, or varieties, which survived the occupation as did so many of their vegetable introductions.

The Elizabethans ate fresh lettuce at the beginning of meals as a spur to appetite, and at the end to soften the effect of alcohol. They also fed lettuce to their goslings to give them a good start.

Sixteenth-century herbals refer to two types; *Lactuca sativa*, which was the Cabbage lettuce, and *Lactuca oblongo folio acuto*, the Cos, but gardening works name nine varieties. It was valued as a sedative, for treating headaches and indigestion, and for nursing mothers. John Parkinson thought it an excellent bromide, and one detects a note of mischievousness when he wrote:

It abateth bodily lust and therefore both it and rue are commended for Monkes, Nunnes and the like of people to eat, and use to keep them chaste; it represeth also venerous dreams, and applyed to the Cods with a little Campfire [camphor], abateth the pride and heate of lust which some call the Coltes evill.

An earlier herbalist asserted that 'Garden lettuce eaten in meate, engendereth better better (sic) bloud, and causeth a better digestion than the other woort or pot-hearbe, specially being boyled, and not eaten rawe.'

The Garden lettuce, Curled lettuce, Small Curled lettuce, Savoy lettuce, Cabbage lettuce, and Lumbard (Lombard) lettuce, were normally found in Tudor gardens, and were boiled, or if raw, dressed with vinegar, oil and salt.

By the eighteenth century, lettuce was essential in every kitchen garden, and there were no less than fifteen varieties, of which the most popular were the Egyptian Green Cos, and the Versailles, or White Cos, the Cilicia, and Black Cos. The Royal and Imperial Lettuces were commonly grown.

Tremendous care was taken in selecting only the best and strongest plants for seed, a process which eventually led to over 127 named varieties being grown at the beginning of this century, although many of them were remarkably similar.

The eighteenth century also saw the lettuce being prepared and served in imaginative ways. Lettuce fritters were popular, and it was regularly cooked with peas or as an individual dish such as Cabbage Lettuce Pie:

> Take some of the largest and hardest cabbage-lettuce you can get, boil them in salt water till they are tender, then lay them in a colander to drain dry; then have your paste (pastry) laid in you pattipan (baking dish) ready, and lay butter on the bottom; then lay in your lettuce and some artichoke-bottoms, and four large pieces of marrow (bone marrow), and the yolks of eight hard boiled eggs, and some scalded sorrel; bake it, and when it come out of the oven, cut open the lid, and pour in a caudle made with white-wine and sugar, and thickn'd with eggs; so serve it hot.

So important were lettuces that in order to have a supply during the winter, plants were pulled up, roots and all, in the autumn and packed in sand in barrels.

From very ancient times the lettuce was recognised as the most important ingredient in a salad. The Emperor Augustus raised an altar to the lettuce, and the Roman gardeners watered their plants with wine and honey, which must have made them very sticky. To be quite correct in the past it was only eaten raw, dressed with orange or lemon juice, mixed with a little sugar. A dressing of vinegar, pepper and oil was permitted in moderation. One wonders what our forefathers would have made of salad cream.

Most people have now reverted to using lettuce exclusively as a raw salad vegetable. However, it should not be disregarded as a cooked vegetable, and it is a good way of using up a surplus before it runs to seed.

It can be boiled like spinach, using only the water clinging to the leaves after washing, and thickened in the pan with a little flour, butter, top off the milk, and flavoured with nutmeg.

Stuffed lettuce is an interesting variation. Large, firm heads must be chosen which are blanched, and afterwards part of the heart is scooped out. That part of the lettuce is finely chopped and mixed with minced chicken and mushrooms which have been cooked in butter. The mixture is bound with a rich white sauce, seasoned and laid into the cavities. Each stuffed head is tied up and braised in stock and butter.

Celtuce, the so-called cross between celery and lettuce, was introduced from the wild in China in 1938. It is hardly grown in Britain, but it quite popular in America, where it is cultivated for its thick fleshy stem, which is peeled and eaten raw, or sometimes boiled.

MARROWS, PUMPKINS, SQUASHES and GOURDS are all of the same family, *Curcurbitaceae*, and the arguments for their country of origin are as varied and interesting as their shapes and colours, although China and America are hot favourites, as well as Africa. For the student of the kitchen garden there is further confusion in the way the old authors muddled them together under their rather prettier popular names of Pepo and Pompion.

There is the vague concensus that marrows originate from the Americas, but this is hard to reconcile with the fact that the Romans used the vegetable marrow in their cuisine. Indeed, it was one of the vegetables served raw at the beginning of a meal with mulsom, the dressing made from grape juice and honey. They were also cooked and seasoned with cumin, coriander seed and fresh mint, or with a sauce made from *liquamen*, vinegar, pepper, cumin and rue.

A favourite Roman dish was Stuffed Marrow, which was prepared by cutting out a wedge from the side of the vegetable so that the seeds could be scooped out. The cavity was filled with minced brains, pepper, lovage, oregano blended together with raw eggs and *liquamen*. The wedge was replaced and tied in, and the whole marrow boiled. When tender it was sliced and fried, and served with a spicy sauce.

Pumpkins were certainly grown in Saxon gardens, and were to be found with gourds in Tudor times, and in the early eighteenth century they were popular salad vegetables.

When John Parkinson was writing about pompions in 1629 it seems clear that he was using it as a generic name for marrows, pumpkins and gourds, for he describes the fruit as 'very great, sometimes of the bigness of a man's body, and oftentimes less, in some ribbed or bunched, in others plaine, and either long or round, either green or yellow, or gray, as Nature listeth to shew herself...' In all he listed seven varieties, and said they were boiled in salt and water, powdered beef broth, or milk, and eaten with butter. Pumpkins were stuffed with pippins and baked.

Gourds were called Melopepo in the seventeenth century, and were picked young and boiled with meat like turnips. Pumpkins were stuffed with apples and sugar, baked in the oven, and then eaten spread on bread and butter, but were considered fit only for country and labouring people.

The crushed seeds and juice of the marrow were mixed with meal into a paste and used as a beauty preparation to remove freckles and spots from the face.

In recent years the passion for growing massive marrows and pumpkins for the show bench has done little to improve their culinary image, although the growing popularity of courgettes and zucchinis is helping to put that right.

The little apple-sized squashes are far too rarely grown in Britain, which is odd since they are extremely easy, and there are few more delicious supper dishes than a squash baked in the oven, served with pepper, salt and butter and eaten from the shell with a spoon.

Another excellent squash or marrow is the so-called Spaghetti marrow. They need to be picked when they are ripe, that is when the rind is hard and the vegetable gives of a hollow sound when it is rapped. Then it is boiled until the flesh shreds into strands like spaghetti. The marrow should be cut in half longways, the seeds removed and the cavity filled with a good Bolognese sauce.

Ordinary Vegetable marrow boiled and served with a white sauce is a delicious accompaniment to roast lamb; and old marrows should be used to make marrow and ginger jam.

The ONION (*Alium Cepa*) must be the most ubiquitous of all kitchen garden vegetables, and has been so for thousands of years. The Ancient Egyptians regarded it as a sacred plant, although that did not prevent them eating vast quantities, and it is said that the great slave army that built the pyramids lived off them. The Children of Israel mourned the loss of them during their long trek in the wilderness and even contemplated returning to Egypt and servitude for their sake.

Onions featured largely in Roman cookery, being used in black puddings, and in an oil and wine dressing for salads. They were also used with fish, crayfish and prawns.

Large quantities were grown in twelfth- and thirteenth-century gardens. They were grown with chives in the fifteenth century. It can be said with certainty that onions have an unbroken history of cultivation from about 3000 B.C. Not only were they popular as vegetables, but they also acquired an important place among the medicinal herbs.

Tudor doctors had ten different medical uses for them: the treatment of urinary problems, haemorrhoids, swellings, poor eyesight, hearing difficulties; for purging the brain, dog bites, rashes and blistered feet.

The Elizabethans also ate onions with honey for breakfast as an aid to good health. They rubbed the juice into their bald heads and sat in the sun, believing that the treatment would restore their hair. They used them as a plaster to treat burns, mixed onions and vinegar to stem nose bleeds, and roasted the bulbs with sugar, oil and vinegar as a cough cure.

At least four varieties were cultivated at that time; the red and the white, the round and the long. The long onions were called St. Omer's onion, and sometimes, incorrectly, St. Thomas onions. They were grown either as a crop of their own, or mixed with lettuce, parnsips or carrots.

While many people ate them raw like an apple, especially the sweet Spanish onions, they were also cooked in a number of different ways: in pottage; sliced and served as a salad with pepper, salt, oil and vinegar; made into a sauce for mutton and oysters; and as a stuffing for roast meat. Farm workers made a meal of roast onion, parsley, bread and salt. They are delicious roasted round a joint.

By the late seventeenth century onion culture had obviously been brought to considerable refinement, and single bulbs weighing as much as eight pounds were described.

In the eighteenth century the common cold was treated with onions in a pleasant manner by making them into a palatable gruel. You boil four large bulbs, cut up, in a quart of water for four hours, then add two ounces of oatmeal, and boil gently for two hours more, adding water if need be, and stirring from time to time. Strain through a fine sieve, add a little salt. A yolk of egg or a little cream may be beaten in at the last moment.

But by the 1830s, twenty-seven varieties, which included four Spanish, three Dutch, and two Strasburgh were being grown. This increased to sixty-four varieties by the turn of the nineteenth century.

Apart from the conventional onion, there are a number of others that deserve a place in the kitchen garden. Head of the list is the shallot, which is an essential for any good cook. Moules Marinère would not be the same without finely chopped shallots, and they are perfect used whole in stews, and in steak and kidney pudding. As pickling onions they are far superior to the somewhat anaemic silver-skinned pickling variety, that only a few years ago the EEC tried to designate as the official pickling onions.

The Welsh onion, Perpetual onion or Ciboule is extremely useful. It is said to come from Siberia, and is certainly hardy enough, standing any amount of harsh weather, and forming dense clumps, which can be used when normal supplies are low, or have run out.

Chives are a tiny Clumping Onion grown for their grass-like leaves which are chopped into salads or used as a garnish. The foliage dies down in the winter, and the evergreen Welsh onion leaves can be used in their place.

Almost more of a curiosity than anything, but useful for all that, is the Tree or Egyptian onion, which produces clusters of tiny bulbs at the top of its leaves. These drop off to grow into mature plants, but if they are picked they make a splendid addition to mixed pickles. Spring onions should be grown for salads and Chinese cookery.

The Catawissa onion seems to be merely a variation on the Tree onion. There is also the Potato onion, which produces clusters of bulbs underground.

The Rocambole, which is sometimes known as the Sand Leek, is grown less now than it was in the past, and was mainly used for flavouring.

Relatively new, for Britain at least, and very useful is the Japanese onion. It is sown late in the season, over-winters, and produces small, firm bulbs which are eaten fresh from the soil at the time when most of the stored harvest from the previous year has been exhausted.

ORACHE (*Atriplex hortensis*) or Arrach is a vegetable which has gone from the kitchen garden, although for centuries it was as familiar as onions and cabbage. The seeds of the familiar Common orache (*Atriplex patula*) have been found by Palaeobotanists on prehistoric sites, which testify to its long use as a food. The garden form originates from Asia and

Europe, and was an important vegetable in the twelfth-century gardens. It was still being grown towards the end of the seventeenth century but by the middle of the eighteenth century it was clearly out of fashion for Philip Miller wrote that orache was 'formerly cultivated in the kitchen-gardens, as a culinary Herb, being used as Spinage . . .'.

White and purple orache were grown and boiled and eaten in salads. Alternatively it was boiled and buttered, with sugar and spices added to give it flavour. The young tender leaves could be used in salads, but generally it was regarded as a more useful pottage vegetable, and this was its main function.

In British gardens now the red form tends to be grown as an ornamental in flower borders, but in France it is produced as a vegetable. Certainly it is a handsome plant capable of growing five or six feet high. Since it tolerates hot, dry weather, and is a useful spinach substitute, a corner ought to be found for two or three plants.

Probably because it is of relatively recent introduction into British kitchen gardens, the TURNIP-ROOTED PARSLEY (*Petroselinum crispum* var. *tuberosum*) is still quite rare, although it is popular on the Continent, and deservedly so, because it is quite delicious. It is also remarkably easy to grow and the roots will stand the winter in the ground. In the third and last edition of *The Vegetable Garden* published in 1920 it is said to be a vegetable 'taken in hand and introduced into cultivation at a comparatively recent date'.

This is not completely accurate since Philip Miller described it in his *Gardener's Dictionary* in the eighteenth century as the Broad-leav'd garden parsley, with a large sweet edible root, and added an even more resounding Latin name, *Apium hortense latifolium, maxima, crassissima, suavi & edula radice.*

'The great Garden Parsley' he wrote, 'is now more known to us in England than it was some years ago: in Holland it is very common in all their Markets.' He added that it was used in a popular Dutch dish which he named Water Souche, but must have meant Water Zooi, a substantial soup using a whole chicken, eggs and root vegetables, including parsley.

Turnip-rooted parsley, which is also known as Hamburg parsley, has a unique flavour; a delicate mingling of parsley and anise. It is a splendid vegetable on its own, boiled until tender, and tossed in melted butter.

Another aromatic and unusual root vegetable is TURNIP-ROOTED CHERVIL (*Chaerophyllum bulbosum*), a native of Southern Europe, apparently hardy, but virtually unheard of in British gardens. In cooking it is treated in the same way as Turnip-rooted parsley. Unlike the parsley, the chervil roots should not be peeled, but well scrubbed. Parboiled roots can be roasted round a joint, or the boiled roots, which tend to become a little floury, make a good puree.

If PARSNIPS (*Pastinaca sativa*) could get up and walk off in a huff they probably would, for they have been subjected throughout the centuries to rudeness ranging from disparaging comments to downright abuse, yet they have endured as one of our most familiar inhabitants of the kitchen garden. They are easy to grow, weather tolerant, and an outstandingly delicious vegetable if properly treated.

In the past many authors considered the skirret, now no more than a curiosity, as a superior vegetable, and in those distant days this might well have been the case, because the parsnip is a native plant and had been brought in from the wild, but probably not greatly improved for a very long time, so it would have been coarse and strongly flavoured.

The Romans ate them raw with salt, oil and vinegar, but when they cooked them they were flavoured with cumin sauce.

Historically they were mainly used in pottage, and from the time of Edward I to Henry VIII were part of the diet of rich and poor alike. John Gerarde, in 1597, was one of the few people to have something polite to say about parsnips, which he described as a good and pleasant food, more nourishing than carrots or turnips. In his time they were boiled until tender and then stewed in butter. They were used for fattening up people who were under-weight, as an aphrodisiac, and as a treatment for snake bite.

By the end of the seventeenth century parsnips were being served at table in more imaginative ways. One was to take large roots, peel and boil until tender. Cut into strips, flour and fry until golden brown. Serve with melted butter, sugar and cinnamon. They were also mashed and tossed in butter, sugar, raisins and lemon juice. They were the vegetable to serve with salt cod.

Elizabeth Smith in *The Compleat Housewife* has a recipe for Parsnip Fritters which could easily be made today:

Boil your parsnips very tender, then peel 'em and beat them in a mortar and rub them through a hair sieve, [a blender is quicker], and mix a good handful of them with some fine flour, six eggs, some cream and new milk, salt, sugar, and nutmeg a little, a small quantity of sack (sherry) and rose-water; mix all well together a little thicker than pancake batter; have a frying-pan ready with a good store of hog's-lard very hot over the fire, and put in a spoonful in a place until the pan be so full as you can fry them conveniently, fry them a light brown on both sides. For sauce, take sack and sugar, with a little rose-water or verjuice, strew sugar on them when they are in the dish.

Parsnips are very good as a puree, or parboiled and finished off around a joint.

If any vegetable can claim to have no enemies it must be the PEA (*Pisum sativum*), which, second to cereals, has been a staple food source from the most distant times. Along with lentils, wheat and barley they were domesticated in the Near East, and introduced into Europe before 5000 B.C. The evidence points to it being cultivated at prehistoric sites, and the variety has been identified by paleobotanists as the Field Pea, *Pisum sativum* var. *arvense*. Alphonse de Candolle in his *Origin of Cultivated Plants* says that seeds discovered at a Bronze Age site in Switzerland are a smaller version of the garden pea.

Peas in prehistoric times and for many centuries to come would not have been grown principally as a green vegetable, but to be harvested and dried for winter use, either to adulterate cereal flour, or for use in pottages. This use remained important until relatively recent times, and dried peas still are the basis of Pease Pudding, and the splendid mushy peas in the North of England. Because they preserve so easily by drying they were always included in ships stores. When the Royal Navy vessels *Isabella* and *Alexander* were exploring Baffin's Bay and searching for the North-West Passage, they carried over 552 bushels of dried peas.

The Romans, of course, grew and ate peas, and served them with salted whale meat. Known as pisan, they were a kitchen garden crop in Anglo-Saxon times.

A variety which remained popular for a very long time was the Rouncival, believed to have originated from Roncesvalles in the Pyrenees, and along with asparagus was one of the most favoured Elizabethan vegetables. Henry Lyte, in 1619, mentions only three types, 'the great, the meane, and the small', and really has little to say about them, beyond the fact that they 'engender windinesse', while later herbalists believed they sweetened the blood and were an anti-scorbutic.

Parkinson in *Paradisi* names nine varieties; 'the Runcival, the Green Hasting, the Sugar Pease, Spotted Pease, Gray Pease, White Hasting, the Pease without skins, the Scottish or Tufted Pease, sometimes called the Rose Peas, the Early or French Pease, sometimes called the Fulham Peas.' In his time they were eaten green. At Lent dried peas were made into a broth flavoured with thyme, mint, savory and other strong herbs. Some confusion is created by early writers referring to the English Sea Pease, and Suffolk Sea Pease, which were boiled in water to make a treatment for scurf. The Sea peas were considered to have grown from peas cast up from a shipwreck. Philip Miller was closer to the mark believing them to be a species in their own right. He wrote in his *Gardener's Dictionary*: 'The English Sea Pea is found wild upon the Shore in Sussex, and several other Counties in England. This was first taken notice of in the Year 1555. Between Orford and Aldbrough, where it grew upon the Heath, where nothing, no not Grass, was ever seen to grow; and the poor People, being in Distress, by reason of the Dearth of that Year, gathered large quantities of the Peas, and so preserv'd themselves and Families.' He called it *Pisum spontaneum maritimum Anglicum*, a name emphasising the apparent mystery of its origin. It is not a *Pisum* at all, but a relative of the sweet pea, and is now known botanically as *Lathyrus maritimus*, and has become very rare.

Including the Sea Pea, there were twenty-one varieties of peas grown in the eighteenth century, but writers like William Cobbett did not believe in growing a vast range of different kinds.

'As to sorts of peas' he wrote in *The English Gardener*, 'the earliest is the early-frame, then comes the early-charlton, then the blue-prussian and the hotspur, then the dwarf-marrowfat, and the tall-marrowfat, then knight's pea. There are several others, but here are quite enough for any garden in the world.' Peas were, he declared 'one of those vegetables which all people like. From the greatest to the smallest of gardens, we always find peas . . .' During the reign of George III it became a matter of pride among gardeners to pick the first from the garden (not those forced on hot-beds) on the King's birthday, June 4th. It was regarded as proof of an indifferent gardener to fail to produce the first boiling on that date.

Even in America, where the King's name was a term of abuse, eating green peas on the King's birthdays was a tradition. Cobbett, who bounced to and fro across the Atlantic, usually just a step ahead of a writ for his arrest, recalled an old Republican officer who had fought in the revolution who always had his peas ready for 'old Uncle George's birthday'.

Such was the popularity of green peas that in the eighteenth century they were preserved for Christmas by being parboiled, dried, put in glass jars and covered with melted mutton fat and sealed. The jars were kept in cool cellars, and when they were needed they were turned out into boiling water with a spoonful of sugar, and a large lump of butter.

Mangetout or sugar peas, which are eaten in the pod when they are immature (if they get beyond the stage of being eaten in the pod, leave them on the plant and let them develop. The tiny, sweet peas are as good as petit pois), were popular three hundred years ago and more. The raw peas were used in salads. Thanks to freezing, mangetout is becoming a widely popular vegetable again. It is certainly well worth growing, especially in a garden where there simply is not room for crops of Early, Middle and Late Peas.

Another 'pea', which really is not a pea at all, is the Asparagus pea (*Lotus tetragonolobus*), which produces curious winged pods. They have a delicate nutty flavour, slightly similar to asparagus. It is a low-growing bushy plant, a little untidy, with pretty rusty-red flowers. The pods must be picked very young when they are an inch to an inch and a half long. If they are allowed to mature they become woody and inedible, but when small, boiled or steamed and tossed in butter, they are a delicious vegetable. They freeze well. The roasted seeds are a coffee substitute.

Cooking peas was an elaborate business in the eighteenth century, according to a contemporary recipe:

Take five pints of young green peas, put them into a dish with a little spring water; savory, some sweet marjoram and thyme, and an onion; a few cloves, and a little whole pepper; melt half a pound of sweet butter, with a piece of fat dried bacon the bigness of an egg, in a stew pan, and let it boil until it is brown; take the white part of three hard lettuces cut very small, and put them into the butter; set it again on the fire for half a minute, stirring the lettuces four or five times; then put in the peas, and after you have given them five or six tosses, put in as much strong broth as will stew them; then add half a pint of cream, and let them boil till the liquor is almost wasted; bruise them a little with a spoon, and put a quarter of pint more cream to them; toss them five or six times, and dish them.

Pea soup was a culinary marathon:

Take the broth of a leg of beef, and boil in it a piece of bacon and a sheep's head, to mash with a good quantity of peas; strain the broth from the husks, then take half a nutmeg, four cloves, a race [root] of ginger, some pepper, a pretty deal of mint, some sweet-marjoram and thyme; bruise the spice, and powder the herbs, then put them into the soop; boil leeks in two or three waters till they are tender, and the rankness out of them; put in what other herbs you please, as spinage [spinach], lettice, beets etc., forget not to boil an onion or two in the broth at first; some will burn butter in a stew-pan, and when it is boiling put in a large plate of sliced onions; let them boil until they are tender, keeping them stirring all the time, and boil them in a soop, others will scrape a little Cheshire-cheese, and strew it in the butter and onions; it ought to be old Cheshire-cheese; if you put in the onions mentioned last, they must be fry'd in brown butter before they are put in the soop; when you put them in the frying-pan flour them well, put in sallery [celery] and turnips, if you like the taste, but strain the turnips out: to throw an old pigeon in with the meat at first, gives a high taste, or a piece of lean bacon dry'd.

By the turn of this century peas were so popular that Vilmorin-Andrieux in *The Vegetable Garden* was able to describe no less than 173 English, French, German and American varieties, and 21 types of mangetout.

The average seedsman's list now offers a total of around twenty varieties, and many of the popular old types have been outlawed by the Common Market. Commercial growing for freezing has placed the emphasis on conformity.

Although green peas can be made into delicious mousses and purees, it is difficult to improve on boiling them quickly with a sprig or two of mint and a little sugar and tossing them in butter before serving.

A French recipe is an excellent way of using up old peas: simmer the peas, a large cabbage lettuce, a chopped onion, parsley, four ounces of butter mixed with flour, a pinch of salt and sugar for about three-quarters of an hour in a covered pan.

No vegetable is better known or more widely grown than the POTATO (*Solanum tuberrosum*), and yet in terms of history it is a relative newcomer to Europe, and once in Europe it took a very long time to reach popularity and universal use. Long before it was introduced it was grown and used as a staple diet in those parts of South America where it grows wild.

In nature it is a plant that will survive quite high altitudes, and was adopted by Indians living in mountainous areas where it was impossible to cultivate maize, the other staple of that part of the world. The theory is that the maize-growing Indians of the forest migrated into the mountains and found the potato flourishing where their grain crop failed. Colombia, Ecuador and Bolivia are the historic potato areas, and there is evidence to suggest that the plant was being cultivated thousands of years before the birth of Christ. The plant itself may well have originated in Mexico, simply because it is a country rich in species of Solanum.

Funeral urns and pots in the shape of potatoes depicting highly stylized acts of sex, have been discovered by archaeologists, and that would tend to prove that the tuber was of such importance in the whole business of life and death that it was a sacred object to the Indians, as well as their main source of food. Even today in South American countries religious and quasi-religious ceremonies attend the potato crop at planting, harvest, and various stages of its development.

Most of us have been brought up to believe that Sir Walter Raleigh introduced the potato from Virginia, in the days when that American state was part of the Empire, and many of the sixteenth-century writers refer to it as the potato or *batata* of Virginia. The fact is that it was never a native of Virginia, and neither was it introduced by either Sir Walter, or Sir Francis Drake, the other Elizabethan credited with its discovery.

It was the Spanish invaders of South America who first saw it growing in the fields and gardens of the Indians they subjugated. Their first contact with it was in 1536 in Chile, and they actually introduced it to Europe from Colombia at some point between 1550 and 1573. In 1573 there is certain evidence that it was being fed to the patients in the Sangre Hospital in Seville, so tubers must have been grown in Spain for at least a year or two before that. Clusius wrote that potatoes were being cultivated in Italian gardens in 1588.

John Gerarde, called them Bastard Potatoes, to distinguish them from the Sweet Potatoes (*Ipomea batatas*), which were so highly regarded by the Elizabethans. He includes them in the list of plants he was growing in his garden in Holborn in 1596. It is most likely that the tubers he first acquired were among those that had been taken on as ships stores by Drake returning from his second expedition to Virginia in 1585, thus creating the confusion.

The Conquistadors used potatoes as food for their slaves, and throughout Europe they were considered fit only for working people, although they did appear on dining tables of the rich boiled, baked and roasted and eaten with butter, salt, vinegar and a little sugar.

Like most new plant introductions the potato was instantly endowed with remarkable, almost magical, curative properties. William Salmon declared them to be: 'moderately Diuretick, Stomatick, Chylisick, Analeptick and Spermatogenick. They nourish the whole body, restore consumption, and provoke Lust.' His enthusiastic endorsement was not shared by everyone. In Burgundy they were banned as being a source of leprosy, and a Swiss doctor linked them with scrofula.

Down the centuries has come the belief that rheumatism can be prevented by a carrying a dried tuber in your pocket, and a peeled potato was used as a cure for toothache. A sixteenth-century recipe included potatoes in a tart eaten to build up strength and health after an illness. The tart included two quinces, two or three Byrre (Burr) roots, and a potato, all of which were cooked in wine with dates, eggs, the brains of a cock sparrow, rose water, sugar, cinnamon, ginger, cloves and mace.

The Swiss shared the view that the vegetable was strengthening, and to this end served them with a fatty sauce. They considered them as particularly good food for elderly people. They were used in a complicated potato pie served during Lent. Although some of the ingredients are costly, a modified version can be made.

Make first your forc'd meat, about two dozen of small oysters just scalded, and when cold chopt small, a stale rowl [roll] grated, and six yolks of eggs boil'd hard, and bruis'd small with the back of a spoon; season with a little salt, pepper,

170

and nut-meg, some thyme and parsley, both shred small; mix these together well, and pound them a little, and make it up in a stiff paste, with half a pound of butter and an egg work'd in it; just flour it to keep it from sticking, and lay it by till your Pye is fit, and put a very thin paste in your dish, bottom and sides; then put your forc'd-meat, of an equal thickness, about two fingers broad, about the sides of your dish, as you would do a pudding-crust; dust a little flour on it, and put it down close; then fill your Pye, a dozen potatoes, about the bigness of a small egg, finely pared, just boil'd a walm [a short period of boiling] or two, a dozen yolks of eggs boil'd hard, a quarter of a hundred of large oysters just scalded in their own liquor and cold, six morels [morello cherries], four or five blades of mace, some whole pepper, and a little salt butter on the bottom and top; then lid your Pye, and bake it an hour; when it is drawn, pour in a caudle made with half a pint of your oyster liquor, three or four spoonfuls of white-wine, thicken up with butter and eggs, pour it in hot at the hole on the top, shake it together, and serve it.

A simpler recipe was for Potato, or Lemon-Cheese-Cakes: 'Take six ounces of Potatoes, four ounces of Lemon-peel, four ounces of sugar, four ounces of butter; boil the Lemon-peel till tender, pare and scrape the potatoes, and boil them tender and bruise them; beat the Lemon-peel with the sugar, then beat all together very well, and melt the butter in a little thick cream, and mix all together very well, and let it lie till cold: Put crust in your pattipans and fill them little more than half full. Bake them in a quick oven half an hour, sift some double-refin'd [caster] sugar on them as they go into the oven; this quantity will make a dozen small pattipans [a bun baking tray will do as well].'

The supposed health-giving properties of potatoes were probably the reason why in the sixteenth century they were also known as the Apples of Youth. In Ireland they might more accurately have been called the Apples of Life, because they rapidly became the main source of protein for the peasant class. In that country it is very likely that they were introduced indirectly through Sir Walter Raleigh, who owned large estates there.

Redcliffe N. Salaman, author of the classic *History and Social Influence of the Potato*, argued that Sir Walter gave tubers to one of his tenants, Thomas Southwell, and that it was he who began their culture. It is also feasible that they were washed ashore from the stores of Armada ships wrecked on the West Coast of Ireland.

171

It is a terrible irony that this life-supporting vegetable was to become the people's executioner when the crops were destroyed by blight in the devastating Irish famine of 1845–6. Because it was so important to the country some curious ceremonies were developed for planting and harvesting. In Mayo the tubers were dressed with a pinch of salt and human excrement. Good Friday was the day set for planting, and on Ascension Day holy water was sprinkled on the crop. In Galway it was considered unlucky to plant on the fourth day following Christmas, which anyway seems pretty early.

In England, Scotland and Wales, the potato made slow progress, despite some landowners urging their tenants to plant them as a hedge against food shortages. The Puritans condemned the vegetable because it is not mentioned in the Bible.

William Cobbett, who in his reforming zeal was always concerned for the plight of the poor, sneered at them as 'Ireland's lazy root', and 'The root of extreme unction'. Wherever he discovered them being grown and eaten in any quantity he instantly assumed that the people were being oppressed. His loathing of the potato bordered on the fanatical. He saw it as a threat to wheat and bread.

In *Cottage Economy* he develops an elaborate case against their culture:

Suppose a bushel of potatoes to be cooked every day in order to supply the place of this bread, then we have nine hundred boilings of the pot, unless cold potatoes be eaten at some meals; and in that case the diet must be cheering indeed! Think of the labour, think of the time, think of all the peelings and scrapings and washings and messings attending these nine hundred boilings of the pot! For it must be a considerable time before English people can be brought to eat potatoes in the Irish style; that is to say, scratch them out of the earth with their paws, toss them into the pot without washing, and when boiled turn them out upon a dirty board, and then sit round that board, peel the skin and dirt from one at a time and eat the inside.

Again in *The English Gardener* he writes:

I am going to speak here of this vegetable, as a thing to be used merely in company with meat; and not to be used as a substitute for bread, having proved, in

172

various parts of my writing, and proved it beyond all contradiction, that, as a substitute for bread, it is the most wasteful thing that can possibly be used.

The Royal Society in 1662 tried to popularize potatoes by asking its Fellows to grow them. A good deal of mystery surrounded their production because people were accustomed to cultivate from seeds, cuttings or by grafting and budding, but growing from tubers was baffling. At Horsted Keynes in Sussex a man had to come from a neighbouring village to plant the potato crop.

It was not before the end of the eighteenth century that the vegetable came into general use, and this was dictated to some extent by the high price of flour.

By 1770 named early varieties were being grown (the first potatoes to be introduced were late maturing), the Howard or Cluster and the Irish Apple. They were followed by The Manly, White Kidney, Ox Noble, The Yam, The Cups, The Ashleaf, Lapstone Kidney and The Lumper. The latter was the tuber that became blighted and caused the Irish famine. The popularity of the potato was reflected in its nicknames in Ireland, England, Wales and Scotland; pratie, fata, taters, murphy, crockers and spud.

Elsewhere in Europe the names are markedly different from the English potato. This is due to the fact that originally they were considered to be some kind of truffle, the underground fungi. In Italy they were called tartuffle; *cartoufle* in seventeenth-century French; *kartoska, katopha, kartocle* and *kartovka* in Russian; *karrofla* and *karczofle* in Polish. The French later adopted the more familiar *pomme de terre* (Apple of the Earth), which seems to have influenced the Malay and Sri Lankan name, *artappel*, and the Iranian, *sib-i-zamini* (Earth Apple).

By the late nineteenth and early twentieth century the potato was attracting enormous attention from hybridizers, and from one of the most distinguished, Archibald Finlay, came Majestic. In 1903–1904 there was a brief potato boom that was reminiscent of tulipmania, during which enormous prices were paid for seed tubers. Finlay introduced a variety he named Eldorado, which had earlier been known as Evergood, and declared it to be the perfect potato. Fourteen pounds of seed tubers were sold for £1,400. Based on the cost of living index that would be £46,200 today, or £3,300 a pound.

King Edward VII, now known as King Edwards, was raised by a Northumberland gardener, who originally called it Fellside Hero.

By the turn of the century there were 63 named first earlies, 65 second earlies, and 144 maincrop. Often they had splendidly colourful names: Goldfinger, Red-nosed Kidney, Red Streak or Lancashire pink-eye, Black Skin and Bread Fruit.

Growing techniques improved, but one intriguing method of producing very early new potatoes was discovered accidentally by George Stanton, the Head Gardener at Park Place, Henley-on-Thames. He stored the maincrop in a chalk cave. After a while he noticed that the stored crop was sprouting fresh, young tubers. He then spread the old tubers on the floor and partly covered them with finely-sifted potting soil, and in that way was able to harvest new potatoes throughout the autumn and winter. Clearly it helped to have a chalk cave, but anyone with a cellar or dark frost-free shed could try the experiment.

Despite Cobbett's fears for bread and the end of civilisation as he knew it, there are few vegetables better than a dish of almost transparent earlies cooked with fresh mint, and served with an abundance of melted butter.

T. W. Sanders, the late famous horticultural journalist, believed that mature potatoes should be baked in their skins and served in a clean napkin. But if they were to be boiled, he said they should be peeled as thinly as possible, put into boiling water with a little salt. When a little over half cooked all the water with the exception of enough to cover the bottom of the saucepan should be poured off, and the vegetables finished over a low heat. They would be transferred into balls of flour he claimed.

RADISHES (*Raphanus sativus*) were among the vegetables grown in the kitchen gardens of the ancient Egyptians two thousand years ago or more, and were valued by the Romans who ate them with a sauce made from *liquamen* and ground pepper. They probably brought them to Britain, where they became firmly established, and were to be found in Anglo-Saxon gardens. Indeed, it is a vegetable that has come to our tables without a break for hundreds of years. They were eaten by the rich before meals to stimulate the appetite, and by the poor as a meal with bread and salt.

While radishes were not considered to be of any nutritional value, the herbalists were in agreement that they were a valuable anti-scorbutic, and doubtless this contributed to their enduring popularity. It was also believed that eaten after a meal they acted as a digestive, while the peel mixed with honey and vinegar sharpened the mind and the wit.

Radishes were also used to prevent drunkenness, to sweeten bad wine, as well as a cure for spots. For hair loss they were mixed with powdered sheep's heart.

From the earliest times the familiar so-called French Breakfast radish, the Black Spanish radish, the White radish and the London radish were grown, although not necessarily under those names.

In very ancient days it was a venerated plant, and there was a radish cast in solid gold in the Delphic Temple.

More recently the seedling leaves and roots were raised on hot-beds almost all round the year for use in salads. The Black radish was a valuable anti-scorbutic during the winter months. It was mixed into mustards, but more normally eaten grated.

A popular eighteenth-century relish which deserves to be re-introduced was pickled radish seed pods. The pods were picked while they were still young and green and soaked in salt and water for twenty-four hours, then drained. A pickle of vinegar, cloves, mace, and whole pepper was brought to the boil and poured over the pods. A bruised clove of garlic was added.

I agree with the old authorities who asserted that the Spanish Black radish is the most valuable of the tribe, simply because it is so versatile. It is very good as a cooked vegetable, either in a stew, or boiled, glazed with a garlic butter and served as a separate vegetable. Peeled, grated or sliced and marinated in a good French dressing it is a delicious winter salad. China Rose, another winter radish with a long, thick red-skinned root is very succulent, but does not stand the cold as well as the Spanish Black, and tends to fall victim to slugs.

HORSE-RADISH (*Armoracia rusticana*) is not a radish at all, though like the radish is a member of the wallflower family (*Cruciferae*), and has an extremely hot flavour. In the sixteenth century it was only thought fit to be used as a sauce by country people and was popular with labourers in Britain and Germany. While being shunned by genteel palates it was prescribed for treating gout and rheumatic pains. In Germany it is traditionally eaten in a sauce for fish, while in Britain it is essential with beef, as well as smoked mackerel.

Some recipes say that the root should be cooked before being made into a sauce. I think this would remove too much of the flavour. The fresh roots must be washed and scraped, and either grated, or shredded in a mechanical chopper. It should then be mixed with single-cream, white wine, vinegar, sugar and a little salt and allowed to stand for an hour or so before use.

Probably now only to be found in specialist collections, RAMPION (*Campanula rapunculus*) was once a fairly common salad vegetable. At one time it was to be found growing wild in hilly parts of Kent and Sussex, and around Croydon in Surrey, which gave rise to the belief that it is a native plant, which it is not.

The roots, which were eaten either raw or boiled, were believed to stimulate the appetite. They were also mixed with lupin seeds and used externally as a skin cleanser. The juice extracted from the leaves and stalks was mixed with mother's milk to produce eye drops.

A widely grown plant in medieval gardens, its popularity was slipping in the sixteenth and seventeenth centuries, although the young roots were eaten like radishes in salads in the spring until relatively recent times.

In France, where it is known as *Raiponce,* both leaves and stalks are used in salads, seed is planted in June to ensure a supply throughout the winter.

ROCKET (*Eruca sativa*) is a salad vegetable that deserves to be grown far more than it is. Apart from being easy to cultivate in the kitchen garden, it is a delicious addition to summer salads. Originating from the Mediterranean region, it is sometimes known as Italian Cress, but flourishes like a native in Britain, and for many centuries was a common annual crop.

The Elizabethans considered it a most virtuous plant, first as a salad to be eaten with lettuce and purslane, but also as an aphrodisiac, although there was some argument about that attribute. The seeds were given as an antidote to scorpion stings and bites from shrews, which were considered to be poisonous. They were also made into a beauty preparation with honey and gall from cattle.

Pliny claimed that a drink made from wine and rocket taken just before a whipping rendered the punishment painless, but, as John Parkinson wrote, and many a bruised and battered victim must have thought: '. . . I wish that Pliny had beene a true relator hereof by his owne experience first, that others might have believed him the better.'

A drink made from rocket was also supposed to act as a deodorant, and the leaves boiled and mixed with sugar were given to children to relieve coughs.

It was still being recommended as a salad vegetable at the turn of the eighteenth century, but by the middle of the century it had fallen into disuse.

The distinctive smell and flavour of rocket may well put some people off, but providing the leaves are picked when young and tender, it is a perfectly delicious addition to any salad served with a good French dressing. Regular watering will prevent the plants from becoming tough too quickly, and successional sowings ensure succulent leaves.

SALSIFY (*Tragopogan porrifolius*) compared to vegetables like leeks and lettuce is a newcomer to the kitchen garden. Introduced into Britain from Italy, it enjoyed a period of popularity, and then slipped quietly into semi-obscurity, despite being given the alluring name of 'vegetable oyster'. Originally it was known as Goat's Beard, or Joseph's Flower.

At the beginning of the eighteenth century it was still listed as one of the plants to be included in the kitchen garden, but by the middle of the century Philip Miller wrote that 'the Goat's beard with a leaf like Leeks, and a purple-blue Flower, commonly call'd Salsaffy, or Sassafy . . . was formerly more in Esteem than at present: this was brought from Italy, and cultivated in Gardens for Kitchen-use, the Roots being by some People greatly valued: but of late there is but little cultivated for the Markets; tho' several Gentlemen preserve it in Gardens to serve their Tables.'

Now it is beginning to reappear in greengrocers shops, and is often served in good restaurants. It is an easy vegetable to grow, although care should be taken not to plant it in recently manured soil, since it has a tendency to fang. It will stand in the ground through the winter, and in the spring the young foliage can be blanched and used in salads. But normally it is grown for its roots. Because the thick white sap discolours rapidly after scraping or peeling, the cleaned roots should be put straight into cold water to which vinegar or lemon juice has been added. To enjoy the flavour thoroughly it is enough to boil them until tender and serve without a sauce.

SCORZONERA (*Scorzonera hispanica*) is related to salsify, and somewhat similar in flavour. It was introduced during the sixteenth century, but more as a medicinal herb than a vegetable since it had a remarkable reputation as a cure for snake bite, thus becoming known as Viper-grass. Some of the old writers claimed that it was not only an antidote to snake bite, but if a snake was touched with the juice it would die, and that a man could safely handle the most venomous types if his hands were first dipped in the thick, milky sap of the plant.

The story goes that a Moor, who was living in Spain, learned in North Africa that the plant was a cure for snake bite. Armed with this knowledge he grew scorzonera secretly in the mountains, and waxed rich on the charges he made for curing snake bite, particularly during harvest time. When he was followed into the mountains the secret of his magical plant was discovered. A specimen of the plant was sent to John Melchion, the Queen of Bohemia's doctor, and he sent it to the great botanist Matthioli.

In France the plant was developed for its edible roots, and during the seventeenth and early eighteenth century it became a popular vegetable in British kitchen gardens. But like salsify if was being grown less and less by the middle of the eighteenth century, and cannot be said to be a particularly common vegetable today. Like salsify it is quite simple to grow, and has the added advantage of having less of a tendency to fang. The long black roots are very brittle, and have to be almost excavated out of the soil. If they do snap off they will come up with the persistence of a dandelion, and in the past root cuttings were a recommended method of culture. However, it is better to grow them from seed.

They can be boiled and served plain, or after boiling can be dipped in batter and fried in deep, hot fat; or boiled, sliced and served in a scallop shell with a cheese sauce.

According to the herbalist John Gerarde 'The root being eaten, either roasted in embers, sodden (stewed) or raw, doth make a man merry and removeth sorrow.' What more could one want from a vegetable.

178

SEAKALE (*Crambe Maritima*) is a peculiarly English vegetable, a native which was originally gathered in the wild by the poor, but was domesticated and became a luxury. It is not now common in kitchen gardens, but once established it is as easy to manage as rhubarb.

A coastal plant, it grows naturally on the seashore in gravel and sand, and even tolerates being doused in sea water. At one time it was found in many places, particularly the Sussex and West Country coast where local people used to look for tell-tale humps in the sand and shingle formed by the young shoots in March and April, which were cut before they appeared through the surface. It was a local delicacy, but according to George Lindley, writing in 1831, was being sold commercially in the middle of the eighteenth century, although he says 'the plant has not long been introduced into public use as a dinner vegetable'. One eye-witness insisted that he saw bundles of seakale being offered for sale in the market in Chichester in West Sussex in 1753. The Rev. Gilbert White was growing it at Selborne in 1751.

It did not come into general kitchen garden use until 1767 when it was grown by a Dr Lettsom of Grove Hill, London.

The popularity of seakale must have been pretty swift, for Philip Miller listed no less than three varieties, although they were doubtless *Crambe maritima*, with slight variations in appearance. He said that in the wild it grew most plentifully in Sussex and Dorset 'where the Inhabitants gather it in the Spring to eat, preferring it to any of the Cabbage Kind, as it generally grows upon the gravelly Shore, where the Tide flows over it.'

Given an open soil in the kitchen garden, the plants will develop rapidly. In autumn, they should be covered by four or five inches of gravel or sand, and this should be sufficient to blanch the young stems. More recent authorities insist that the plants need a deeply dug soil, richly manured, ideally with rotted seaweed. Clearly it does need to be well drained. The young shoots are normally forced and blanched in the same way as rhubarb, and for an early crop plants can be lifted and forced on in a greenhouse. Some growers say that it is better brought on in the open under a thick covering of ashes.

Seakale is raised from seed, which is readily available, but it is two years before the plants are fit to cut. The stock is easily increased by root cuttings.

It should always be cooked in the simplest way, that is boiled for twenty to twenty-five minutes, and served on its own in the manner of asparagus with Normandy butter, which is equal quantities of butter and cream heated without boiling, with a dash of lemon juice added just before serving.

Another rarity which at one time was as common as carrots is SKIRRET (*Sium sisarum*). Believed to be a native of China, it was for centuries grown and valued but by the middle of the eighteenth century was beginning to disappear, a fact bemoaned by Philip Miller, who wrote:

> This is one of the wholesomest and most nourishing Roots that is cultivated in Gardens; and yet it is at present very rare to meet with in the Gardens near London: What may have been the Cause of its not being more commonly cultivated, I can't imagine, since there are many Kitchen-gardens which are proper for this Plant.

By the first half of the nineteenth century it was hardly known or grown at all. Its almost total demise is curious since it was fulsomely recommended by all the authorities as being wholesome and well flavoured. The Emperor Tiberius valued it so highly that he accepted it as a tribute. Normally it was boiled, roasted or baked in pies. Cold cooked skirret was eaten in salads.

It seems very probable that it was brought to Britain by the Romans, was certainly being grown in medieval gardens, and by the turn of the eighteenth century was still being recommended for the well stocked kitchen garden.

Henry Lyte, who called them skirwurts, said they were an aid to appetite, while Culpeper recommended them for urinary problems and jaundice. They were also considered to be an effective aphrodisiac.

Skirret Pie was a rich eighteenth-century delicacy, but quite simple to make:

> Boil your biggest Skirrets, and blanch them, and season them with cinnamon, nutmeg, and a very little ginger and sugar. Your Pye being ready, lay in your Skirrets; season also the marrow of three or four bones with cinnamon, sugar, a

little salt and grated bread. Lay the marrow in your Pye, and the yolks of twelve hard eggs cut in halves, a handful of chestnuts boiled and blanched, and some candied orange-peel in slices. Lay butter on the top, and lid your Pye. Let your caudle be white-wine, verjuice, some sack and sugar; thicken it with the yolks of eggs, and when the Pye is baked, pour it in, and serve it hot. Scrape sugar on it.

Skirret is easy enough to grow from seed, and the stock of the plant can be increased by root cuttings. The roots, which are the only part eaten, are formed in bunches, and perhaps its unpopularity is due to the fact that they are fiddly to clean, and sometimes it is necessary to remove the central core, which can become woody. They could be treated like asparagus, being boiled, served with melted butter and eaten with the fingers.

No good kitchen garden should be without its patch of SORREL (*Rumex acetosa*), which is easy to raise from seed in the first place, and then will produce an abundance of leaves in a trouble-free and obliging manner for years. I have only sown sorrel once in my gardening career; that was fifteen years ago, and those same plants never fail to provide me with all the foliage I need.

The old herbalists used sorrel extensively to treat a considerable catalogue of illnesses, including upset stomachs, sore throats, boils, ringworm and other skin complaints, and scurvy. Common sorrel seeds have been found in Bronze Age settlements in Britain.

As far as John Evelyn was concerned no salad could be called a salad without sorrel, which he said: '... aswages Heat, cools the Liver, strengthens the Heart; is an Antiscorbutic, resisting Putrefaction, and imparting so grateful a quickness to the rest, as supplies the want of Orange, Limon, and other Omphacia [oil or sour grape juice], and therefore never to be excluded.'

The best variety is the so-called French sorrel with its large, succulent leaves. Even in the depths of winter it is always possible to find some to include in a salad.

Although it boils down it can be cooked in milk, not too much, pureed, with cream folded in at the last minute.

Using a good chicken or veal bone stock, it makes a delightfully refreshing soup. Sweat the sorrel, a cubed potato and a finely chopped onion in butter, season well, when soft add the stock, liquidise. It can be eaten hot or cold with single cream added before serving

SPINACH (*Spinacea oleracea*) is a vegetable which has been grown in the kitchen garden for centuries. It is one of those you either love or loathe, but on balance its popularity has been pretty constant. William Cobbett, in his idiosyncratic way, declared: 'Every one knows the use of this excellent plant. Pigs, who are excellent judges of the relative qualities of vegetables, will leave cabbages for lettuce, and lettuces for spinage.'

It was certainly being grown in fifteenth-century gardens, and may well have been around for longer than that. The Elizabethans used it in rich tarts which were filled with chopped veal, kidney, herbs, spices, sugar and dried fruit.

Although it is now considered to be a health-giving vegetable, the old herbalists, because they could not detect any medicinal use for it, were somewhat dismissive. They did not consider that it had any nutritional value, and believed it was inclined to make people sick. Despite this it was popular as a cooked vegetable or raw in salads.

Cooking advice given over two hundred years ago is still valid today. That is, it should be cooked whole in the moisture adhering to the leaves after washing, and no more water should be added. After being boiled for about ten minutes, the leaves should be squeezed dry, and then tossed in hot butter, which is just turning brown. Cream, sugar and seasoning should be added before serving. Spinach is also delicious as a puree.

Only three varieties, the Common Prickly, Narrow leaved and Common Smooth-Seeded, were grown up to the nineteenth century, when the numbers grew to nine.

Spinach is susceptible to dry conditions, and unless well watered will tend to run to seed. The so-called New Zealand spinach (*Tetragonia expansa*), which is a good substitute, is drought resistant. Its only problem is that it tends to spread and ramble, taking up a large amount of room.

The TOMATO (*Lycopersicon esculentum*) arrived in Europe at roughly the same time as the potato, and took about as long to achieve popularity, particularly in Britain. It went by a variety of names: Love Apples, Golden Apples, *Pomum amoris majus* (The Greater Love Apple), Apple Bearing Nightshade, and Peruvian Apples, the latter being a reference to the fact that they grow wild in the lower Andes.

They were boiled and eaten with pepper, salt and oil, or mixed into a kind of sauce with oil, salt and vinegar but not considered particularly nourishing, although they were believed to be a powerful aphrodisiac. The quality owed more to the power of suggestion than anything else, but it did lead them to be eaten raw, boiled, sliced and dipped in flour and fried in butter or oil.

There was also a wide-held belief that tomatoes were poisonous, probably because they do bear some likeness to nightshade, and many people took the view that they were only fit to be grown as an ornamental plant.

Although they were not a popular item of food, eight varieties were grown in the eighteenth century with both red, yellow and white fruit, being cultivated in British gardens. The variety called *Lycopersicon Galeni, fructu rubra* (Love-Apple with a red fruit) was the most cultivated. Phillip Miller wrote: 'The Italians and Spaniards eat these Apples, as we do Cucumbers, with Pepper, Oil and Salt; and some eat them stew'd in Sawces, etc. and in Soups they are now much used in England ... This Fruit gives an agreeable Acid to the Soup; though there are some Persons who think them not wholesome, from their great Moisture and Coldness, and the Nourishment they afford must be bad.'

This attitude had grown out of ignorance. Henry Lyte describing the Amorous Apple, or Golden Apples in 1619 said there were two types, one yellow and one red, and that 'The complexion, nature, and working of this plant is not yet known, but by that (sic) I can gather of the taste, it should be cold of nature, especially the leaves, somewhat like unto Mandrake, and therefore, also it is dangerous to be used.'

By the nineteenth century all the fears and old wives' tales about tomatoes had gone, and in 1920, thirty-seven varieties were described including purple coloured fruits. Methods of serving them also became more enterprising than being confined to salads and soups. Cooks discovered that they could be baked, souffleed, pureed, stuffed, stewed, made into a mousse, a fondu or jellied.

An excellent summer luncheon dish requires the middle to be scooped out of a ripe tomato and the cavity to be filled with minced chicken and mayonnaise, and served on rounds of cold fried bread in a bed of aspic. Green tomatoes left over at the end of the summer can be stewed in butter or baked. First peel and slice them, and then lay them in alternate layers with slices of bacon and parmesan cheese. Moisten with stock, cover with breadcrumbs and bake until golden brown.

TURNIPS (*Brassica rapa*) certainly must be counted among the ancients of the kitchen garden. Although their country of origin cannot be defined with certainty, they are not native to Britain as some authorities claim. They probably came from the Mediterranean region, and were well known to the Romans, who served them with a sauce of myrtle berries and honey, or with a dressing of vinegar, mustard and salt. Cumin was also used in preparing them for the table.

It is possible that the Romans brought turnips to Britain and that they escaped into the wild giving rise to the belief that they were originally a local plant. They were regularly grown in fifteenth century gardens, and in the seventeenth were the standard accompaniment to boiled beef. By the eighteenth century turnips were being grown in huge quantities, because they were adopted as a vital animal feed to bring stock through the winter. Surprisingly this did not have the effect of diminishing their popularity as a table vegetable.

The Elizabethans valued the roots as both medicine and food. They were a nourishing and vital food, and even eaten raw, although this practice was discouraged, as in excess raw turnips caused stomach upsets.

A poultice made from turnips boiled in milk was used to ease the pain of gout; a root hollowed out, filled with oil of roses and roasted 'healeth the kibed heels [chillblains]'. The seeds made into a treacle, presumably with honey, was an antidote to poison, and an oil expressed from them was used to kill intestinal worms. According to the herbalists turnips were an aphrodisiac, and could also be used as a beauty preparation and to improve sight. The juice was used to temper steel. A favourite Elizabethan dish was turnips stuffed with minced meat.

John Gerarde wrote of the Great turnip and the Small turnip in the sixteenth century, and said: 'It groweth in fields, and divers vineyards, or hop gardens in most places in England. The small turnip groweth by a village near London (called Hackney) in a sandy ground, and brought to the Cross in Cheapside by the women of that village to be sold, and are the best that I ever tasted.'

The turnip was held in high esteem for salads, especially the long rooted form, which was eaten when they were not larger than a radish. Turnip bread, appeared at the tables of the wealthy and was hardly distinguishable from the best wheat flour bread.

A seventeenth-century recipe instructs:

> Let the Turneps first be peel'd, and boil'd in Water till soft and tender; then strongly pressing out the Juice, mix them together, and when dry (beaten or pounded very fine with their weight of Wheat-meal), season it as you do other Bread, and knead it up; then letting the Dough remain a little to ferment, fashion the Paste into Loaves, and bake it like common Bread.'

Turnips were also wrapped in damp paper, roasted in hot embers, and eaten with sugar and butter.

By the mid-eighteenth century the long rooted form, known as the Mouse-Tailed Turnip in Hampshire, had gone out of fashion, and the round white- and purple-rooted varieties were most widely grown, and by the nineteenth century the White or Stone-Turnip dominated the kitchen garden scene.

Most of the old authorities say that turnips should not be sown before July or August, and this is sound advice. The spring-sown turnips eaten when they are about the size of a golf ball are delicious, but they tend to come in at a time when there is an abundance of other early vegetables. If they are sown later in the summer they will stand through the winter, when they are a valuable fresh vegetable, particularly with stews and dishes such as boiled beef and boiled mutton. They are good with all game, especially wild duck.

Because it is a member of the cabbage family, the leaves of the turnip can be eaten, although they are pretty vile if badly cooked. The best way of treating them is as a puree blended with butter and cream. When the roots are young they are quite delicious boiled and glazed, and a variation on the Elizabethan practice of stuffing them with minced meat, is to make up a stuffing of breadcrumbs, tomatoes, or tomato concentrate, hard boiled egg yolks and herbs. Bake them in a pan with a little stock, and serve them with a creamy sauce.

The swede or Swedish turnip, as it was known, is easy to grow, and a satisfying winter vegetable, mashed with butter, salt and pepper.

10
The Fruits

While the popularity of vegetables has waxed and waned over the centuries, fruit has always remained popular. Ancient man gathered them in the wild, and fruit seeds have been discovered in prehistoric sites all over Europe. By the early Bronze Age, apples, pears, cherries and plums were being cultivated. Centuries later the Romans brought the culture of fruit to a fine and sophisticated art. A little more than thirty years before the birth of Christ, Virgil wrote of raising trees, including fruit trees, in The Georgics:

One man takes suckers off the tender stock of the mother
And plants them in trenches: another fixes sets in the field
By notching stakes cross-wise or sharpening the wood to a point.
Some forest trees there are prefer the pinned-down arches
Of the layer, that make a nursery alive in the parent's earth.
Some need no root, and the pruner
Can safely commit to the soil cuttings from off a high branch.
What's more – and this is a marvel – if you take a saw to the trunk of
An olive, a root will come pushing out from the dry wood.
Often again we observed the boughs of one tree change
Without harm into another's – grafted apples growing
On a pear, and stony cherries reddening upon a plum tree.
So come, you countrymen, learn the correct training of each
In its kind, domesticate wild fruits by your cultivation,
And let not the earth be lazy!

So there were the Romans grafting, layering and growing fruit trees from cuttings at a time when in Britain we were still living a relatively primitive existence.

Over the centuries fruit has stirred the imagination and imagery of poets, not least of all Robert Herrick, who in the seventeenth century used them in the most sensual allusions in poems to his many mistresses. In *Upon the Nipples of Julia's Breast* he wrote:

Have ye beheld (with much delight)
A red-Rose peeping through a white?
Or else a Cherrie (double grac't)
Within a Lillie? Centre plac't?
Or ever mark't the pretty beam,
A strawberry shewes halfe drown'd in Creame?
Or seen rich Rubies blushing through
A pure smooth Pearle, and Orient too?
So like to this, nay all the rest,
Is each neate Niplet of her breast.

Such was the allure of fruit that ever since orchards were first planted small boys have risked fear and punishment to steal fruit from the bough.

John Clare in *The Shepherd's Calendar* describes just such a country boy who breaks off from leading the cart-horse home from the harvest field to go scrumping:

Oer garden pales or orchard walls to hie
When sleeps safe key hath locked up dangers eye
All but the mastiff watching in the dark
Who snufts and knows him and forbears to bark
With fearful haste he climbs each loaded tree
And picks for prizes which the ripest be
Pears plumbs or filberts covered oer in leams
While the pale moon creeps high in peaceful dreams
And oer his harvest theft in jealous light
Fills empty shadows with the power to fright
And owlet screaming as it bounces nigh

That from some barn hole pops and hurries bye
Scard at the cat upon her nightly watch
For rats that come for dew upon the thatch
He hears the noise and trembling to escape
While every object grows a dismal shape
Drops from the tree in fancys swiftest dread
By ghosts pursued and scampers home to bed
Quick tumbling oer the mossy mouldering wall
And loses half his booty in the fall
Where soon as ere the morning opens its eyes
The restless hogs will happen on the prize
And crump adown the mellow and the green
And makes all seem as nothing ne'er had been

From the very earliest times the APPLE was treasured, not only for its fruit but for its blossom as well. Henry Ward Beecher expressed the delight of a tree in full bloom when he wrote:

What if you have seen it before, ten thousand times over? An Apple-tree in full blossom is like a message, sent fresh from heaven to earth, of purity and beauty!

In the most ancient times the wild crab apples were gathered for cider brewing. The resulting drink must have been incredibly rough and sour, and this gave rise to the harvesters searching for trees producing the sweetest fruits, and through this process of selection the best were brought into orchard cultivation. No doubt the Romans brought their favourite varieties with them.

At the beginning of the thirteenth century named varieties were being mentioned. The most famous were Pearmain and Winter Pearmain, both sweet, yellow-skinned apples, flushed with scarlet. The Costard, which lent its name to Coster-mongers, was a very common apple in 1292. During the reign of Henry VIII the Gold Pippin was raised in Sussex, and became so famous throughout Europe that it attracted no less than one hundred and sixteen synonyms. Other early named varieties were the Devonshire Quarrenden, Juneating, and Golden Russet. Sadly these have either disappeared altogether, or at best are preserved in collections like Britain's National Fruit trials.

For a long time new varieties came along more or less by chance. The Ribston Pippin was grown from three apple pips sent to Sir Henry Goodricke of Ribston Hall at Knaresborough in Yorkshire from Normandy in 1709. Only one germinated and matured. The original tree was blown down in 1810, but was propped up and lived on, and a seed from one of its progeny produced Cox's Orange Pippin.

During the ninteenth century and early in the present century a torrent of new apples arrived from the nurseries of American hybridisers. The most famous was Northern Spy, which was raised in 1800 at East Bloomfield, New York, from a seed of an apple grown at Salisbury, Connecticut. In recent years there has been a rapid reduction of the number of varieties in cultivation due, as much as anything, to the demands of commercial standardisation. Golden Delicious is possibly the most controversial example of this trend, although it is not so new and original as the French would have us believe, having been raised as a chance seedling in Clay County, West Virginia in 1890.

When he published the fourth edition of *Fruit and its Cultivation*, T. W. Sanders was able to recommend 130 different eating and cooking apples for selecting a well-stocked orchard. Only eleven of those are still in general cultivation, although happily a great many of them are still in collections.

Crab apples have always been valued for making jelly, and the very attractive ornamental varieties such as Dartmouth, John Downie, Scarlet Siberian, The Orange and The Transparent make fine garden plants as well as producing good jelly fruit.

The APRICOT is generally believed to have been introduced into Britain from Italy by John Woolf or Wolff, who was gardener to Henry VIII. It is a little surprising that it was so late in arriving at these shores since it had been cultivated by the Chinese from 3000 B.C., and grown extensively in Tibet, Northern India, and by the ancient Greeks and Romans. A favourite Roman dish was a stew made from apricots, mint, pepper, honey, *liquamen*, and *passum* (a sauce made from old wine, dried grapes and water). The stew was thickened with cornflour, and the whole concoction was sprinkled with ground pepper before serving.

Until relatively recent times apricots, or 'apricocks' as they were often more generally known, were widely grown. In August 1790 Parson Woodforde was able to enter into his diary: '... Sent one Dozen and one very fine Apricots from my best Tree called the Anson Apricot, to Mr. and Mrs. Custance by my Maid Betty.' Even at the turn of this century many a cottage boasted a good tree on a warm wall, when there were at least fourteen varieties to choose from, of which today Moorpark is usually all the nurserymen now have to offer.

A favourite eighteenth-century winter dessert was Preserved Apricots.

Take your Apricocks, stone and pare them, and take their weight in double-refin'd sugar beaten and sifted, and put your Apricocks in a silver cup or tankard, and cover them over with the sugar, and let them stand all night; the next day put them is a preserving-pan, and set them on a gentle fire, and let them simmer a little while; then let them boil till they are tender and clear, taking them off sometimes to turn and scum; keep them under the liquor as they are doing, and with a small clean bodkin or great needle jab them sometimes, that the syrup may penetrate into them; when they are enough take up and put them in glasses, boil and scum the syrup and when it is cold put it in on your Apricocks.

CHERRIES have never been the victim of changing fashions. They have been consistently popular from the most ancient times, and often feature in sixteenth-, seventeenth- and eighteenth-century paintings, particularly portraits and family groups, almost as though they represented wealth and success. Herrick, of course, used them in an allusory sense in his pretty little verse 'Cherrie-Ripe':

Cherrie-Ripe, Ripe, Ripe, I cry,
Full and faire ones; come and buy:
If so be, you ask me where
They doe grow? I answer, There,
Where my Julia's lips doe smile;
There's the Land, or Cherry-Ile:
Whose Plantations fully show
All the yeere, where Cherries grow.

The first cherries are said to have originated from Turkey and were grown in a city called Cerasus.

Unlike apples they do not flourish everywhere: Kent, Berkshire, Buckinghamshire and Hertfordshire are the best counties. Possibly because of this they were highly esteemed for a guest. Sir Francis Carew was said to have held back cherries by draping the tree with damp canvas so that they would be perfect when Queen Elizabeth paid him a visit at his seat, Beddington.

Many of the old varieties like Early Rivers, Florence, Frogmore and Governor Wood are still available from nurseries.

Now grown as an ornamental shrub or small tree, *Cornus mas*, or the Cornelian Cherry, was always included in old orchards for its bright red edible fruits, which were a popular dessert either fresh or preserved. It grows wild from Russia right through Europe, and Palaeoethnobotanists have discovered that it was part of the diet of Neolithic people. Apart from eating it fresh or dried, the Romans also employed the fruits in winemaking.

FIGS, usually the Brown Turkey, are still to be found in old gardens. Fine examples grow in the London Parks, and outside the National Gallery in Trafalgar Square. The Romans almost certainly brought them with them, and more recently plants were imported from Italy by Thomas a Becket in the twelfth-century, and later still by Cardinal Pole and Archbishop Cranmer.

The Romans preserved the fruit in honey, and they also used the thick white sap as a rennet in cheese-making, as did the Elizabethans who also hung peacocks from a staff cut from a fig tree because they believed it acted as a tenderiser. At Lent they were served as a dessert with blanched almonds and raisins. On other occasions they were eaten fresh with pepper and salt.

MEDLAR is another fruit of antiquity which has been largely dropped from gardens. It is a good looking small tree with large single white flowers, and warm autumn colours. A Roman introduction, it established itself like a native and is still to be found growing wild in some parts of the country. The fruits, about the size of a tomato have a rough brown skin, and an unusual form which has attracted names like Hollow Berry, Openers, and the unattractive Open-ars tree. To add to its eccentricity, the fruit cannot be eaten until it is beginning to go off, because only then is the flesh soft enough to bite into. They are either left lying on the ground until they are fit to eat, or brought indoors for the ageing process.

MULBERRY (*Morus nigra*) is not only a lovely, long-lived tree, but produces, in my opinion at least, one of the most delicious fruits it is possible to grow. It was introduced to Britain in 1458, and planted in the garden of Syon House. James I boosted its popularity when he tried to establish a silk industry. That was a failure, due to the fact that it was *Morus nigra* which was grown, and not *Morus alba*, which silkworms are said to prefer.

In Elizabethan times it was appreciated for its medicinal use. The roots, which are somewhat fleshy, were boiled in vinegar and rose water to relieve toothaches, and both mulberry seeds, and the roots steeped in vinegar for five days, dried and ground into a powder, were used to anchor loose teeth.

There was some resistance to eating the fruit because it can stain the fingers and lips, although the unripe fruit was eaten to ease sore throats. In the eighteenth century the fruits were preserved in syrup, and they were also made into a wine.

The belief that it takes a lifetime for a mulberry to mature to the fruiting stage is not so; my tree began fruiting when it was just ten years old.

The PEACH (*Prunus persica*), and its smooth-skinned twin, the nectarine have always been sought after by lovers of fruit. John Milton saw the nectarine as one of the bounties of the Garden of Eden, and wrote in 'Paradise Lost':

> They sat them down; and after no more toil
> Of their sweet Gard'ning labour than sufficed
> To recommend cool Zephyr, and made ease
> More easy, wholesome thirst and appetite
> More grateful, to their supper fruits they fell,
> Nectarine fruits, which the compliant boughs
> Yielded them, side-long as they sat recline
> On the soft downy bank damask'd with flow'rs.
> The savoury pulp they chew, and in the rind,
> Still as they thirsted, scoop the brimming stream

Peaches will grow and fruit against a warm wall in the open, but nectarines do need protection, and both really do better under cover. Ever since they were introduced to Britain (some say by Henry VIII's gardener Woolf, although it seems the fruit was here earlier because King John was supposed to have hastened his death by a surfeit of peaches and ale), gardeners have devoted much skill and ingenuity to their culture.

The Romans grew peaches which they prepared for the table in typically eccentric fashion by soaking them in brine for twenty-four hours, sponging them dry, and then coating the fruit with a mixture of salt, vinegar and savory.

PEARS have a long history of cultivation, stemming from the wild forms gathered by prehistoric people and dried for winter use. Their sound keeping qualities have always made them particularly useful. Good cultivated varieties were grown by the Romans. Virgil speaks of the Pound-pear, the Crustumine, which came from the Sabine town of Crustuminium, and the Bergamot. They introduced the latter to Britain.

The Warden, or Wardon, and sometimes known as or confused with the Black Worcester, referred to by Herrick in his poem to Anne Soame: 'Of rosted warden, or bak'd peare' held its popularity as a long-keeping cooker.

Another ancient variety is Catillac. When *The Herefordshire Pomona* (1876–85) was being compiled, it was known that this large cooker had been in cultivation for at least two hundred years.

The hybridisers increased the choice from eighty varieties in the eighteenth century to over six hundred in the ninteenth century. Today the Conference and William pears are probably the most popular.

PLUMS in one form or another, either the sloe (*Prunus spinosa*), the bullace (*Prunus institia*) or the wild plum (*Prunus communis*) have been eaten by man since the earliest times. Stones of the bullace and wild plum have been found at prehistoric sites in Switzerland and Germany, and sloe stones at Whitehawk Camp in Sussex, and Bryn Celli Ddu in Anglesey.

The best eating plums probably originated in Damascus, Syria, Armenia, Transjordan, Iran and the Caucasus. Damascus gave us the damson, which for centuries was known as the Damascene plum. From Armenia came the succulent gages. The earliest variety was Reine

Claude, named after the Queen of Francis I of France, who reigned during the early sixteenth century. It was introduced to Britain by the Gage family and thus acquired its Anglicised name, Green Gage.

Prunus cerasifera, the pretty Cherry plum came from the Caucasus, and China produced the Salicine plum (*Prunus triflora*), which is particularly popular in America.

Like apples, many of the best varieties have come from chance seedlings. The Victoria plum was found in a garden at Alderton in Sussex, and the Farleigh Damson and the Pershore were Worcestershire seedlings.

In the eighteenth century plums, damsons and green gages were preserved in syrup or an apple jelly for winter use. They were also dried.

The QUINCE (*Cydonia oblonga*) is a lovely tree with a truly exquisite fruit which has been disgracefully neglected by gardeners for the greater part of this century. It thrives in damp conditions, and forms a small tree which is beautiful for its large pink-tinged flowers, its golden-green leaves lined with fine silver hairs, and large fruit that ripens to a rich, perfumed gold.

Believed to be the Golden Apples of Hesperides, it was worshipped by the Greeks, and in many countries, including Britain, played an important part in wedding ceremonies. Prolific in Mediterranean countries, it was probably first brought to this country by the Romans. Certainly it adapted readily, and in relatively recent times orchard escapers grew wild in the Sussex Weald.

John Parkinson, the sixteenth-century herbalist, wrote: 'There is no fruit growing in this Land, serving as well to make many dishes of meate for the table, as for banquets, and much more for the Physicall vertues.'

He named six varieties: The English or Apple quince, the Barbary quince, the Lyons quince, and the Brunswick quince. They were all used either baked, preserved in sugar, made into marmalade, jelly or paste. However they were prepared they were considered to be good for the stomach, and a salve made from the seeds was used to ease sore breasts after childbirth. It was even thought that the smell of quinces reduced the potency of poisons. An old remedy for bilious attacks was a quince sweet made by boiling the pulp of the fruit with sugar until it coagulated into a thick paste, and was then rolled out and dried.

A variety, Bereczki, or Vranja, which is grown in commercial orchards in Yugoslavia, is particularly well suited for small gardens. It forms a good plant, and once established and cared for should produce heavy crops of fruit.

Quince cream was an eighteenth-century delicacy. The fruit is cooked until soft, peeled and pulped. To every pound of fruit add a pound of caster sugar and egg white. Mix in a blender until white and foaming, serve in individual dishes.

To preserve quinces, choose the largest and greenest fruits and cook them until they are soft, peel and core; with an equal weight of sugar, make a syrup, but only using half the sugar. Using pippins make a quantity of liquor in the same way you would make any apple jelly, and add the remaining sugar. Boil the quinces in the syrup until they are clear, then transfer them to the pippin liquor, simmer gently until the fruit is quite white. Put them in jars, let the jelly set, and seal.

A sliced quince greatly improves an apple pie, and quince jelly is excellent as a jam or with cold meat such as lamb or game.

THE SERVICE TREE (*Sorbus domestica*) finally went out of fashion as a fruit tree at the beginning of the century, and its use before that had been quite rare. But in medieval times it was extensively grown, and would be an attractive addition to a mixed orchard. The small red-flushed fruit were treated like medlars, that is 'bletted' or allowed to go off before eating.

BARBERRY (*Berberis vulgaris*), a British native, was once an important fruit plant, although that use has long since disappeared and its place in gardens has been superseded by the more decorative exotic species. The sharp, acid berries were used in sauces, made into a piquant jelly, and the unripe berries were pickled as a relish to go with cold meats.

BILBERRY, BLUEBERRY OR WHORTLEBERRY form neat little bushes which could well be used to edge beds in the kitchen garden. The native form is *Vaccinium myrtillus*, and the American Blueberry is *Vaccinium corynbosum*. They both produced rich blue berries which are used to make tarts and jellies.

The BLACKBERRY (*Rubus*) is so familiar in hedgerow and thicket, and as a noxious weed, that it hardly seems necessary to describe it. It is a native represented by about four hundred species, which includes the raspberry. A few are worth growing for their fine soft fruits.

Parsley-leaved Blackberry, sometimes called the American Black-berry, was in fact found growing wild in Surrey. It produces large, sweet, juicy fruit. The so-called Himalaya Berry originated in America, as did the King's Acre Berry.

Whatever else he did in life, Judge Logan of Santa Cruz in California will remain immortalised by the Loganberry, which he claimed to have produced in 1882 from a cross between the American Dewberry and a raspberry. It now seems more likely that it is a native Californian Blackberry called *rubus vitifolius*. However, the Laxtonberry is a true cross between a loganberry and a raspberry call Superlative.

Another phoney hybrid is the Strawberry-Raspberry, which in 1900 was claimed in Ware's Catalogue of Hardy Plants to be a 'fruit of Japanese origin . . . a hybrid between the Strawberry and the Raspberry'. It is a wild species that grows in China and Japan.

Veitchberry is another raspberry-blackberry cross, while a Wine-berry, a delicious golden-yellow fruit, is a native of China.

Raspberries are the most widely grown of the *Rubus* family because of their fine flavour and more disciplined manner of growth. Eighteenth-century cooks used to preserve them in jelly. They freeze remarkably well.

RIBES is another large soft fruit family which embraces the familiar black, red and white currants, and the even more familiar gooseberry, all of which have been grown without a break for centuries.

Apart from being a very popular dessert fruit, gooseberries also became the special preserve of the show-bench gardener, and there are records of giant berries.

Elizabeth Smith has an interesting eighteenth-century version of Gooseberry Fool:

Take two quarts of Gooseberries, put to them as much water as will cover them; let them boil all to mash, then run them through a sieve with a spoon; to a quart of the pulp, you must have six eggs well beaten, and when the pulp is hot, put in it an ounce of fresh butter, sweeten it to your taste, and put in your eggs, and stir them over a gentle fire till they grow thick; then set it by, and when 'tis almost cold, put into it two spoonfuls of juice of spinage [spinach], and a spoonful of orange-flower water or sack, stir it well together, and put it in your basons; when 'tis cold serve it to the table.

Gooseberry and mint jelly is an excellent relish to go with cold meat, particularly lamb, as is gooseberry and sage jelly.

All the currants go well together, particularly in Queen of Summer pudding, but red currants are good for jellies to be eaten as a relish. A particular favourite of mine is red currant and marjoram jelly.

For anyone who has a surplus of soft fruit on their hands, Arthur Young, the nineteenth-century agriculturist, has the solution in a recipe for 'Family Wine':

Take Black currants, red currants, white currants, ripe cherries (black hearts are best), raspberries, each an equal quantity, or nearly so: if the black currants be the most abundant, so much the better. To 4lb. of the mixed fruit, well bruised, put one gallon of clear soft water. Steep three days and nights in open vessels, frequently stirring up the mass; then strain through a hair sieve. The remaining pulp press to dryness. Put both liquors together, and to each gallon of the whole, put 3lb. of good, rich, moist sugar of a bright yellowish appearance. Let the whole stand again three days and nights, frequently stirring up as before, after skimming the top; then turn it into casks, and let it remain, full and purging at the bung-hole, about two weeks. Lastly, to every nine gallons put one quart of good brandy, and bung down. If it does not soon drop fine, a steeping of isinglass may be introduced, and stirred into the liquor, in the proportion of about half an ounce to nine gallons.

Gooseberries, especially the largest, rich-flavoured, may be used in the mixture to great advantage: but it has been found the best way to prepare them separately, by more powerful bruising or pounding, so as to form the proper consistence in pulp, and by putting in six quarts of fruit to one gallon of water, pouring on the water twice, the smaller quantity at night, and the larger the next morning.

This process, finished as aforesaid, will make excellent wine, unmixed; but this fluid added to the former mixture, will sometimes improve the compound.

The origin of RHUBARB (*Rheum rhaponticum*) seems to be a bit of a mystery. Some authorities say that it comes from Siberia, others name Mongolia, while there is a story that it is a native of China and that the first seeds to reach Britain were smuggled out in the seventeenth century. What does seem likely is that the succulent varieties we now grow are the result of a chance cross between *Rheum rhaponticum* and the American *Rheum undulatum*. Support for this theory is offered by the fact that in the years following its introduction it was grown only as a medicinal plant, and widely used as a laxative.

Although a bit of a space invader in the kitchen garden, it is a very useful plant, and once established needs very little care beyond keeping weed-free and feeding well with manure. The flavour is greatly enhanced if a leafy branch of angelica is included in the cooking.

From the earliest times the WILD STRAWBERRY (*Fragaria vesca*) was valued, and plants were carefully selected from woodlands and grassy banks for the size and flavour of their fruits. The Hautbois (*Fragaria moschata*) was introduced from Europe, as well as one which John Parkinson called the Bohemia strawberry, which was probably an Alpine form. The tiny, delicious wild strawberries were served with claret, cream or milk, and sugar. The leaves were used in cooling drinks, and for gargles, and the fruit was distilled for heart complaints. John Gerarde recommended the boiled leaves for sore gums.

When the Virginia strawberry (*Fragaria virginiana*) was introduced in the early seventeenth century it was not a success, but later it was crossed with the Chilean Strawberry (*Fragaria chiloensis*) and the union produced the first in the large family of modern strawberries which we now grow in huge quantities.

The little Woodland and Alpine strawberries should not be ignored. They are neat in habit and exceptional in flavour.

Epilogue

The last ten years has seen a marked increase in kitchen gardening, which is more than a mere fad. There is a genuine enthusiasm for fresh, home-grown food, which is really a reaction against mass production that does not seem to offer a real choice.

It was understandable that there was a sharp decline in home vegetable and fruit growing in the post war years. Six years of shortages, queues, and the 'Dig for Victory' campaign, all part of the conflict, left a desire to forget the hardships and hostilities. By the mid-1950s the shops were full, jobs were plentiful, and people had money to spend. Unless they were enthusiasts they did not want to spend their spare time digging and hoeing, watering and weeding. There was a brief, quirkish return to the land towards the end of the 1960s when it became rather trendy to take on an allotment or start a vegetable patch. But that did not last. From the middle of the 1970s, however, the mood has changed. Kitchen gardening has become more closely linked, and very properly so, with the widening interest in cooking which is shared by both women and men. It is an interest that can be inhibited by the uniformity which has been introduced by supermarkets and mass marketing in general. The European Economic Community has not helped with its obsession for standardisation, and neither has government-subsidised market swamping, immortalised in the awful Golden Delicious apple from France. By pleasant contrast variety has increased in exotic fruits and vegetables, mainly thanks to Asian and West Indian immigrants, and gardeners are now growing sweet peppers, aubergines and chilli peppers in greenhouses.

It is scarcely surprising that people have turned to their gardens to ensure variety, and seedsmen are responding with seeds, sets and tubers of a good choice of vegetables, particularly hardy vegetables, even if the number of varieties of each has been reduced.

Modern techniques and developments have also helped to encourage the amateur. Disappointments are fewer thanks to the range of pesticides and herbicides, and relatively cheap artificial fertilizers. There are excellent machines and inexpensive irrigation systems to take the backache out of digging and watering, and cultivation in general. Better design and lightweight materials have improved hand tools.

F1 hybrids, pelleted seeds, and seed dressings; frames and greenhouses tailored for small gardens; pre-mixed seed and potting soils have all done an enormous amount to help ensure good crops.

No doubt when it is made a little simpler, fluid sowing will be more widely adopted. This is the technique by which seeds are germinated on damp absorbent paper, like kitchen towelling. The tiny seedlings are mixed with a gel, a diluted non-fungicidal wallpaper glue is ideal, and put into a sealed plastic bag, such as a freezer bag. A corner of the bag is snipped off, and the mixed seed and gel squeezed out into a drill. It is a method which guarantees a particularly good take, and is claimed to bring crops on early. In a small garden where it is necessary to achieve a quick turnover it has a particular value, especially as rapid harvesting has been made possible with the availability of freezers.

Sterile micropropagation, in which all kinds of material, leaves, seeds, shoots, bulbs and plant tissue, are started in clinically controlled conditions in high protein 'soups', will probably be quite commonly used by amateurs even by the end of the present decade. Home units are being developed, and the work is particularly well advanced at the University of Cork in Southern Ireland. It is a technique that guarantees success at the propagation stage.

Along with the useful developments there are the crackpot notions. One which enjoyed a brief period of attention was non-digging cultivation, called by some, chemical digging. The idea was that you cleared your beds with herbicides and then sowed the crops, but you never touched the soil with spade or fork, except to lift root vegetables. No doubt it was intended to appeal to the idleness in all of us, but it was poor advice. Indeed in the face of these new ideas it is as well to remember the examples of the past. The simple techniques of cultivating a kitchen garden originated hundreds of years ago have changed very little, and those functional rules are as good today as they ever were.

The old gardeners understood that the soil is a living element, even if they did not know its composition; they knew that it needed to breathe, to be fed and watered, and cherished if it was to flourish.

Although power cultivators can undoubtedly do a good job, I do not believe that they should be used exclusively. As far as tenacious weeds like couch-grass, bindweed, docks, dandelions and nettles are concerned, a cultivator will actually encourage their growth and proliferation, since they grow so eagerly from root cuttings, and the cultivator tends to chop the roots into neat lengths. Plantains and buttercups, if they are turned under will simply do a U-turn and come up again. At least once a year the ground should be hand-dug and weeded.

Herbicides are all very well for effortless weed control, but if they are used between crops they leave the ground barren and impacted. Hoeing is cheaper and far more beneficial. I recall being told by an old, and infinitely wise and experienced gardener, that regular hoeing was as good as a shower of rain.

Artificial fertilisers like Growmore are a very useful boost to growing plants, but they should be used secondarily, as a back up, to good organic material, whether farm or stable manure, or compost. There is a very encouraging movement in favour of organic gardening, and, while it can, like so many things, be taken to absurd lengths, and even become somewhat fetishist, it is a movement that can do nothing but good. The rule should be to use herbicides, pesticides and artificial manures as sparingly as possible.

Compost-making methods are becoming increasingly refined. In some cases the instructions are so complex and time-consuming that people are simply put off. This is unhelpful, because perfectly good compost can be made with virtually no effort at all. I have a kind of pen constructed from five-foot chestnut posts supporting galvanised, rigid small-mesh pig-netting. Sometimes I do turn the material a bit, but very rarely, and no doubt the purists would be horrified. However, everything that will rot down goes into it from household waste, including eggshells, fish bones and shellfish shells, to weeds, spent crops, twiggy clippings, leaves and lawn-mowings. I usually dig it in every other year because I depend on the natural rotting process, but that can be accelerated with the aid of chemical agents. It is astonishing just how much compost can be produced from a normal household and garden. I find it extraordinary that people do not have a compost heap, and I can only imagine they have a distorted view of neatness, like the individual who twice a year dumps plastic sacks of garden rubbish on the side of the road near my home.

The future does look good for kitchen gardening, but there is one threat to choosing what you want to grow: standardisation.

Commercial growers, processors, distributors and retailers want a standard product. The EEC backs this by outlawing hundreds of vegetable varieties, many of them old and treasured favourites. One reason that has been advanced is that these varieties are the genetic source of disease. The real reason is that the food industry wants types that are reliably uniform and tailored for large scale processing. Many respected scientists, however, argue that the elimination of old varieties is denying plant breeders access to an absolutely essential genetic reservoir. Despite the dictats of the EEC civil servants, a few enthusiasts, such as the members of the Henry Doubleday Institute, are keeping the old varieties going. This rescue operation could very well turn out to be the single most important function of the twentieth-century kitchen gardener.

When the gardeners of the past tended their kitchen and herb gardens, orchards and fruit enclosures, they were not looking for a standard shape or size. They were seeking flavour and colour that would enrich their tables. It is that principle which must continue to inspire the modern kitchen gardener.

Bibliography

Bacon, Francis, *Of Gardens: an Essay*, 1625.

Bennett, H. S., *Life of the English Manor, 1100–1450*, 1937.

Boniface, Priscilla, *The Garden Room*, H.M.S.O., 1982.

Burton, Robert, *The Anatomy of Melancholy* (Edited by the Rev. A. R. Shilleto), G. Bell and Sons, 1920.

Capek, Karel, *The Gardener's Year*, George Allen & Unwin, 1946.

Cecil, Hon. Mrs. Evelyn, *A History of Gardening in England*, 1910.

'Sidney Chave's War Diary, 1939–1942', Imperial War Museum Mss.

Clare, John, *The Shepherd's Calender*, Oxford University Press, 1983.

Cobbett, William, *Cottage Economy*, 1822.

Cobbett, William, *Rural Rides* (1830), Penguin Books, 1979.

Cobbett, William, *The English Gardener* (1833), Oxford University Press paperback, 1980.

Cousins, H. S., 'Second World War History of Hersden Temporary Council School', Imperial War Museum Mss.

Crisp, Sir Frank, *Medieval Gardens*, 1924.

Crompton, Margaret, 'Journal of the War Years, 1939–1945', Imperial War Museum Mss.

Culpeper, Nicholas, *Culpeper's Complete Herbal & English Physician*, 1826.

'Dig for Victory' Leaflet No. 1, Ministry of Agriculture, Fisheries and Food, 1941.

Drummon, J. C. & Wilbraham Anne, *The Englishman's Food: A History of Five Centuries of English Diet*, Jonathan Cape, London, 1939.

Earle, Mrs. C. W., *Pot-Pourri from a Surrey Garden* (1897), Century Publishing Co. Ltd., 1984.

Evelyn, John, *Acetaria. A Discourse on Sallets*, 1699.

Evelyn, John, *Diary of John Evelyn, 1677–1683.*

Evelyn, John, *Kalendarium Hortense, or Gardeners Almanac*, 1685.

Flower, B. and Hosenbaum, E., *Apicius: The Roman Cookery Book. A Critical translation of the art of cooking*, 1958.

Forsyth, Alastair, *Yesterday's Gardens*, H.M.S.O., 1983.

Gardener, Master John (Ed. Hon. A. M. T. Amherst), *The Feate of Gardening*, 1894.

Gerarde, John, *The Herbal or General Historie of Plantes Gathered by John Gerarde of London, Master in Chirurgerie*, 1597.

Greenoak, Francesca, *Forgotten Fruit*, André Deutsch, 1983.

Hammond,R. J., *Food Vol. 1 The Growth of Policy*, H.M.S.O. & Longman Green & Co., 1951.

Harvey, John H., *Mid-Georgian Nurseries of the London Region*, Transactions of the London & Middlesex Archaeological Society, Vol, 26, 1975.

Hayward, Joseph, *The Science of Horticulture, including a Practical System for the Management of Fruit Trees*, 1818.

'Herbs in the Kitchen', Ministry of Agriculture, Fisheries and Food Pamphlet, 1943.

Herrick, Robert, *The Poetical Works of Robert Herrick*, Oxford University Press, 1921.

The Herefordshire Pomona, 1876–1885.

How Britain Was Fed in War Time. Food Control 1939–1945, Ministry of Agriculture, Fisheries & Food, H.M.S.O., 1946.

Johns, Rev. C. J., *Flowers of the Field*, George Routledge & Sons Ltd., 1913.

Journal of the Royal Horticultural Society, 1940.

The Kitchen Front, BBC, 1942.

Lewis, Marjorie A., *A Letter from Provincial England, Accent on Danger*, The Catholic World, New York 1941.

Lindley, George, *A Guide to the Orchard and Kitchen Garden*, London, 1831.

London, G. and Wise, H., *The Retir'd Gardener*, 1706.

Lucas, Elizabeth, *Vegetable Cookery*.

Lyte, Charles, *Sir Joseph Banks*, David and Charles, 1980.

Martin, W. Keble, *The Concise British Flora*, George Rainbird, 1969.

The Complete Poems of Andrew Marvell, Penguin Books, 1983.

Mawe, Thomas & Abercrombie, John, *Every Man: His Own Gardener*, 14th edition 1794.

Meager, Leonard, *The New Art of Gardening*, 1670.

The Poems of John Milton, Frederick Warne & Co., 1888.

Minns, Raynes, *Bombers & Mash*, Virago, 1980.

Nilsen, Angela & Weatherall, June, compiled by, *Just Like Mother Used to Make*, Circle Books, 1980.

Organ, John, *Rare Vegetables for Garden & Table*, The Garden Book Club, London, 1960.

The Oxford Book of Food Plants, Oxford University Press, 1982.

Parkinson, John, *Paradisi in Sole, Paradisus Terrestris*, 1629.

Parkinson, John, *Theatrum Botanicum*, 1640.

Parry, W. E., *Journal of a Voyage for the Discovery of a North West Passage from the Atlantic to the Pacific*, 1821.

'Diary of Nurse Katherine Phipps, 1939–1945', Imperial War Museum Mss.

'Second World War Channel Island Account by Mr. Queree', 1940–1945, Imperial War Museum Mss.

Renfrew, Jane M., *Palaeoethnobotany: The Prehistoric Food Plants of the Near East and Europe*, Methuen & Co. Ltd., 1973.

Rhind, William, *A History of the Vegetable Kingdom*, 1872.

Robinson, William, edited by, *Flora & Sylva*, London, 1903–1905.

Rohde, Eleanour Sinclair, *A Garden of Herbs*.

Rohde, Eleanour Sinclair, *Unusual Vegetables*.

Ross, John, *A Voyage of Discovery* (Baffins Bay), 1819.

Salaman, Redcliffe N., *The History and Social Influence of the Potato*, Cambridge University Press, 1949.

Sanders, T. W., *Fruit and its Cultivation*, Collingridge, 4th edition, 1926.

Sanders, T. W., *The Book of the Potato*, Collingridge, 1905.

Scott-James, Anne, *The Cottage Garden*, Allen Lane, 1981, Penguin Books, 1982.

Smith, Elizabeth, *The Compleat Housewife or Accomplish'd Gentlewoman's Companion*, Twelfth Edition, London, 1744.

Smith, Muriel, W. G., *National Apple Register of the United Kingdom*,

Ministry of Agriculture, Fisheries & Food, 1971.

Steele, Arnold F., *The Worshipful Company of Gardeners of London, A History of its Revival 1890–1960*, London, 1964.

Switzer, Stephen, *Ichonographis Rustica or, The Nobleman, Gentleman, and Gardener's Recreations*, 2nd edition, 1742.

Switzer, Stephen, *The Practical Kitchen Gardener*, 1729.

Taylor, H. V., *The Plums of England*, Crosby Lockwood & Son Ltd., London, 1949.

Tergit, Gabriele, *Flowers Through the Ages*, Oswald Wolff, London 1961.

Thompson, Flora, *Lark Rise to Candleford*, Penguin Books, 1973.

'The Thorpe Report' (Department Committee of Inquiry into Allotments), H.M.S.O., 1969.

Vilmorin-Andrieux, Mme., *The Vegetable Garden*, English edition, published under the direction of W. Robinson, Third edition, John Murray, London 1920.

Virgil, *The Eclogues & The Georgics* (translated by C.Day Lewis), Oxford University Press, 1983.

Ware's Catalogue of Hardy Plants, Spring 1900.

Webber, Ronald, *Market Gardening The History of Commercial Flower, Fruit and Vegetable Growing*, David & Charles, 1972.

White, Gilbert, *The Garden Kalendar, 1751–1771*, The Scolar Press, 1975.

Wilson, C. Anne, *Food & Drink in Britain from the Stone Age to Recent Times*, Penguin Books, 1976.

Wilson, E. J., *West London Nursery Gardens*, The Fulham & Hammersmith Historical Society, 1982.

Woodforde, Rev. James, *Diary of a Country Parson, 1758–1781*.

Woodward, Marcus, *The Countryman's Jewel: Days in the Life of a Sixteenth-Century Squire*, Chapman & Hall, 1934.

Wright, Thomas, *The Homes of Other Days: A History of Domestic Manners and Sentiments in England from the Earliest Known Period to Modern Times*, Trubner & Co., London, 1871.

Wright, Richardson, *The Story of Gardening from the Hanging Gardens of Babylon to the Hanging Gardens of New York*, George Routledge and Sons Ltd., London, 1934.

Young, Arthur, *A Six Months Tour through the North of England*, 1771.

Young, Arthur, *The Farmer's Calendar*, 10th edition, 1815.

Index

Index

Index

Index